EXCHANGE-RATE REGIMES AND CURRENCY UNIONS

Exchange-Rate Regimes and Currency Unions

**Proceedings of a conference held by
the Confederation of European Economic
Associations at Frankfurt, Germany, 1990**

Edited by

Ernst Baltensperger
Professor of Economics
University of Bern, Switzerland

and

Hans-Werner Sinn
Professor of Economics
University of Munich, Germany

St. Martin's Press

© Confederation of European Economic Associations 1992

First published in Great Britain 1992 by
THE MACMILLAN PRESS LTD
Houndmills, Basingstoke, Hampshire RG21 2XS
and London
Companies and representatives
throughout the world

This book is published in association with the Confederation of European Economic Associations.

A catalogue record for this book is available from the British Library.

ISBN 0–333–56943–1

Printed in Great Britain by
Billing and Sons Ltd
Worcester

First published in the United States of America 1992 by
Scholarly and Reference Division,
ST. MARTIN'S PRESS, INC.,
175 Fifth Avenue,
New York, N.Y. 10010

ISBN 0–312–08101–4

Library of Congress Cataloging-in-Publication Data
Exchange-rate regimes and currency unions / edited by Ernst
Baltensperger and Hans-Werner Sinn.
p. cm.
Based on papers presented at a conference held in Frankfurt,
Germany, in Feb. 1990.
"In Association with the Confederation of European Economic
Associations."
Includes bibliographical references and index.
ISBN 0–312–08101–4 (New York).— ISBN 0–333–56943–1 (London)
1. Monetary unions—Europe—Congresses.   2. Foreign exchange–
–Europe—Congresses.   3. European Monetary System (Organization)–
–Congresses.   I. Baltensperger, Ernst.   II. Sinn, Hans-Werner.
III. Confederation of European Economic Associations.
HG925.E98   1992   92–7179
332.4'5'094—dc20   CIP

Contents

v

4 Floating Exchange Rates and Capital Mobility

Esko Aurikko   **64**

**5 Monetary Integration of Eastern Europe Into the
World Economy**

Christoph Buchheim   **86**

PART II   FLEXIBLE EXCHANGE RATES AND CENTRAL
          BANK POLICY

PART III EUROPEAN MONETARY UNION

List of Figures

List of Tables

Preface

This volume contains the proceedings of a conference of the Confederation of European Economic Associations (CEEA) held at Frankfurt, Germany, in February 1990 on the theme of 'Exchange-Rate Regimes and Currency Unions'. It includes a variety of papers devoted to theoretical and empiral analyses of systems of fixed and flexible exchange rates; to the role of Central Bank behaviour and other government policies in such systems; to the prospects, workings, and effects of a European Monetary System (EMS); and to topics of capital mobility and economic and monetary integration in general.

There is no need to emphasise the topicality of these subjects. Among issues of special current interest, the volume includes discussions of the entry of Southern countries into the EMS, the monetary integration of Eastern Europe into the world economy, the possibility of fiscal policy independence in a European Monetary Union (EMU), and the role of Central Bank independence. An introduction by Pierre Maillet (Chapter 1) gives an overview of all the papers presented in the book, and the volume also includes a discussion of each paper by one conference participant (except for the paper by Artus and Dupuy). The contributors to the proceedings represent diverse European countries, and include leading writers in the areas of monetary and international economics.

We wish to thank all those who have made the conference and this book possible. The conference was organised by the Verein für Socialpolitik for the CEEA. We are especially indebted to the Deutsche Bundesbank, our generous host in Frankfurt, for providing a stimulating atmosphere for the conference, as well as financial support. We also gratefully acknowledge financial help by BHF-Bank and Deutsche Bank AG. Special thanks go to Wolfgang Schill, Kai Konrad, Thomas Jordan, Stefan Wolter and Ruth Parham for the great help they have given us in organising the conference and preparing this book.

ERNST BALTENSPERGER
HANS-WERNER SINN

Notes on the Contributors

Professor Patrick Artus, Caisse des Dépôts et Consignations, Paris, France

Dr Esko Aurikko, Bank of Finland, Helsinki, Finland

Professor Ernst Baltensperger, Department of Economics, University of Bern, Switzerland

Dr Christoph Buchheim, Seminar für Wirtschaftsgeschichte, University of Munich, Germany

Professor Rolf Caesar, Seminar für Wirtschafts- und Finanzpolitik, University of Bochum, Germany

Dr Olivier Davanne, Direction du Trésar, Paris, France

Professor Slobodan Djajić, Graduate Institute of International Studies, Geneva, Switzerland

Dr Hermann-Josef Dudler, Deutsche Bundesbank, Frankfurt a.M., Germany

Dr Claude Dupuy, Caisse des Dépôts et Consignations, Paris, France

Dr Sylvester C.W. Eijffinger, Department of Economics, University of Tilburg, the Netherlands

Dr John S. Flemming, Bank of England, London, Great Britain

Professor Giancarlo Gandolfo, University of Rome, Italy

Professor Charles A.E. Goodhart, London School of Economics and Political Science, London, Great Britain

Noud P.D. Gruijters, Department of Economics, University of Tilburg, the Netherlands

Professor Antonie Knoester, Department of Applied Economics, Catholic University of Nijmegen, the Netherlands

Dr André M.M. Kolodziejak, Department of Applied Economics, Catholic University of Nijmegen, the Netherlands

Professor Pierre Maillet, Université de Lille 1, Paris, France

Professor Guus Muijzers, Department of Applied Economics, Catholic University of Nijmegen, the Netherlands

Professor Pier Carlo Padoan, Faculty of Economics and Commerce, University of Urbino, Italy

Professor Jürgen Siebke, Alfred Weber Institut, University of Heidelberg, Germany

Professor Hans-Werner Sinn, Seminar für Versicherungswissen-schaft, University of Munich, Germany

Professor Erich W. Streissler, University of Vienna, Austria

Professor Vasumathi Vijayraghavan, Department of Finance–ESSEC, Cergy Pontoise, France

Professor Georg Winckler, University of Vienna, Austria

List of Abbreviations

AP	Associated Press
CMEA	Council for Mutual Economic Assistance (see Comecon)
Comecon	Russian Acronym for CMEA
CSSR	Czechoslovak Socialist Republic
DNB	De Nederlandsche Bank
EC	European Community
ECs	European countries
ECB	European Central Bank
Ecu	European currency unit
ECBS	European Central Bank System
EFMC	European Finance Ministers' Council
EFTA	European Free Trade Association
EMPC	European Monetary Policy Committee
EMS	European Monetary System
EMU	European Monetary Union
EPU	European Payments Union
ERM	Exchange-rate Mechanism
ESCB	European System of Central Banks
FAZ	*Frankfurter Allgemeine Zeitung*
GDP	Gross Domestic Product
GDR	German Democratic Republic (former East Germany)
IMF	International Monetary Fund
NFA	Net foreign assets
NIC	Newly-industrialised countries
NNI	Net national income
NZZ	*Neue Zürcher Zeitung*
OECD	Organisation for Economic Cooperation and Development
PPP	Purchasing power parity
SZ	*Süddeutsche Zeitung*
WRR	Netherlands Scientific Council for Government Policies

1 Introduction

Pierre Maillet

In international economic life, the issue of the exchange-rate system is a perennial concern; the way of looking at it, however, has radically changed over the past decade.

In the 1950s and 1960s, attention focused on external trade. At an international level, economists were concerned with the best exchange-rate system for stimulating commercial transactions between countries, with the ultimate goal of favouring improved specialisation among countries and an increased use of possible economies of scale. It seemed obvious that the best system was that of fixed exchange rates. That system was adopted at Bretton Woods; it was also the system underlying the efforts to create a European common market, where the main preoccupation was with the impact on the efficiency of the economy. Indeed, such a system worked well and Europe experienced a fairly high increase in output, in *per capita* output, and an even higher increase in the volume of trade. Numerous academic studies concentrated on the real side of the balance of payments in order to explain the evolution of trade and the ratio of exports or imports to GDP for each country was an important indicator.

All that broke down in the early 1970s. First, the collapse of the world monetary system – and its death certificate issued by the Nixon decisions in August 1971 – brought about a huge amount of turbulence on the exchange markets, resulting in the adoption of a flexible exchange-rate system by many countries. The European Community (EC) attempted to maintain a fixed-rate system, but was only partly successful until the European Monetary System (EMS) was created in early 1979 (in the absence of some members).

The coexistence in the OECD of two systems of exchange has given rise to a great many difficulties, and a number of studies on the pros and cons of either system have been written. A second major cause for change was the liberalisation of capital markets and the creation of new financial instruments exerting a great impact on the effectiveness of interventions by Central Banks. Two aspects of this development must be especially mentioned, concerning the volume of flows and the nature of actors. Globally, on the exchange market,

1

the daily volume of financial transactions is about fifty times higher than that of payments related to commercial transactions: the daily rate of exchange and the daily equilibrium of the market is influenced to a far greater degree by finance than by trade. A second characteristic is the heterogeneous nature of the actors on the exchange market, enhanced by the success of new financial instruments. One may distinguish, on the one hand, between fundamentalists and chartists and, on the other, between players with different planning horizons and with different expectations: on one and the same market we have a wide variety of actors with fairly different goals, fairly different planning horizons and fairly different types of behaviour. Hence the need for a detailed analysis of exchange markets, carefully distinguishing between operators and operations.

Let us finally note that the EC is deeply involved in a process of creating complete economic and monetary union, whose main lines were sketched in the Delors report of April 1989, and whose progressive implementation was decided at the meetings of the European Council in June and December 1989. Hence the value and topicality of this conference, organised for the Confederation of European Economic Associations by the Verein für Socialpolitik.

The eleven papers presented and discussed may be grouped under three main headings: first, the working of the EMS and the general process of European monetary integration (Chapters 2–5); second, the policy of the Central Banks, especially under a system of flexible exchange rates (a situation which particularly concerns the relations between the EC and the USA) (Chapters 6–8); finally, the process aimed at creating a full European Monetary Union (EMU) (Chapters 9–12).

1.1 EUROPEAN MONETARY SYSTEM AND MONETARY INTEGRATION

Four papers deal with the EMS, touching various aspects but, in each case, referring to and illustrating the actual situation of one particular country (member or non-member of the EC). This way of proceeding, albeit having the great advantage of relying on real situations, evidently leads to results which should be extrapolated only with some degree of caution.

The paper by Artus and Dupuy (Chapter 2) focuses on the choice of debt currency, foreign or domestic. For that purpose, the authors develop three models – with external financing in foreign currency, financing in domestic currency with flexible exchange rates, and financing in domestic currency with fixed exchange rates, respectively. The working of these three models is illustrated by the empirical examples of Spain and Portugal in the 1980s, with three successive periods – financial-market isolation until 1984, the opening of the financial markets, and finally the decision to join the EMS. The authors reach the conclusion that the decision to join had a favourable effect on the economies of these Southern countries.

The purpose of Gandolfo and Padoan in Chapter 3 is to set up a continuous time macro-econometric model for evaluating the impact of financial liberalisation in advanced open economies. Indeed, even if the existing literature gives some interesting results – among others, that the removal of capital controls may give rise to speculative attacks forcing parity realignments – it does not say anything about the *speed of the adjustment*. Hence the need for dynamics instead of comparative statics, taking due account of various forms of expectations (extrapolative or normal – i.e., regressive), associated with two types of agent. It can be shown that those forecasting for shorter periods display extrapolative and destabilising expectations, while those operating with relatively longer planning horizons tend to have regressive and stabilising expectations. Bearing in mind these two types of agent, Tobin (1978) suggested putting a tax on all capital flows to discourage the spot traders. Gandolfo and Padoan's paper shows that the introduction of such a Tobin tax provides a crucial contribution to the stabilisation of a system with full capital liberalisation. This conclusion is very important, and will certainly be explored further in the future.

Some European countries, although not belonging to the EC for various reasons, are nevertheless strongly influenced by its economic situation and policy, and must find the best way to adapt their own policy. This applies to Finland; the paper by Aurikko (Chapter 4) is concerned with the classical contrast between pegging the exchange rate to a currency index (or, more concretely, to the EMS currencies) and maintaining a higher degree of autonomy in domestic monetary policy by allowing the currency to float. A quantitative simulation, using the Bank of Finland's macro-economic model which pays particular attention to the working of the labour market, leads the author to conclude that, with increasing capital mobility, the economy is better off if insulated from most shocks by allowing the currency to float.

The Conference took place at a time when political events in Eastern Europe were inducing Western European economists to have a special look at the possibility of enlarging European economic integration (this topic was examined more carefully in the Third Integration Symposium of the Confederation, organised in October 1991 by the Società Italiana degli Economisti, on the subject of Europe between East and South). In Frankfurt an initial paper was presented on some monetary aspects of these Eastern European countries. The paper by Buchheim (Chapter 5) deals with the evolution of payments within the Comecon, and tries to draw from the experience of Western European countries in the 1950s some conclusions for a Comecon which would, as today, include the six existing Eastern European countries and the USSR. The main goal is a restructuring and modernisation of the economies of those countries which, for their part, will have to import more goods from Western countries. In order to avoid huge financial assistance from the West, the scenario suggested by Buchheim is to introduce into this Comecon a high degree of multilateralisation, using a procedure inspired by the European Payments Union (EPU) in Western Europe in the 1950s, which could lead progressively to full convertibility. Naturally, the political situation of these countries is developing rapidly: with German monetary unification, the Comecon of the seven is vanishing, and the position of the five remaining Eastern countries positioned between the EC and the USSR is unclear. In Western Europe, and even more in Eastern Europe, a desire is being voiced for a rapid intensification of economic relations, with the ultimate goal of full integration; perhaps, given this situation, one ought to concentrate more on the experience of the Marshall Plan than on that of the EPU. The great importance of Buchheim's paper, however, was to force discussion on this extremely topical issue.

1.2   EXCHANGE RATES AND CENTRAL BANK POLICY

The crucial point of the effectiveness of interventions by the Central Bank is investigated in one theoretical paper and in two applied analyses.

The paper by Djajić (Chapter 6) gives a careful insight into the path of a floating exchange rate in the face of non-sterilised intervention. Many cases are explored, differing mainly in the existence or absence of pre-announcements by the Central Bank as to its policy, and in the content of this policy (level of depreciation which induces intervention, influence of the rate of depreciation on the quantity of reserves offered for sale). One important policy conclusion is drawn from this analysis: 'the central bank has an incentive to sell a smaller-than-expected quantity of reserves at the first critical level of e'. The paper also confirms that 'the prospect of unsterilised intervention *does* serve to keep the market in check'.

The paper by Eijffinger and Gruijters (Chapter 7) is rather exceptional, for the authors had the possibility of knowing, on a confidential basis, daily data of official intervention by the Deutsche Bundesbank and the Federal Reserve. These authorities intervene to 'counter disorderly market conditions'; but this criterion may be interpreted in various ways, in particular fighting against erratic short-term exchange rate fluctuations or pushing towards an equilibrium value based on 'fundamentals'. A distinction has also to be made between coordinated and non-coordinated interventions. The authors also emphasise the importance of market signals.

Theory suggests that if an intervention provides the market with new information or a signal about the future course of either exchange-rate or monetary policy, and if the market is highly efficient, then the exchange rate will immediately change after the intervention. The empirical analysis suggests a far less favourable conclusion: the effectiveness of exchange-market intervention is *limited, and depends heavily on the specific circumstances under which the intervention takes place*. By way of contrast, the authors show the overwhelming importance of the monthly announcements of US trade balance figures. In the light of the fragility of such statistics (and, more generally, of the statistics on the balances of payments in the world, confirmed yet again by the IMF), one cannot help being frightened by the strong influence the world exchange market exerts on the management of our economies. Nevertheless, as stressed by Georg Winckler, the discussant, the conclusion arrived at in the study may be overrated, due to the authors' imperfect knowledge of the exact time of intervention.

The answers given to the issue of the exchange-rate system and the management of this system by the Central Bank have an *impact on some other goals or policies*, and these links have to be considered when both a better system and the best way of intervening in the exchange market have to be chosen. On the issue of inflation, the paper by *Davanne and Vijayraghavan* (Chapter 8) – building on the hypothesis that long-term expectations and long-term investment are a stabilising and short-term speculation a destabilising factor on the exchange market – concludes that diminishing the investors' uncertainty arising from inflation probably stabilises the exchange rate. Two instructions for the Central Bank derive from this: to reveal its long-term inflation targets and to restrict its objective function, as far as the long term is concerned, to stabilising inflation.

Most of the papers in Parts I and II have in common that they use models differentiating between various types of actor or various types of operation on the exchange market. This process of differentiation is one of the main values added by these papers. But, naturally, when one starts such a process of disaggregation it is difficult to know what level is appropriate. It is, therefore, not surprising that the discussion aroused some objections concerning an alleged insufficient degree of detail; it will be left to the reader to make up his or her own mind on this point which, naturally, may affect the validity of the specific conclusions.

1.3 EUROPEAN MONETARY UNION

Political union and full monetary union are the two main great challenges Europe is now facing at the beginning of the 1990s. Europe's main choice is indeed between merely a largely unified market of twelve, extended as a free-trade area to other European countries (especially the EFTA countries, so setting up the European economic area) or a more ambitious goal, the creation of an economically and politically integrated area, but concerning (at the beginning at least) only part of Europe as a whole. Political decisions were taken in various European councils at the turn of 1989–90 to embark on the road towards this goal, and the Conference devoted four papers and much discussion to the topic of European monetary union, two papers dealing mainly with monetary aspects, the others expanding the field to include other issues.

There is a large consensus (even in the Delors report) that Europe should sooner or later have a *single currency*. But what currency should that be? Streissler's paper (Chapter 10) distinguishes itself by being quite frank and concentrating on the only real alternative: the German Mark or some kind of Ecu (although Streissler does not mention the name). Following a refreshing historical discussion, he concludes that the only feasible solution is the adoption of the

German Mark. He puts it quite clearly: 'we are . . . witnessing the establishment of a currency union in Europe by the forces of the market and by currency competition: the process of the Deutsche Mark becoming the common currency in Europe . . . In face of this rare and happy occasion of a better currency actually establishing itself, it appears quite incomprehensible that at the same time attempts should be made to create another common European currency by artificial means'. The ensuing lively discussion showed that this conclusion was not fully accepted by all participants, partly for economic and partly for political reasons.

This brings us to the next point, the *independence of the Central Bank*, an old issue, but again highly topical. Caesar (Chapter 11) begins by defining the expression 'independence' (he prefers 'room for manoeuvre', showing that today's discussions in member countries arise at least in part from differing interpretations of this concept). He provides a well-balanced analysis of the pros and cons of various solutions, arguing that the Central Bank should have a wide room for financial manoeuvre and be fully independent of political pressure, subject only to legal constraints. The subsequent discussion showed a large degree of agreement among the participants. However, it should not be forgotten that all those present were economists, and it is not certain that this presentation will be sufficient to convince political decision-makers in countries with Central Banks which enjoy a lower degree of independence. Seen from this perspective, the main question concerns the attribution of competence for deciding the main priorities between the macro-economic goals of the 'magic triangle', with two issues: first, the distribution of competence between the government and the parliament (this issue is particularly acute in the Community itself, where the European Parliament feels frustrated); second, is it pertinent to add to the three classical powers (i.e., legislative, executive and judiciary) a fourth (i.e., the monetary power)? To what extent is this compatible with a democratic system embedded in a parliamentary system? And what form will this parliamentary system take in the politically unified Europe of tomorrow? Here again, an old issue, but one of great topicality. In the 1950s, Winston Churchill spoke of this system as being the worst, excepting all others. The political difficulties experienced in Western Europe in recent years and the current political breakdown in Eastern Europe place European countries under an obligation to concentrate their efforts on the best institutional framework for tomorrow, and this question of the independence of the Central Bank may provide an opportunity to think carefully about the organisation of tomorrow's political Europe.

A further delicate and very controversial issue concerns the link between *fiscal policy and European monetary union*. Academic circles are strongly divided on the amount and content of a necessary coordination of fiscal policies across countries, while governments and national administrations are naturally very reluctant to abandon part of their sovereignty in this field.

As a matter of fact, the discussion is somewhat confused, for at least two issues are involved: in an EMU, is it possible to leave each country entirely free to define and implement its fiscal policy, or is some kind of coordination necessary? If so, does that mean that national policies may differ according to individually differing national situations, or that there must be a common fiscal policy, in the same way that common policies in the fields of agriculture or commercial external trade are pursued?

On the first issue, the answer given by the Werner report of 1970 advocated only the need for a certain coordination on the general magnitude of the budget. The Delors report of 1989 went much further, by advocating a statutory ceiling on deficit spending and, more generally, by repeatedly insisting that national fiscal policies must be constrained by binding rules.

Apart from comments on the official UK view on EMU, Goodhart devotes a good part of his paper (Chapter 9) to this issue, concluding in favour of a mixture of some degree of national fiscal policy independence and some coordination. His main argument refers to the imperfection of markets (especially labour markets), which hampers speedy adjustments: an alternative mechanism is required to restore the economy's equilibrium (i.e., the use of fiscal policy and fiscal deficits). Even though the author is aware of the numerous valid arguments in favour of some kind of common fiscal policy (or, rather, of the drawbacks of totally independent national fiscal policies), he nevertheless considers the above-mentioned argument based on imperfections of markets to be more important and therefore concludes that coordination is possible only to a certain degree, leaving open the possibility of substantial differences between individual countries.

Finally, the well-documented paper by Knoester, Kolodziejak and Muijzers (Chapter 12) broadens the view on the whole subject of economic policy and European integration. The main message may perhaps be summed up in the two sentences, at the beginning and the end of this paper:

– '[the present] process of negative integration should be followed by a process of positive integration (i.e., harmonisation of national policies)'.
– '[this process being uneasy, and at the moment not being accepted by all member countries, we must] opt for a two-speed Europe . . . rather than acquiescing in minimum progress or even stagnation'.

References

Delors, J. *et al.* (1989) 'Committee for the Study of Economic and Monetary Union: Report on economic and monetary union in the European Community; Luxembourg.
Tobin, J. (1978) 'A Proposal for an International Monetary Reform', *Eastern Economic Journal* (July–October).
Werner: Commission of the European Communities. Report to the Council and the Commission on the Realization by Stages of Economic and Monetary Union in the Community (Werner Report), *Supplement to Bulletin of the European Community*, no. 11 (Brussels, 8 October 1970).

Part I
European Monetary System and Monetary Integration

2 The Entry of Southern Countries Into the European Monetary System*

Patrick Artus and Claude Dupuy

2.1 INTRODUCTION

Spain and Portugal became members of the EC in 1986 and joined the EMS at the Madrid European summit of 26–27 June 1989. This paper explores how these Southern European countries may benefit from involvement in EMS mechanisms and, subsequently, in a European monetary union.

Some of the arguments for their integration have already been applied to the countries t᷉ ᷉ng part in the concerted-float agreement: by joining the EMS, th᷉ ᷉outhern European countries 'import' the Bundesbank's reputation and limit the loss linked to the non-credibility of their resolve to curb inflation (Giavazzi and Pagano, 1988; Giavazzi and Giovannini, 1989; Melitz, 1988; de Grauwe, 1989). EMS membership, the argument runs, is a substitute for a policy precommitment on their part. Similarly, Spain and Portugal's acceptance of EMS discipline can be seen as a statement of their refusal to play a non-cooperative game aimed at exporting inflation via their exchange rates (Hamada, 1985). In our analysis, however, we shall disregard these arguments, which are based on Central Bank reputation and announcement effects.

Alternatively, one could make a case for the drawbacks of joining a fixed exchange-rate mechanism (Dornbusch, 1988; Drazen, 1989; de Kock and Grilli, 1989). The floating exchange-rate regime allows governments to finance their deficits through seigniorage – that is, inflation. As monetary integration rules out this option, it would make the governments of these high domestic-debt countries insolvent; as a result, integration would be pernicious. This argument is hard to accept, for it implies that such countries must be allowed to

13

pursue bad policies by financing their growth through inflation.

A more constructive approach would be to tackle the issue from the opposite end: do monetary integration or fixed exchange rates facilitate a non-inflationary development? We shall discuss the subject from this angle, taking as an example the economic development of Spain and Portugal over the past several years.

The brisk growth of the Southern countries (Table A2.1, p. 32) exhibits two distinctive characteristics: heavy imports of capital goods and large-scale recourse to external financing. The rapid capital accumulation of recent years was made possible only by the intensive use of imported investments. In Spain, they represented more than a third of total investments in 1988 (Table A2.2, p. 32), and they formed a decisive component of the current-account balance. It should be noted that the investment demand was mainly directed toward northern EC countries.

Similarly, an examination of Spain and Portugal's capital accounts shows that their imports were largely financed by foreign-capital inflows in the form of credit from non-residents or direct investments (Table A2.3, p. 33). As with imports, northern European countries were the main contributors to this external financing.

The specific features of these countries' growth lead us to frame the question of their EMS membership in terms of the opportunities for external financing available for their development. In other words, in what conditions can Spain and Portugal most effectively tap the European savings needed to offset their capital-goods imports?

In the exchange-rate policy alternative, choosing a fixed rate clearly restricts the range of economic policy options available. Since we have disregarded the notion of the 'reputation effect', this loss must be compensated by greater discretion elsewhere. In the case of external indebtedness, this means securing an optimal level of financing.

The debate is complicated, however, by the often-overlooked fact that debtor countries can borrow in lending-country currencies, avoiding the payment of an exchange-risk premium. Indeed, the Southern EC countries have resorted almost exclusively to loans in foreign currencies (Table A2.5, p. 33).

It is commonly argued that EMS membership would benefit Spain and Portugal by enabling them to reduce the risk premium charged by their creditors, and therefore the debt cost. But the argument is invalid when the borrowing takes place in foreign currency. It would apply only to loans in domestic currency. This possibility, in turn, cannot be envisaged unless the debtor countries modernise their domestic financial markets, inducing non-residents to hold securities there.

In weighing the foreign- or local-currency financing alternatives, one must assess the gain that would be achieved in terms of economic policy discretion to offset the loss of exchange policy freedom. With foreign-currency loans, the exchange rate is exogenous and freely determined by the Southern countries. With domestic-currency loans, the rate is endogenised, depriving the authorities of the exchange-rate weapon. Consequently, the latter alternative entails a loss of freedom *a priori* that can be compensated only by the ease with which solvency can be obtained – a constraint that is binding on any debtor. This constraint can be satisfied through spontaneous economic mechanisms. If, however, it is not met naturally, the authorities must adjust their policies to comply with it. One may then ask if solvency is not more easily reached by altering economic policies in the endogenous exchange-rate scenario. Here, the authorities would be induced to give up their exchange-rate freedom, too costly in terms of economic regulation.

The authorities can also deprive themselves of the exchange-rate weapon voluntarily. Financing in domestic currency reduces the risk premium and increases capital substitutability and international mobility – with potentially favourable effects on the domestic economy.

In short, we must examine three issues: (1) the choice of debt currency; (2) the compliance with the solvency constraint; (3) the degree of freedom (discretion) in economic policy. Section 2.2 presents three models for the functioning of an economy representative of the Southern EC countries, defined according to the three types of external financing envisaged: foreign-currency loans (Model 1); domestic-currency debt with exchange-rate flexibility (Model 2); domestic-currency borrowing with fixed exchange rates (Model 3). In Section 2.3 we conclude by examining Spain and Portugal's external debt policies in the light of all three models.

2.2   THE MODELS

Before defining the content of the three models, we shall set forth the theoretical framework of our description of Spain and Portugal.

Representation of the Spanish and Portuguese economies

The three models are based on a common set of macro-economic features, financing patterns, economic policies and solvency criteria.

Macro-economic features

We describe an economy with the following four features (for the equations, see Figure 2.1 (equations (1)–(5)) and Figure 2.2 (equations (6A), (6B) and (7)).

Southern countries' output

$$y_t = \alpha_t k_t = c_t + x_t + g_t \tag{1}$$

y = South's output log

e = exchange-rate log (ratio of Southern currency to Northern currency)
k_t = log of Southern capital (at the start of period t)
g_t = exogenous demand component
c = log of Southern consumption

Southern countries' consumption

$$c_t = \beta_0 y_t - \beta_1 r_t - \beta_2 (e_t - \varrho_t + f_t) \tag{2}$$

$$\beta_0 < 1$$

c = Southern consumption log
e = Southern production price log
r = Southern nominal interest log
f_t = log of Southern external debt at the start of period t in Northern currency

Southern exports

$$x_t = \gamma(e_t - \varrho_t) \tag{3}$$

x_t = log of Southern exports; $\gamma > 1$

Southern monetary equilibrium

$$m_t = \varrho_t + \eta_0 y_t - \eta_1 r_t \qquad (4)$$

m_t = log of Southern money supply

Capital dynamics

$$k_{t+1} = k_t(1 - \delta) + \delta_t \qquad (5)$$

δ = capital scrapping rate (= equilibrium ratio of investment to capital)

Figure 2.1   The model: real sector

Case A   Non-substitutability between Southern and Northern securities: financing in Northern currency
Dynamics of Southern external debt (in Northern currency)

$$f_{t+1} = r_t^a + (1 + r) f_t - \varepsilon_0 (x_t + \varrho_t - e_t) + \varepsilon_1 i_t \qquad (6A)$$

ε_0 = equilibrium ratio of exports to debt
ε_1 = equilibrium ratio of investment to debt
i = investment log
r_t^a = Northern interest rate (r = its highest value)

Case B   Imperfect substitutability financing in Southern currency
Dynamics of Southern external debt (in Northern currency)

$$f_{t+1} = r_t + (1 + r) f_t - \varepsilon_0 (x_t + \varrho_t) + \varepsilon_1 (i_t + e_t) \qquad (6B)$$

Northern portfolio choice

$$r_t = r_t^\bullet + (e_{t+1} - e_t) + \theta(f_t + e_t) \qquad (7)$$

Figure 2.2   The model: financing

- The government and firms are aggregated and invest to accumulate fixed capital, including plant, equipment and infrastructure (equation (1)). This investment is entirely imported, and indeed constitutes the only import. Consumer goods must be produced locally. The standard model for analysing the effects of EMS membership typically distinguishes between monetary policy and fiscal policy (de Grauwe, 1989; Cohen, 1989). We exclude fiscal policy, whose role is restricted to cyclical stabilisation, whereas – in our model – government expenditure and that of firms are the engines of supply. We take a highly *dirigiste* view of Spain and Portugal's spending on plant, equipment and infrastructure, since these are economic policy tools here, not an endogenous variable as in the standard literature on exchange-rate determination in open economies (Borenzstein, 1989; Brock, 1988; Murphy, 1986; Murphy, 1989). This interpretation seems justified by the share of investment in vital infrastructure. Indeed, Aschauer (1989) shows that even in the USA the level of public-sector capital goods has a very strong influence on labour productivity throughout the economy.

- The supply of goods depends on the capital accumulated previously (equation (1)); the price achieves the competitive equilibrium of the market for goods.
- Demand for domestic producers' goods includes consumption, exports and an exogenous component, but excludes imported investments. Consumption grows with output and decreases with the interest rate and external debt (equation (2)). The country's households possess cash and securities issued in the national currency by firms and the government. From the latter, they receive incomes that decrease with the external debt – the source of interest payments to the rest of the world. Hence the presence of external debt in consumption. Exports grow with competitiveness (equation (3)).
- Households' trade-off between cash and domestic securities is represented by the monetary equilibrium (equation (4)).

Financing of investment expenditures

We distinguish between two situations:

- In case A, the securities issued in the Southern countries' currencies are not accepted by the Northern countries. Corporate and government debt consists of: (1) a portion in domestic currency (of the Southern countries) held by local residents; (2) a portion in foreign currency (Northern currency) held by the rest of the world.

No substitution is possible between these two types of debt, and the interest rates on Northern and Southern currencies are independent. The external-debt dynamics are given by equation (6A). Interest is paid at the northern rate.

• In case B, the financial markets are globalised, and the Northern countries agree to finance the Southern ones in the latter's currency. Debt is consequently expressed in Southern currency (equation (6B)). Interest rates are not independent here, for they are interrelated via the portfolio choices (equation (7)) of Northern-country residents. If substitutability is weak (high θ), a rise in the South's external debt expressed in Northern currency will drive up the Southern interest rate sharply. If substitutability is perfect ($\theta = 0$), exchange-rate expectations are assumed to be perfect.

Economic policies

In theory, the Southern countries have three economic policy instruments at their disposal: the exchange rate, monetary policy (money supply, hence domestic interest rates) and the investment level (hence capital-goods imports). The countries have three economic policy objectives: the output level (hence employment), the consumption level (hence welfare) and zero inflation. As we mentioned in the introduction, we consistently assume the absence of deliberately inflationary policies. The analysis is confined to long-term goals, corresponding to the stationary solution of our model. We ignore adjustment paths, except to verify their effective convergence toward the long-term solution.

Solvency

We identify solvency and dynamic stability of the external debt. These two notions are different in theory, but the most satisfying, in our view, is the non-divergence of the debt/GDP ratio obtained under stationary equilibrium if the debt is stable. We know that these two notions can differ. Solvency implies that the underlying growth rate of debt is slower than that of the nominal interest rate (Buiter, 1986). If the latter exceeds the nominal growth rate of output, the debt/GDP ratio may diverge even though solvency is guaranteed. This guarantee does, however, apply since the debt interest/GDP and taxes/GDP ratios diverge in parallel, making this situation implausible. We shall therefore use the stability of the debt/GDP ratio – that is, the equivalent of the economic stability of debt, the concept used in studies such as (Hamilton and Flavin, 1986; Kremers, 1989).

The solvency condition is fairly stringent. It implies that a rise in debt reduces private demand – and therefore lowers prices – while improving foreign trade enough to offset the 'snowball' effect of interest payments.

What scope does the model allow for handling foreign investment (of the direct or portfolio type), which does not appear directly? Foreign investment represents either (1) a capital-goods purchase financed by a domestic loan by the Northern European firm investing in the Southern country, or (2) an acquisition by non-residents of securities issued by Southern-country firms. In both cases, these modes of external financing are neutral with respect to the debt.

However, foreign investors – who are normally attracted by the capital returns in the Southern countries (Hamada and Iwata, 1989) – demand a yield at least equal to the Northern interest rate. Our formalisation may therefore minimise interest payments on the current account and the outstanding external loans.

Model 1: external financing in foreign currency

In Model 1, where capital-goods imports are financed solely by foreign-currency loans, the Southern countries' financial markets are open to local residents alone. This is due either to regulatory restrictions on foreign investment or to lack of confidence in these countries' currencies, with the result that Northern creditors will agree to lend only in their own currency.

Direct consequences of borrowing in foreign currency

We can identify three major consequences:

- There is no exchange risk for lenders. External debt is denominated in Northern currency and can in principle accumulate at market rates until a solvency risk emerges.
- Northern and Southern interest rates are completely disconnected. As regards their debt, the Southern countries are therefore in a fixed-rate regime. So long as solvency is ensured, capital inflows from Northern countries finance the South's current deficit. Since this involves no exchange risk or default risk, capital mobility must be perfect. Capital inflows play the role of Central Bank intervention in the standard fixed-rate model. Moreover, borrowing in foreign currency spares Southern countries the opportunity

cost of holding currency reserves (Frenkel and Razin, 1987).
● The endogenisation of the exchange rate due to foreign-currency borrowing allows the domestic economies of the South to be emancipated from external constraints. In principle, this gives the Southern countries free use of their three instruments: exchange rates, monetary policy and investment levels. However, the economic performance of this debt option depends on whether or not the solvency conditions are met.

The foreign-currency loan option does not seem to have received the attention it deserves. Most studies on external debt are guided by models derived from Mundell and Fleming, where countries borrow in their own currency (see, for example, Dooley and Isard, 1983). If the loans are in foreign currency, there is normally no crowding-out or rigid link between investment and national saving such as the one identified by Feldstein and Horioka (1980) and Feldstein (1983). Borrowing in foreign currency is in effect equivalent to a loan in domestic currency followed by a sterilising intervention by the Central Bank – which explains the similarity with the fixed-rate regime (Golub, 1989).

Debt equilibrium and economic policy freedom

The dynamic solvency of countries borrowing in foreign currency can be achieved through an internal self-balancing mechanism: the debt is stabilised by a natural levy on internal demand. An increase in external debt has a negative effect on national income. It therefore reduces private demand. This in turn drives down domestic prices, improving foreign trade and ultimately restoring the debt position.

In this case, solvency removes the constraints on Southern countries' economic policy freedom. They can set their exchange rates to make their balance of trade compatible with their output and consumption targets. If the former are high compared with the latter, the exchange rate falls and the trade account posts a real surplus. Exchange-rate movements thus absorb fluctuations in demand for goods.

Investment policy is set with the aim of reaching the level of capital required to fulfil the output target. Monetary policy is defined with the objective of neutralising inflationary pressures; if demand rises, monetary policy will therefore be restrictive.

If solvency is ensured and the three targets are met, the country's situation is perfect and cannot be better than that obtained in the other scenarios. However, this requires compliance with the solvency conditions – which, as we saw, are very strict. To secure long-run debt-ratio stability, the external surplus allowed by deflation must offset the additional interest charge resulting from the increase in debt expressed in local currency. This current-account equilibrium therefore depends on the downward mobility of domestic demand and its repercussions on prices and exports.

Debt stabilisation through economic policy constraints

It is quite possible that solvency may not be achieved spontaneously. The authorities will then have to constrain their domestic policies to obtain it. If domestic demand does not fall automatically to a level that permits dynamic debt stability, the country must seek external competitiveness by depreciating its currency, so as to improve its balance of trade and stabilise its external debt.

The pursuit of such an exchange policy is costly in terms of economic objectives, since it prevents the joint fulfilment of targets for growth, prices and consumption. We assume – here and throughout the rest of our study – that the consumption target is the first to be sacrificed.

In the three cases of debt instability – increase in the output target, rise in Northern interest rates and exogenous shock on domestic demand – the return to equilibrium can be achieved only by reducing overall domestic consumption. A larger levy will be raised on output volume to make output available for export:

- If the output target is increased, the debt equilibrium will be threatened by the larger imports of capital goods. This threat requires an exchange-rate depreciation to promote exports, coupled with a restrictive policy to curb consumption.
- An exogenous rise in Northern interest rates will aggravate the debt burden, requiring consumption to be sacrificed for exports.
- Thirdly, for the same reason, a positive shock on domestic demand will also necessitate a cut in consumption. In this case, however, it should be noted that the compliance with indebtedness criteria is achieved without exchange-rate movements. The increase in demand is neutral on the current-account balance, as only capital goods are imported.

Thus, in the case of foreign-currency borrowing, if solvency is not reached spontaneously (the most favourable scenario), the need for debt stability leads authorities to constrain their policies and depart from the optimum consumption level achieved. In this case, borrowing in local currency might be a more cost-effective way to meet the solvency target.

Model 2: financing in domestic currency with flexible exchange rate

Indebtedness in domestic currency implies that Southern countries' financial markets are open to non-residents. It will be recalled that this requires Spain and Portugal to modernise their markets in order to attract foreign investors. An effort in areas such as quotation procedures, hedging instruments and the security of transaction closes should lead to an increased presence of Northern countries, providing the Southern markets with the necessary liquidity.

Direct consequences of domestic-currency borrowing

Financing in domestic currency differs from the previous scenario as regards external solvency criteria. Exchange-rate movements do not affect the domestic-currency value of the external debt. As a result, with interest rates being expressed in Southern currency, the consumption level and debt dynamics no longer depend on exchange-rate fluctuations.

Residents of Northern European countries can arbitrate between their domestic securities and those issued by Southern countries. Interest rates are therefore linked by the equilibrium condition of portfolio choices (equation (7) in Figure 2.2): Southern interest rates will rise all the more strongly compared with Northern rates as the external debt is greater and currency substitutability is weaker.

Here, capital inflows do not play the role of non-sterilised intervention and the Southern countries do not operate under a fixed – or an exogenous – exchange-rate regime. The exchange-rate dynamics being endogenous (a condition that follows from equation (7)), and all other factors being equal, a rise in external debt entails the expectation of an appreciation that encourages creditors to increase their lendings.

The dynamics of this scenario therefore involve the exchange rate, external debt and capital. We assume rational exchange-rate expectations. The dynamics must accordingly be of the 'saddle path' type, with only one divergent eigenvalue. The exchange rate will thus follow a stable path. This effectively occurs when one of the equations (not reproduced here) is fulfilled.

Is solvency more easily reached in the domestic-currency indebtedness scenario than with foreign-currency borrowing? To answer this question, we begin by analysing the situation in which the Southern countries adopt a flexible-exchange regime (outside the EMS).

Flexible exchange rates and dynamic debt equilibrium

We base our analysis on an economic situation in which the effect of debt fluctuations on exchange rates is mediated by the market. In general, increased borrowing leads to an expected – and therefore actual – appreciation of the exchange rate, with imperfect capital mobility due to portfolio choices. A higher debt drives up the domestic currency rate, reduces import costs and makes exports more expensive in foreign currencies. If the consequences of a fall in import prices outweigh those of a rise in export prices, the trade account will improve and the debt will therefore be reduced. A Southern country with large imports of capital-goods and weak export price-elasticity will thus be better off borrowing in its own currency since it will meet the solvency criteria more easily.

Flexible exchange rates and the conduct of economic policy

(a) We begin by looking at the case of economic policies conducted when solvency conditions are met. Compared with borrowing in foreign currency, the decision to contract external loans in domestic currency reduces the authorities' degree of economic policy freedom. Governments are left with only two policy instruments at their disposal – money supply and investment – which they apply in order to meet their price and output targets.

Nevertheless, it is interesting to compare the conduct of policies (1) with foreign-currency borrowing when dynamic debt stability is not obtained spontaneously and with domestic-currency borrowing when the stability is obtained. In both cases, the authorities can exercise two degrees of freedom in pursuing their objectives.

In the case of a higher output target, the induced increase in capital-goods imports causes the exchange rate to appreciate. In the long run, this reduces the debt, offsetting the deterioration of the trade account. Similarly, the effects (in absolute value) of domestic demand shocks and foreign interest-rate shocks on consumption are weaker when the debt is denominated in domestic currency. To cope with these shocks, the Southern countries should modernise their financial markets and borrow in their currency if this stabilises their external debt.

As explained earlier, in the foreign-currency scenario, the demand shocks are levied entirely on consumption. In the domestic-currency alternative, they entail an exchange-rate appreciation that stabilises total demand and increases the share of consumption in demand.

With domestic-currency indebtedness, the effect of a foreign interest-rate rise on the exchange rate and on debt is diluted by imperfect currency substitutability. The rise increases the domestic interest rate but, in the long run, reduces the debt (and therefore the interest rate itself) at portfolio equilibrium. The dilution explains the result.

(b) If the solvency conditions described above are not met, the authorities must constrain their policies to stabilise the debt. Here again, the authorities lose a degree of freedom, since they cannot apply exchange rates or economic policies to meet their output, investment and consumption targets.

In this debt-instability scenario, the effect on consumption may be quite different from that obtained in the similar situation with foreign-currency loans. In the latter case, the output target could be achieved by acting on investment, debt stability by acting on the exchange rate, and price stability by acting on interest rates. The local currency depreciates with the rise in foreign interest rates and in exogenous demand. Consumption falls with steeper foreign interest rates and higher exogenous demand.

With domestic-currency borrowing, the exchange rate ensures debt stability if foreign interest rates and investment increase. Price stability implies that the exchange rate depreciates with the foreign interest rate and investment, and appreciates with exogenous demand.

If imports are strong, the exchange rate will have a greater effect on the debt than in the previous case, since exchange fluctuations modify the nominal domestic-currency value of foreign trade. As a result, small exchange-rate variations will ensure debt stability. Output will therefore decrease with the foreign interest rate, and increase with exogenous demand.

To sum up, external debt is less sensitive to exogenous demand when borrowing takes place in the domestic currency. Sensitivity to the foreign interest rate is thus weaker if demand exhibits low interest-rate elasticity. When the debt is in foreign currency, the output level does not enter into the equation, as it is controllable.

Model 3: financing in domestic currency with fixed exchange rates

As in Model 2, this external financing policy implies the opening of financial markets to non-residents, with the same direct consequences. It should be noted that domestic-currency financing provides a much stronger incentive than foreign-currency borrowing for the authorities to stabilise the exchange rate as protection against overshooting in the event of exogenous shocks.

Fixed exchange rates and debt dynamics

With fixed rates, higher indebtedness leads to an anticipated market appreciation of the exchange rate. The authorities must therefore tailor their policies to cancel the effects of this increase on their currency's exchange rate. In particular, they will implement a restrictive monetary policy to raise interest rates, so that foreign capital inflows will have a sterilising effect.

Higher interest rates will, however (1) increase the debt interest charge, promoting debt instability and (2) reduce domestic prices, improving competitiveness and therefore debt control. If the first effect predominates, solvency is harder to obtain. If, instead, external demand is very sensitive to export competitiveness, stable exchange rates will make it easier to meet the solvency constraint.

We should also note that, compared with floating exchange rates – which weaken currency substitutability – adherence to a fixed-rate discipline allows a reduction of risk premiums and an improvement in capital mobility, and hence in exchange-rate stability.

Fixed exchange rates and the conduct of economic policy

How do fixed rates help achieve economic policy goals when the debt is stable? First, let us look at the alternative involving domestic-currency debt under a floating rate and under a fixed rate. Choosing fixed rates means using the monetary policy instrument – that is, raising interest rates. As a result, unlike in the floating-rate scenario, neither the output target nor the consumption target can be met. Naturally, the increase in substitutability amplifies the effect in absolute-value terms of foreign interest-rate changes on consumption. On the other hand, it reduces the influence of exogenous expenditures, at least for a country with sizeable capital-goods imports.

Let us now compare (1) foreign-currency indebtedness with a policy constraint to ensure debt stability and (2) fixed rates with domestic-currency borrowing. In (1), it will be remembered, economic policies were chosen with a view to stabilising the debt. If a foreign interest-rate shock increased the interest charge, a depreciation was required, entailing a levy on output and reducing consumption. In (2), any external interest-rate shock will affect demand and, as before, perfect capital mobility will promote the alignment of domestic rates on foreign rates. However, the effects on consumption here are direct, and consumption must be highly sensitive to foreign interest-rate changes if stability is to prevail. If the debt dynamics are unstable (the solvency condition is not met) and, at the same time, no use is made of exchange rates (fixed-rate scenario), then no economic policy goal can be attained.

We can summarise the findings of our analysis of the three models as follows:

- With an external debt in foreign currency, a Southern country can meet all its objectives, since it can freely determine its monetary and exchange-rate policies. However, the country may have considerable trouble stabilising its debt – that is, reaching solvency – since such stability depends solely on the effects of wealth on absorption. There seems little point in stabilising the exchange rate, since there is no risk premium or overshooting risk.

- With an external debt in domestic currency, a Southern country is more easily solvent if it is a heavy importer of capital goods. This is due to the link between debt, exchange rates and external equilibrium. If the market modernisation needed for foreign-currency borrowing ensures solvency, it will work to the country's advantage: by exposing the exchange rate and domestic interest rate to debt fluctuations, market modernisation will make consumption less vulnerable to shocks affecting domestic demand and world interest rates.

- In this solvency scenario, one can seriously envisage a constraint on monetary policy to avoid exchange-rate fluctuations. In particular, if export price-competitiveness is high, a stable exchange rate will make it easier to meet the solvency constraint owing to the induced link between external-debt level and prices. In principle, this stabilisation should also drive down the risk premiums, further facilitating solvency. If fixed rates allow the country to obtain dynamic debt stability, they will make its consumption less sensitive to exogenous domestic-demand shocks, but more sensitive to changes in foreign interest rates.

• If debt stability is obtained not spontaneously but through economic policy constraints, consumption behaviour will be very different if the debt is denominated in foreign currency or in domestic
currency with flexible rates: fixed rates in case of debt instability
should be avoided, since the authorities will forfeit all freedom
without compensatory gains. In a country that imports large
amounts of capital goods, consumption will probably be less sensitive both to demand shocks and – with flexible rates – to foreign
interest-rate shocks.

2.3   INDEBTEDNESS POLICIES OF SPAIN AND PORTUGAL

The models developed in Section 2.1 will help us to interpret Spain
and Portugal's debt policy options – which, it will be remembered,
are guided by (1) the solvency constraint and (2) the two countries'
room for manoeuvre in domestic economic policy. The Spanish and
Portuguese examples prove fruitful as they encompass all three models.

Financial-market isolation

Until 1984, the economies of Spain and Portugal resembled Model 1.
Their financial markets were isolated because of (1) severe restrictions on capital movements through currency controls; (2) the lack of
appeal of their domestic currencies for investors (as witnessed by the
absence during this period of a Euro-pesetas and Euro-escudos
market, and of Euro-bond or Euro-paper issues denominated in
these currencies). Spain and Portugal consequently enjoyed a distinct
measure of autonomy in the pursuit of their economic policy. Their
short-term management relied almost exclusively on exchange-rate
and monetary policies. The latter combined two elements: (1) the
management of interest rates – kept low by strict regulations, particularly in Portugal – to meet output and consumption targets; (2)
direct administrative curbs on bank-loan growth to meet the price
target.

Thanks to a policy of sliding exchange-rate depreciation against the
currencies of major partners, Spain and Portugal were able to maintain their competitiveness and therefore to check the growth of their
external debt, denominated exclusively in foreign currency (Table
A2.5, p. 33). This management of economic policy instruments,

which made it possible to attain growth and consumption targets in optimal conditions, soon came up against the problem of debt instability.

The levy on output that Portugal should normally have applied to stabilise its debt did not occur. The debt quickly soared to levels reflecting Portugal's total insolvency – $16.68 million in 1985, or 80.6 per cent of GDP. Spain faced the same problem. Its outstanding debt reached $29 million in 1984, although its insolvency was comparatively smaller at 20 per cent of GDP (Table A2.4, p. 33).

The debt explosion dealt a fatal blow to these countries' relative freedom of economic action. The authorities modified their economic policy. In particular, they constrained their monetary policy by raising interest rates and required-reserves ratios. To stabilise their debt, they applied very heavy pressure not only on private consumption but also on investment. This recessionary policy was successful, since the indebtedness ratio in both countries began to fall in 1984–5. However, the pressure became unbearable socially (Portugal's private consumption fell one point in 1983 and three points in 1984) and economically (disinvestment reached six points in Spain in 1984 and eighteen points in Portugal in 1984). As a result, the two countries altered their debt strategy by seeking external loans in domestic currencies – a less costly option in economic policy terms.

The opening of the financial markets

Spain and Portugal abandoned the policy of foreign-currency borrowings, which had become too costly owing to what lenders regarded as excessive indebtedness ratios. In the case of Portugal, creditors had even rationed their loans. The two countries turned to non-resident investment as a potential alternative source of external financing – a move equivalent to opting for domestic-currency borrowing (Table A2.3, p. 33). The spectacular increase in direct investments, and even more so in portfolio investments, was accompanied by a swift modernisation of financial markets beginning in 1984. Spain and Portugal made a far-reaching effort to revamp their stock exchanges, government-bond issue techniques, and banking systems. This increased the attractiveness to non-residents of assets denominated in local currency. In a related development, the two countries began to abolish currency regulations in 1985. The process, completed by 1987, promoted the necessary capital mobility.

Spain and Portugal's choice to borrow in their own currencies allowed them not only to meet the solvency conditions but also to regain a measure of domestic policy discretion, despite their abandonment of the exchange-rate weapon. Indeed, one can observe that solvency remains under control[1] even as investment, consumption and growth are recovering (see Table A2.1, p. 32). In keeping with the mechanisms described earlier, the endogenisation of the exchange rate has made it possible to dampen demand shocks[2] through positive changes in the escudo and peseta rates without undermining the solvency achieved earlier.

Currency appreciation allowed Spain and Portugal to adjust their current-account balances and hence to stabilise their external debt in 1984–7. In this connection, it should be recalled that the two countries' imports exhibited high demand elasticity – greater than 2 for Spain – and that their loss of price competitiveness was largely offset by their joining the EC. The policy of deliberately managed sliding depreciation was thus followed by a steady appreciation – in particular for the peseta – observable on the foreign-exchange market.[3]

The change in debt policy seemed to have enabled Spain and Portugal to solve the traumatic problem of debt (in the broad sense) while maintaining acceptable targets for growth, consumption and prices – a process to which world disinflation contributed. The loss of freedom in exchange-rate policy was therefore largely offset by the easier compliance with reasonable indebtedness ratios. In these circumstances, the two countries' choice to enter the EMS fixed-rate mechanism – that is, to adopt Model 3 – was not an obvious one. Indeed, by maintaining fixed rates, they seemed to be depriving themselves of their main resource for debt stabilisation and to stray from optimal economic targets.

The decision to join the EMS

The decision to join the EMS was justified by the fact that Spain and Portugal, since early 1988, had been facing a specific overshooting problem, of the type mentioned in our discussion of Model 3 above. Market modernisation and the lifting of regulatory barriers considerably increased capital mobility, allowing foreign capital to make quick, very short-term investments determined by yield projections. In practice, foreign investors expected an increased imbalance on the current account, as is normal in a heavy-growth period. They therefore regularly anticipated the demand for pesetas and escudos that would eventually be required to cover external financing needs.

These expectations were instantly realised on the foreign-exchange market, resulting in a steady appreciation of the exchange rate.

Thus, instead of damping exogenous shocks, as in the description of Model 2, the bullish pressures fuelled an internal demand made solvent by a massive inflow of speculative capital. This prevented the fulfilment of the price target and jeopardised monetary policy. The influx, particularly of short-term capital, caused a certain confusion among the authorities. This was reflected in the swings in official Central Bank intervention rates and in the rapid cycle of deregulation/reregulation, more visibly in Spain.

After an attempt to lower interest rates during the first half of 1988 to check the destabilising inrush of foreign capital, the monetary authorities had to contend with the sharp revival of inflation and resigned themselves to lifting the rates (in Spain, this occurred in August 1988). This monetary policy turnaround was not only highly penalising for growth and consumption; it also endangered the debt equilibrium by increasing the interest charge.

Moreover, the steady appreciation of the domestic currency – a positive development in an import-intensive foreign-trade structure – penalised exports heavily. But Spain and Portugal's Central Banks could not afford to cripple their countries' export-oriented industries. They were therefore obliged to take costly measures to sterilise a part of the capital inflows and thus curtail the appreciation of local currencies. These interventions led to a spectacular swelling of official reserves.[4]

The June 1988 reinstatement of restrictions on the inflow of short-term capital could serve only as a temporary measure to combat the destabilising overshooting. Indeed, it runs counter to the general European trend toward market deregulation and liberalisation. This sequence of events helps us to understand why Spain and Portugal decided to join the EMS. Although, by accepting fixed exchange rates, they will lose virtually all room for domestic policy manoeuvre, EMS membership should enable them to put their balance of payments on a sound footing. By entering the EMS, Spain and Portugal will rely no longer on a depreciation of their imports in real terms to solve their debt problem – a tactic that proved ineffective as it made domestic demand uncontrollable – but on their new-found export dynamism. In the short run, joining the EMS will undoubtedly entail a slowdown in private and public consumption. In the longer run, however, it ought to prove more satisfactory than the flexible exchange rate option.

Appendix: Figures for Spain and Portugal

Table A2.1   Gross domestic product and its components (% real change)

	1984	1985	1986	1987	1988
Spain					
Private consumption	0	2.4	3.6	5.5	4.5
Government consumption	2.8	4.6	5.7	8.7	5.0
Gross fixed-capital formation	−6.8	4.1	10	14.6	14
Exports of goods and services	11.7	2.8	1.3	5.9	6.3
Imports of goods and services	−1	6.2	16.5	20.4	15.2
GDP at market prices	1.8	2.3	3.3	5.5	5.0
Current-account balance					
($bn)	(2)	(2.5)	(3.9)	(0)	(−3.6)
Portugal					
Private consumption	3.0	1.0	7.0	6.8	6.5
Government consumption	2.5	1.7	1.0	2.0	3.8
Gross fixed-capital formation	−18.0	−3.0	9.5	20.2	15.5
Exports of goods and services	14.2	11.0	7.0	11.1	7.3
Imports of goods and services	−2.7	3.9	17.2	26.1	17.5
GDP at market prices	−1.6	3.3	4.3	4.7	4.1
Current-account balance					
($bn)	−0.6	0.4	1.1	0.4	−0.6

Source: OECD (1989).

Table A2.2   Capital-goods imports (% real change)

	1985	1986	1987	1988
Spain	13.6	18.1	39.3	29.1
Portugal	3.4	21.0	44.3	21.6

Source: OECD.

32

Table A2.3   Changes in external financing

	1984	1985	1986	1987	1988
Spain (bn pesetas)					
Long-term capital	506	−270	−224	1 283	1 257
of which: − investment	322	413	719	1 039	1 101
− loans	322	−470	−804	246	382
Portugal (bn escudos)					
Long term capital	196	199	−46	33	119
of which: − investment	25	36	23	44	90
− loans	181	166	−79	−76	−37

Sources: Banco de España; Banco de Portugal

Table A2.4   External debt

	1984	1985	1986	1987	1988
Spain					
Debt ($bn)	29.0	28.0	24.0	30.0	33.0
Debt/GDP (%)	19.4	15.6	10.1	10.1	9.5
Portugal					
Debt ($bn)	15.0	17.0	16.0	18.0	16.0
Debt/GDP (%)	90.4	+4.5	53.9	46.1	45.2

Sources: Banco de España; Banco de Portugal.

Table A2.5   External-debt components (% of total)

	Total ($bn)	US$ (%)	Y (%)	DM (%)	Ecu (%)	Domestic currency
Spain						
1985	28	46	13	12	5	2
1986	24	35	17	16	6	3
1987	30	33	16	17	7	4
1988	33	31	15	16	8	6
Portugal						
1985	17	59	12	7	6	−
1986	16	47	17	9	9	−
1987	18	40	19	10	12	−
1988	16	35	20	13	12	−

Sources: OECD, *Portugal* (1988); Banco de España.

Notes

* The findings presented in this paper are based on the resolution of a mathematical model. Space requirements prevented us from including the mathematical derivations of the model here, but we will be happy to provide them on request. Please write to: Patrick Artus, Head of the Department of Economic and Financial Analysis, and Claude Dupuy, Economist, Caisse des Dépôts et Consignations, 195 Boulevard Saint-Germain, 75007 Paris, France.
1. The decisive share of foreign investments in total external financing makes the debt/GDP ratio irrelevant as a yardstick of solvency. The external liabilities/GDP ratio published by Banco de España seems preferable (Table A2.4, p. 000).
2. Demand – negative in 1984 – grew at a real rate of 6.5 per cent and 8.9 per cent in Portugal and 5.2 per cent and 7.8 per cent in Spain in 1986 and 1987 respectively.
3. The escudo appreciated sharply against the dollar and achieved stability against European currencies.
4. Changes in official reserves ($billion).

Spain	*1985* (%)	*1986* (%)	*1987* (%)	*1988* (%)
	−1.9	2.7	14.2	9.7

References

Aschauer, D. (1989)   'Is public expenditure productive?' *Journal of Monetary Economics* (March) pp. 177–200.
Banco de España' *Boletin Estadistico*, various issues.
Banco de Portugal' *Quarterly Bulletin*, various issues.
Borenzstein, E. (1989)   'Fiscal policy and foreign debt', *Journal of International Economics* (February) pp. 53–75.
Brock, P. (1988)   'Investment, the current account and the relative price of non-traded goods in a small open economy', *Journal of International Economics* (May) pp. 235–53.
Buiter, W. (1986)   'Fiscal prerequisites for a viable managed exchange rate: A non-technical eclectic introduction', NBER Working Paper, no. 2041 (October).
Cohen, D. (1989)   'Monetary and fiscal policy in an open economy with or without coordination', *European Economic Review. Papers and Procedings* (March) pp. 303–9.
De Grauwe, P. (1989)   'The cost of disinflation and the European Monetary System', Working Paper, University of Leuven (April).

De Grauwe, P. (1986) 'Fiscal policies in the EMS: a strategic analysis', International Economics Research, Paper, no. 53, University of Leuven.

De Kock, G. and Grilli, V. (1989) 'Endogenous exchange-rate regime switches', paper given at the Deuxièmes Journées Franco-Américaines, Paris (June 21–22).

Dooley, P. and Isard, P. (1983) 'The portfolio balance model of exchange rates and some structural estimates of the risk premium', *IMF Staff Papers* (December) pp. 683–702.

Dornbusch, R. (1988) 'The EMS, the dollar and the yen', in Giavazzi, F., Micossi, S. and Miller, M. (eds), *The European Monetary System*, Cambridge, Cambridge University Press.

Drazen, A. (1989) 'Inflation tax revenue in open economies', in de Cecco, M. and Giovannini, A. (eds), *European Central Bank*, Cambridge, Cambridge University Press.

Feldstein, M. and Horioka, C. (1980) 'Domestic saving and international capital flows', *Economic Journal* (June) pp. 314–29.

Feldstein, M. (1983) 'Domestic saving and international capital movements in the long run and in the short run', *European Economic Review* (March–April) pp. 129–51.

Frenkel, J. and Razin, A. (1987) *Fiscal Policies and the World Economy*, Cambridge, Mass., MIT Press.

Giavazzi, F. and Giovannini, A. (1989) *Limiting Exchange Rate Flexibility: The European Monetary System*, Cambridge, Mass., MIT Press.

Giavazzi, F. and Pagano, M. (1988) 'The advantage of tying one's hands: EMS discipline and central bank credibility', *European Economic Review*, no. 32 (June) pp. 1055–74.

Golub, S. (1989) 'Foreign currency, government debt, asset markets and the balance of payments', *Journal of International Money and Finance* (June) pp. 285–90.

Hamada, K. (1985) *The Political Economy of International Monetary Interdependence*, Cambridge, Mass., MIT Press.

Hamada, K. and Iwata, K. (1989) 'On the international capital ownership pattern at the turn of the twenty-first century', *European Economic Review* (May) pp. 1055–85.

Hamilton, J. and Flavin, M. (1986) 'On the limitation of government borrowing: a framework for empirical testing', *American Economic Review*, vol. 48, pp. 201–12.

Kremers, J. (1989) 'US Federal indebtedness and the conduct of fiscal policy', *Journal of Monetary Economics* (March) pp. 219–38.

Melitz, J. (1988) 'Monetary discipline and cooperation in the EMS: a synthesis', CEPR Discussion Paper, no. 219 (January).

Murphy, R. (1986) 'Productivity shocks, non-traded goods and optimal capital accumulation', *European Economic Review* (October) pp. 1081–95.

Murphy, R. (1989) 'Stock prices, real exchange rates and optimal capital accumulation', *IMF Staff Papers*, March, pp. 102–29.

OECD (1988/1989) *Spain*, Etudes Economiques, Paris.

OECD (1988/1989) *Portugal*, Etudes Economiques, Paris.

3 Perfect Capital Mobility and the Italian Economy[1]

Giancarlo Gandolfo and Pier Carlo Padoan

3.1 INTRODUCTION

The problem of modelling capital liberalisation has not yet been satisfactorily solved in the theoretical literature, nor do suitable empirical studies exist for the industrialised world.

As regards economic theory, on the one hand we have the traditional Mundellian analysis (Mundell, 1963) of perfect capital mobility and its subsequent refinements, on the other the recent literature on foreign-exchange crises. For the reasons explained in Section 3.2, neither seems fully satisfactory for telling us what is going to happen in the macro-economic system when full liberalisation of capital movements is introduced. A related problem is how to model capital liberalisation as a dynamic process, in particular the transition from a situation of capital controls to a situation of perfect capital mobility. These theoretical problems will be examined in Section 3.2.

As regards empirical research, only limited empirical work is available on the effects of capital liberalisation on the macro-economic system. Most if not all of this research has been carried out in relation to the problems of the developing countries, where the issue of opening up the domestic economy to the world economy through the liberalisation of trade and capital movements has been of perennial concern to policy-makers in the developing world.

We are thus in the paradoxical situation that the empirical studies on the capital liberalisation problem are fairly advanced as regards developing countries and almost absent as regards the industrialised world. We plan to show in Sections 3.3 and 3.4 that our continuous time model of the Italian economy (Gandolfo and Padoan, 1987; 1990) is well suited for this study. In fact, given that international capital movements are modelled – according to the 'modern' or portfolio view – as the flow deriving from the adjustment of the actual to the desired stock of net foreign assets, one needs in the first place a

36

rigorous estimation of the relevant speed of adjustment independently of the time interval inherent in the data. This estimation can be obtained only through the continuous time approach to econometric modelling. In this context, capital liberalisation takes the form of an increase in the adjustment speed of net foreign assets to their (partial) equilibrium value, and the analysis is carried out at two levels. First, stability and sensitivity analysis about the steady state of the model identify a source of instability in the increase in this adjustment speed. Possible stabilising factors are also considered. In the second place, the systematic consequences of capital liberalisation are considered by carrying out a number of simulations and comparing the behaviour of the variables of the model with that obtained in the base run.

3.2 MODELLING PERFECT CAPITAL MOBILITY

As is well known, the Mundellian analysis examines the effectiveness of monetary and fiscal policy under fixed and flexible exchange rates and perfect capital mobility. Under fixed exchange rates, perfect capital mobility implies the ineffectiveness of monetary policy and the full effectiveness of fiscal policy, while the opposite is true under flexible exchange rates (ineffectiveness of fiscal policy and full effectiveness of monetary policy). These propositions are almost thirty years old, but subsequent studies have not added much to them (refinements include the distinction between perfect capital mobility and perfect asset substitutability, the reintroduction of some effectiveness of fiscal policy through changes in the real money supply due to exchange-rate changes, etc., see Gandolfo, 1987, para. 16.6).

The literature on the relationships between capital controls and crises of the foreign-exchange markets points out that, in a regime of fixed but adjustable parities, the removal of capital controls may give rise to speculative attacks capable of exhausting official reserves, thus forcing parity realignments. Besides, in the presence of perfect capital mobility, accommodating realignments (i.e., realignments that completely offset the cumulated loss of competitiveness) may give rise to undesirable oscillations in the exchange rate and to vicious-circle phenomena (see Wyplosz, 1986; Driffill, 1988; Obstfeld, 1988). This will increase the frequency of realignments and hence undermine the credibility of the exchange-rate arrangements. The conclusion is that one cannot rely solely on realignments of real exchange rates to eliminate external disequilibria. But, again, nothing is new under the sun: these problems and propositions are, in fact, well known to every student of the Bretton Woods system.

As regards empirical research, it is not possible to apply the results of the studies on developing countries to the problem that interests us, given the intrinsic differences between the two categories of countries. There is, however, one point that deserves attention in the literature on liberalisation in developing countries. This is the fact that a liberalisation of capital movements not accompanied by the full liberalisation of trade flows may destabilise the economic system (Khan and Zahler, 1983; 1985). This leads to an only apparently technical point – i.e., how to model capital controls (and liberalisation). In some cases (Wyplosz, 1986) capital controls are modelled so as to lead to zero capital outflows from residents, as only non-residents' capital movements are allowed. While this way of modelling capital controls partly reflects the Italian experience of asymmetric capital controls (where only capital inflows are freely allowed) – see, for example, Papadia and Vona, 1988; Papadia and Rossi, 1990 – it seems much too extreme especially if the case of developed countries is considered. More accurately, in our view, Khan and Zahler (1983; 1985) assume that, given an equation for capital movements where flows react to covered interest-rate differentials, controls are modelled through the introduction of a coefficient which takes on the value of zero (less than 1) in case of total (partial) controls. A more rigorous specification is the one followed by Gros (1987), who assumes that capital controls are equivalent to a (positive but not prohibitive) adjustment cost that markets have to bear in order to adjust their financial assets to the desired value whose amount does not depend on controls. Such a specification allows one to take into account two features of a world with capital controls: one that capital controls seldom, if at all, lead to a complete elimination of capital movements; the second that capital liberalisation can be clearly understood as an intrinsically dynamic process. In this respect, the view (Palmisani and Rossi, 1988) that capital controls, and any other kind of currency restriction, can be thought of as a tax on interest income, is not fully convincing. In fact, a tax on interest income changes the desired stock of net foreign assets since it alters the interest differential, but has no effect on the speed at which agents adjust the actual to the desired stock. We thus believe that the question of the speed of adjustment and the tax on interest income are two aspects that can coexist, but should be kept distinct.

This brief overview of the state of the art suggests that the study of the effects of the liberalisation of capital movements in an advanced open economy should be carried out along the following lines. (a) It should consider the dynamic nature of the process of adjustment towards a liberalised regime. Technically – as recalled in the general discussion above – this means that we should use dynamics and not comparative statics. (b) It should take account of the role of economic policy, and in particular of the behaviour of the monetary authorities as regards international reserves, exchange rates, etc. (c) It should consider the effects of the liberalisation on the whole economic system. This point has a twofold nature. On the one hand, it would be insufficient to consider only the effects on the foreign-exchange market. On the other, even if one were interested in examining solely the effects on the exchange rate, it should be noted that the liberalisation influences the foreign-exchange market not only directly but also indirectly through the changes in the macro-economic variables induced by the liberalisation. In short, the study should be carried out in the context of economy-wide dynamic macro-econometric models. But the existing models are not suited to this purpose (at least as regards Italy), partly because they do not contain an adequate modelling of capital movements and lack the technical possibility of embodying perfect capital mobility in a rigorous way. According to the modern or portfolio view, capital movements are not pure flows but represent the adjustment of the desired to the actual stock of net foreign assets. Now, the parameter representing the adjustment speed depends not only on the behaviour of economic agents but also on the presence of capital controls, and hence on an institutional arrangement – in the sense that a low adjustment speed is due to the fact that agents are not free immediately to adjust the actual to the desired stock of net foreign assets. To put the same concept in other words, the desired stock of NFA (net foreign assets) depends on fundamentals, the adjustment speed reflects institutional features such as capital controls.

3.3   THE MODEL AND THE CAPITAL MOVEMENT EQUATION

Our model (see Tables A3.1 and A3.2, pp. 54 and 58, for a summary view; for a full description see Gandolfo and Padoan, 1987; 1990) is a medium-term disequilibrium model specified and estimated in continuous time as a set of stochastic differential equations which stresses real and financial accumulation in an open and highly integrated economy. The Mark V version includes a detailed specification of the financial sector as well as the endogenous determination of the exchange rate. It considers stock-flow behaviour in an open economy in which both price and quantity adjustments take place. Stocks are introduced with reference to the real sector (where adjustments of fixed capital and inventories to their respective desired levels are present) and to the financial sector, which includes the stock of money, the stock of commercial credit, the stock of net foreign assets and the stock of international reserves. The exchange rate is endogenously determined in the exchange market, which clears instantaneously. Since we do not promote any one of the competing theories but believe in an eclectic approach, exchange-rate determination is thus related to all the variables present in the model, including policy variables. Policy-reaction functions cover fiscal variables (government expenditure and taxes) and financial variables such as the interest rate, money supply and international reserves.

Let us take a closer look at the equation which most interests us in the present context, namely the capital movements equation, which is specified as follows:

$$DlogNFA = \alpha_{24}log(N\hat{F}A/NFA) + \alpha_{25}log(PMGS_f$$
$$\cdot E \cdot MGS/PXGS \cdot XGS), \quad \alpha_{25} < 0 \qquad (1)$$

where:

$$N\hat{F}A = \gamma_{11}e^{\beta_{19}[i_f + log(FR/E) - i_{TIT}]}(PY)^{\beta_{20}}(PF_f \cdot E \cdot YF)^{-\beta_{21}}$$

Equation 1 has a twofold nature. First of all, the stock of net foreign assets (*NFA*) adjusts to its desired value $N\hat{F}A$. The latter reflects the portfolio view, in which the scale variables are proxied by the domestic (*PY*) and foreign ($PF_f \cdot E \cdot YF$) money incomes. Given the scale variables the level of $N\hat{F}A$ is determined by the interest-differential term corrected for exchange-rate expectations; these are proxied by the ratio of the forward to the spot exchange rate (*FR/E*) for a discussion of this way of modelling expectations, see Gandolfo and Padoan (1987, para. 2.2.3).

The second element in equation (1) refers to capital movements which are not strictly related to portfolio considerations, but rather to trade flows. The ratio of the value of imports to the value of exports is meant to capture the effect of commercial credits on the capital account. A trade deficit – i.e., $(PMGS_f \cdot E \cdot MGS/PXGS \cdot XGS) > 1$; hence log $(\#) > 0$ – is partly financed through commercial credits from abroad, hence an increase in foreign liabilities $(DlogNFA < 0)$.

3.4 CAPITAL LIBERALISATION

The transition to a regime with higher capital mobility is equivalent, in our model, to an increase in α_{24}, the adjustment speed of net foreign assets to their desired value. The effect of an increase in this parameter on the dynamic properties of the model can be ascertained through sensitivity analysis. By 'sensitivity analysis', we here mean the analysis of the effects of changes in the parameters on the characteristic roots of the model. This can be performed in a general way by computing the partial derivatives of these roots with respect to the parameters. If we call A the matrix of the linear approximation of the original non-linear system, we can compute $\partial\mu_i/\partial A$, where μ_i denotes the ith characteristic root of A. Now, the partial derivative of one real root with respect to α_{24} is positive and very large in relative terms, which implies that the model becomes unstable for sufficiently high capital mobility. This is a worrying result, but sensitivity analysis indicates some possible stabilising effects. Both an increase in α_5 (the adjustment speed of imports) and an increase in α_8 (the adjustment speed of exports) has a stabilising effect on the same root. The implication seems to be that the destabilising impact of an increase in capital mobility can be counteracted by an increase in goods mobility: when one frees capital movements one must also have free trade in goods and services. This interesting result confirms some of the insights of the literature on the order of liberalisation mentioned in Section 3.2. A stabilising effect is also displayed by an increase in δ_8, a parameter present in the monetary authorities' reaction function (see equation (16) in Table A3.1, p. 54). This parameter can be interpreted as the weight that the monetary authorities give to the discrepancy between the desired and the actual stock of international reserves when they decide the intensity of their intervention in the foreign-exchange market.

Further indications on the effects of higher capital mobility can be obtained by comparing the behaviour of the model in its basic estimated version (base run or control solution) with that of versions in which some of the parameters have been altered as a consequence of capital liberalisation. These exercises have been performed by using the original non-linear model. In fact, since the parameters being estimated are those of the original non-linear differential model, this non-linear model and not the linear approximation can be used for simulation. The starting point was the first quarter of 1980 in order to have, in principle, five years of in-sample behaviour for comparison. The spirit of the exercise is to 'rerun history', asking ourselves what would have happened if capital movements had been liberalised at that point in time and, hopefully, gathering further information on the adjustment of the Italian economy, as described by our model, to a new institutional regime. Thus point still requires investigation.

The transition to a regime with higher capital mobility has been simulated by imposing an increase in α_{24} (the adjustment speed of net foreign assets to their desired value)[2] and eliminating capital controls from the equation of real imports[3] of goods and services. The value of α_{24} has been set to 90 (i.e., a mean time lag of one day, an assumption of (almost) perfect capital mobility or of 'full' capital liberalisation). It should, however, be noted that the results are qualitatively the same (i.e., the model becomes unstable) even with much lower values of α_{24}: in fact, the bifurcation value of this parameter is about 0.20 (the estimated value is about 0.10). The difference is in the magnitude of the effects only, not in the direction. It should also be stressed, from the purely theoretical point of view, that a very great (let us suppose infinite) speed of adjustment of the net foreign asset position does *not* mean an infinite flow of capital (which, if true, might threaten the non-negativity of the reserves, as pointed out in the Conference discussion). An infinite speed of adjustment, in fact, simply means that economic agents are allowed (and able) to adjust the actual to the desired stock of net foreign assets immediately. The amount of the ensuing capital flow will be equal to the difference between NFA and $N\hat{F}A$, and this difference is finite because $N\hat{F}A$, according to the portfolio view, is a finite amount, as determined by equation (12.1) in Table A3.1, p. 54.

A related problem is that of exchange-rate expectations: the role of these expectations is, in fact, crucial for the onset of possible de-stabilising speculative capital flows. We also considered different hypotheses about the formation of exchange-rate expectations. The literature on foreign-exchange speculation and expectations is enormous, so we decided to consider, in addition to those included in the estimated version of the model, only two other types of expecta-

:ions: extrapolative and 'normal' or 'regressive'. The former simply mean that, if a change has taken place, a further change in the same direction is expected; as regards the latter, they imply that economic agents have an idea of a normal, long-run value of the variable under consideration so that, whenever the current value is different from the normal one, they expect that the current value will sooner or later move towards (or 'regress' to) the normal one. It seems also plausible to assume the PPP value as the long-run normal exchange rate, because the model possesses a steady-state path on which the exchange rate is at its PPP value (see Gandolfo and Padoan, 1990). Hence rational agents, who know the model (and the fact that its steady state is stable) have this normal value in mind.

It is fairly obvious that extrapolative expectations are bound to have a destabilising effect whereas normal expectations will have a stabilising effect. The reason for considering these two types of expectations is related to the argument put forward by Frankel (1988). From surveys of the forecasts of the agents operating in the foreign-exchange market, Frankel concludes that those who forecast at shorter horizons display destabilising expectations because they tend to extrapolate recent trends, while those who operate with relatively longer horizons tend to have regressive, or stabilising, expectations. The reasons for this differing behaviour are to be seen, according to Frankel, in the fact that short-term traders in the foreign-exchange market have to show to their superiors (typically, bank executives) that they are able to make profits over a much shorter time period than that over which the performance of longer-term traders is evaluated. Independently of the reason, we believe that Frankel's distinction is correct, since it corresponds to the distinction between 'occasional' and 'permanent' speculators introduced by Cutilli and Gandolfo (1963; 1972; 1973).

In the light of this distinction, the argument in favour of a Tobin tax on all capital flows (so as to avoid the practical enforcement problem of trying to distinguish between foreign-exchange purchases for 'speculative' purposes and purchases for the purpose of longer-term investments) seems to receive new support. Such a tax, in fact, would not be much of a deterrent to anyone contemplating the purchase of a foreign security for longer-term investing, but it might discourage the spot trader who is now accustomed to buying foreign exchange with the intention of selling it a few hours later. As Frankel notes (1988, p. 184), there has been little if any attempt to appraise the Tobin proposal in the context of an appropriate macro-economic model. This is particularly true of Italy, where the Tobin tax has been

advocated by various authors (see, for example, Basevi and Cavazzuti, 1985) without much empirical support.

The Tobin tax on capital flows is a tax on the relevant foreign-
exchange transactions, but it can be translated into an equivalent tax
on interest income. It is, in fact, equivalent either to a tax on
foreign-interest income at a rate which is an increasing function of the
Tobin tax rate θ, or to a *negative* tax (i.e., a positive subsidy) on
domestic-interest income at a rate which is an increasing function of
θ. To show this, let us consider the standard method of determining
the relative profitability (including the gains due to expected changes
in the exchange rate) of placing funds abroad or at home. This
amounts to comparing $(1/E)(1+i_f)\bar{E}$ with $(1+i_h)$, where the interest
rates and $\bar{E}$ (the expected exchange rate) are referred to the same
time interval. Let us now introduce a tax at the unit rate θ (to be paid
in domestic currency) on both the amount of domestic currency
transferred abroad and the amount that will be repatriated (principal
plus interest) at the end of the relevant period. The first term of the
comparison then becomes

$$[(1-\theta)(1+\theta)^{-1} / E](1+i_f)\bar{E}$$

By simple manipulations[4] one obtains that the relevant interest
differential is

$$[(1-\theta)i_f - 2\theta](1+\theta)^{-1} - i_h$$

or, equivalently,

$$i_f - [2\theta+(1+\theta)i_h](1-\theta)^{-1}$$

It is then easy to simulate the introduction of a Tobin tax in our
model, by appropriately modifying the interest differential that appears in the definition of $N\hat{F}A$ (see Section 3.3).

3.5   ALTERNATIVE DYNAMIC BEHAVIOURS

The basic case

In this simulation we will consider the expectation formulation used
in the original (i.e., estimated) version of the model. The main result

of this simulation is that, after a period of apparently stable behaviour, the dynamic path of some of the variables, notably the exchange rate, assumes an explosive behaviour. We may distinguish between an impact effect and an adjustment mechanism (see Figure 3.1, where only the results relative to a selection of endogenous variables of the model are reported). The increase in α_{24} leads to an immediate increase in *NFA* which causes an appreciation of the exchange rate E (impact effect). This is a well-known effect in portfolio models (see Gandolfo, 1987, Section 18.8.3.3). The change in E, in turn, leads to a decrease in the interest rate (i_{TIT}) and to an increase in the level of international reserves (R). This is the consequence of the 'leaning against the wind' components present in both equations, according to which the interest rate increases (decreases) and international reserves decrease (increase) when the change in the exchange rate $(DlogE)$ is positive (negative). Finally the improvement of the terms of trade associated with the decrease in E produces an improvement in the current account. From this point onwards, a reaction mechanism involving mainly the interest rate and the level of international reserves is set in motion.

The level of R is now too high with respect to its target value which is a function of the value of imports (now lower because of the appreciation of the exchange rate). As as consequence the level of reserves tends to decrease. The level of the interest rate, on the contrary, is pushed upwards by the appreciation of the spot exchange rate relative to the forward rate which increases the target value of i_{TIT}, and the monetary squeeze caused by the decrease in international reserves through the money-supply equation. The increase in i_{TIT} leads to a decrease in the accumulation of net foreign assets.

The decrease in *NFA* pushes towards the depreciation of the exchange rate. This effect is partially offset by the behaviour of the current account (which is improving). At this stage, the economy is apparently following a stable path characterised by a lower exchange rate and a higher interest rate. One important real effect is the relatively lower level of fixed investment produced by the tighter monetary and credit conditions. After about three years, however, the pressure for a higher exchange rate overwhelms the opposing forces. The exchange rate starts a depreciating movement which soon becomes explosive.

The results confirm the widespread view that a decrease in capital controls leads initially to a higher stock of net foreign assets; they seem to confirm also the widespread notion that the economy can be

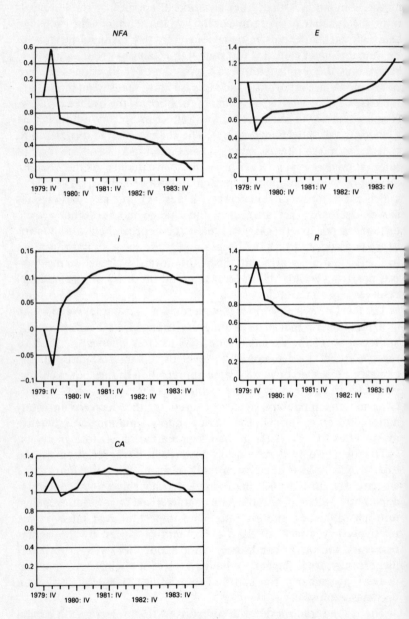

Figure 3.1   The basic case (simulated/base run; simulated-base as regards *i*)

managed to keep on a relatively stable path if appropriate interest-rate and exchange-rate intervention policies are adopted. But this latter notion, though valid for a few years, is no longer valid in the long run. What this exercise shows, in fact, is that the new regime leads to the build-up of market pressures concentrating on the exchange rate, which eventually become unsustainable.

One of the reasons why the model has eventually exploded in the previous simulation is the modelling of exchange-rate expectations which are represented by the ratio of the forward to the spot exchange rate. The forward rate was kept exogenous in the previous simulation, and this fact might have somewhat distorted the results of the exercise.

Different ways out were available, including the possibility of introducing a new equation for the endogenous determination of the forward exchange rate. We decided to adopt another solution, which has the advantage of minimising changes in the structure of the model. Exchange-rate expectations were modelled in two alternative ways to capture the role of 'short-term' and 'long-term' traders respectively (see Section 3.4). In the first case expectations were given an extrapolative formulation, while in the second they were modelled assuming that traders operated according to a 'normal' or 'long-run' expected exchange rate. In both cases, we experimented with alternative runs with and without the introduction of a Tobin tax on capital movements.

Extrapolative expectations

The expected proportional change in the exchange rate is given by $\delta_E D\log E$, $\delta_E > 0$. This coefficient was given values ranging from 0.1 to 1.0. In all cases the model produced an explosive (devaluationary) behaviour of the exchange rate which developed after very few quarters (no more than four). The other variables followed a behaviour quite similar to that observed in the previous simulation. The introduction of a Tobin tax was modelled by multiplying the foreign-interest rate, i_f, by a term $(1-t)$, with $t = 0.3$. This is equivalent to assuming a Tobin tax rate θ approximately equal to 1.6 per cent[5], a large value if one recalls that θ is applied to the principal and on both the outflow and the inflow. This value was chosen after several runs with alternative values of t had shown that, in order to obtain relevant results, t (and hence θ) had to be large. The introduction of the Tobin tax, however, improved the behaviour of the model only slightly. What happened is that the explosive behaviour of the exchange rate developed from two to three quarters later with respect to the cases without the introduction of the tax.

Normal expectations

In this set of simulations the exchange-rate expectations were modelled assuming that traders formed an idea of the 'normal' or 'long-run' exchange rate based on the 'fundamentals' of the system (relative prices). Accordingly, the expected proportional change in the exchange rate was proxied by the log of the ratio of the 'normal' to the spot exchange rate, $\log(\hat{E}/E)$, where $\hat{E} = PXGS/PF_f$ is the ratio of domestic export prices to foreign competitors' export prices in foreign currency (i.e., the exchange rate necessary to maintain price competitiveness). This way of modelling expectations also takes into account the fact that, in the model, monetary authorities adjust international reserves (i.e., intervene in the foreign-exchange market) considering price competitiveness in addition to other targets (see Gandolfo and Padoan, 1990). Normal exchange-rate expectations were introduced in the form $\delta_E \log(\hat{E}/E)$, where δ_E was given a set of values ranging from 0.1 to 1.0. However in what follows we will present only the case of $\delta_E = 1.0$ since the dynamic behaviour of this set of simulations does not change in its main characteristics with a change in the value of δ_E. The following cases also include a change in the value of the parameter δ_8 (i.e., the parameter associated with the desired value of international reserves in the monetary authorities' reaction function), whose value was set to 1.0 (while its estimated value was 0.282). This change, as recalled above, is suggested by sensitivity analysis (see Section 3.4), which indicates that an increase in δ_8 has a stabilising effect on the system. The results of the simulation run are summarised in Figure 3.2.

As in the basic case we can distinguish between an impact effect and an adjustment mechanism. As in the basic case the increase in α_{24} leads to an immediate increase in *NFA* which causes an appreciation of the exchange rate and, consequently, a decrease in i_{TIT}, an increase in the level of international reserves, and an improvement of the trade balance due to better terms of trade. From this moment onwards, the adjustment mechanism develops quite differently from the basic case. The level of international reserves adjusts to a lower desired value determined by the lower value of imports which results from the decrease in E. The higher value of δ_8 strengthens this effect,

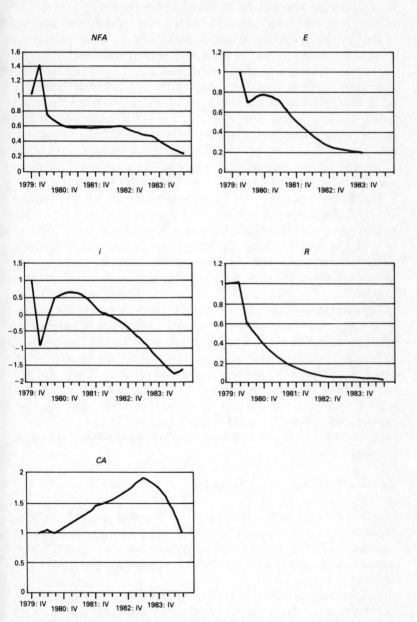

Figure 3.2   Normal expectations (simulated/base run; simulated-base as regards *i*)

thus producing a lower level of R with respect to the basic case. The interest rate is initially higher than the control solution but, contrary to the basic case, it begins taking on lower values after nine quarters. This is the consequence of the fact that long-term exchange-rate expectations indicate an appreciation thanks to the 'virtuous' interaction between the decrease in the spot exchange rate and the decline in domestic prices (and hence in export prices); consequently the target value of i_{TIT} decreases. The initial increase in i_{TIT} leads to a decrease in net foreign assets which continues till the end of the simulation, also as a consequence of the behaviour of exchange-rate expectations. The current account improves, mainly thanks to the improvement in the terms of trade, for more than twelve quarters.

The forces sustaining this apparently stable path begin to lose strength after three years. While the exchange rate keeps appreciating, a pressure towards depreciation develops both from the decrease in *NFA* and from the change in the behaviour of the current account, which starts to deteriorate. After nineteen quarters the exchange rate inverts its course, and starts a depreciating movement which becomes explosive.

The main lesson from this exercise is that the formation of expectations is crucial in determining the dynamic behaviour of the system. The assumption of 'normal' or 'long-run' expectations has dramatically improved the ability of the system to bear the impact of full capital liberalisation with respect to the case of extrapolative expectations. However this was not enough to avoid a final collapse. In this respect what this exercise has shown is that while exchange-rate expectations based on 'fundamentals' (relative prices) do exert a stabilising effect, they cannot fully offset the destabilising effects of financial transactions.

Normal expectations and a Tobin tax

This final exercise replicates the previous one with the addition of a Tobin tax taking on the same value as in the case with extrapolative expectations (about 1.6 per cent, corresponding to a tax of 30 per cent on foreign interest income on a yearly basis). The results are reported in Figure 3.3.
The most relevant result is that the system now follows a stable path throughout the simulation period. In this case, too, we can distinguish between an impact effect and an adjustment mechanism. The impact effect is similar to the previous one, showing an increase

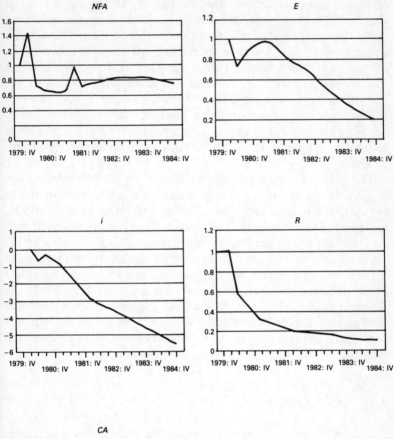

Figure 3.3   Normal expectations and Tobin tax (simulated/base run; simulated-base as regards *i*)

in *NFA* and an appreciation of the exchange rate. The interest rate,
however, decreases steadily over the period. This is due to the fact
that the Tobin tax lowers the target value for the domestic interest
rate. The total effect of the Tobin tax is such that the interest rate
differential is, compared to the previous simulations, in favour of the
foreign rate. This determines a relatively higher accumulation of net
foreign assets (which is, nonetheless, lower with respect to the
control solution). The important element, however, is that, contrary
to the previous simulations, the level of *NFA* fluctuates mildly
around a stable value, rather than decreasing steadily. The exchange
rate tends to appreciate under the pressure of an improving current
account.

The main message from this final exercise is that the introduction
of a Tobin tax provides a crucial contribution to the stabilisation of
the system with full capital liberalisation and exchange-rate expectations geared to relative prices. However, there is more to it than that.
A Tobin tax allows the system to operate with a lower level of the
domestic interest rate, as it makes the constraint represented by the
foreign rate less stringent. This obviously gives more room for
domestic financial policy in terms of (for example) financing of the
domestic public debt, an issue which is of paramount importance for
the Italian economy. The counter-argument for such a tax is that if
not all countries adopted it, then the business would simply go to the
financial centres where the tax was not present.

3.6   CONCLUSION

The main message of this paper is that the effects of perfect capital
mobility ought to be examined in the context of suitable economy-
wide macro-econometric models, where we have suggested a precise
way of modelling capital liberalisation and related questions (such as
a Tobin tax). The results of simulation exercises carried out by means
of our continuous time model of the Italian economy have given
interesting insights in to this issue, which can be summarised as
follows.

First of all, capital liberalisation *alone* has a destabilising effect on
the economy. Secondly, both exchange-rate expectations and a
Tobin tax have a crucial role to play. In fact, the destabilising effects
of capital liberalisation can be *partially* counteracted by a Tobin tax
or by introducing stabilising exchange-rate expectations. These two

measures, however, are not sufficient when considered separately. They turn out to be synergic, in the sense that each alone is *not* able to avoid the final collapse of the system but both together succeed in enabling the economy to bear the impact of full capital liberalisation while remaining on a stable growth path.

Appendix: The Model

Table A3.1   Equations of the model

Private consumption

$$DlogC = \alpha_1 log(\hat{C}/C) + \alpha_2 log\,(M/M_d) \tag{1}$$

where

$$\hat{C} = \gamma_1\, e^{\beta_1 DlogY}\, (P/PMGS_f \cdot E)^{\beta_2}\, (Y-T/P),\ \beta_1 \lessgtr 0,\ \beta_2 \gtreqless 0;$$
$$M_d = \gamma_2\, e^{-\beta_3 i\, TIT}\, P^{\beta_4}\, Y^{\beta_5},\ \beta_3 \geq 0 \tag{1.1}$$

Rate of growth in fixed capital stock

$$Dk = \alpha_3\, [\alpha' log(\hat{K}/K) - k] + \alpha_4 Da \tag{2}$$

where

$$\hat{K} = \gamma_3 \tilde{Y}, \qquad \gamma_3 = \varkappa/u \tag{2.1}$$

Expected output

$$Dlog\tilde{Y} = \eta log(\tilde{Y}/Y) \tag{3}$$

Imports

$$DlogMGS = \alpha_5\, log(M\hat{G}S/MGS) + \alpha_6\, log(\hat{V}/V) + \alpha_7\, PCC \tag{4}$$

where

$$M\hat{G}S = \gamma_4 P^{\beta_6}\, (PMGS_f \cdot E)^{-\beta_7}\, Y^{\beta_8} \qquad \hat{V} = \gamma_5 \tilde{Y} \tag{4.1}$$

Exports

$$DlogXGS = \alpha_8\, log(X\hat{G}S/XGS) - \alpha_9 Da \tag{5}$$

where

$$X\hat{G}S = \gamma_6\, (PXGS/PF_f \cdot E)^{-\beta_9} YF^{\beta_{10}}\, (\gamma_3 Y/K)^{-\beta_{11}} \tag{5.1}$$

Output

$$DlogY = \alpha_{10}\, log(\tilde{Y}/Y) + \alpha_{11}\, log(\hat{V}/V) \tag{6}$$

Price of output

54

$$D\log P = \alpha_{12} \log(\hat{P}/P) + \alpha_{13}Dm + \alpha_{14} \log(M/M_d) \tag{7}$$

where

$$\hat{P} = \gamma_7 (PMGS_f \cdot E)^{\beta_{12}}W^{\beta_{13}}PROD^{-\beta_{14}} \tag{7.1}$$

Price of exports

$$D\log PXGS = \alpha_{15} \log(P\hat{X}GS/PXGS) \tag{8}$$

where

$$P\hat{X}GS = \gamma_8 P^{\beta_{15}}(PF_f \cdot E)^{\beta_{16}} \tag{8.1}$$

Money wage rate

$$D\log W = \alpha_{16}\log(\hat{W}/W) \tag{9}$$

where

$$\hat{W} = \gamma_9 P^{\beta_{17}}e^{\lambda_4 t} \tag{9.1}$$

Interest rate

$$Di_{TIT} = \alpha_{17}\log(M_d/M) + \alpha_{18}[i_f + \log(FR/E) - i_{TIT}]$$
$$+ \alpha_{19} D\log E + \alpha_{20}Dr + \alpha_{21}Dh \tag{10}$$

Bank advances

$$D\log A = \alpha_{22}\log(\hat{A}/A) + \alpha_{23}Dk, \qquad \alpha_{23} \gtrless 0 \tag{11}$$

where

$$\hat{A} = \gamma_{10}e^{\beta_{18}i_{TIT}}M, \qquad \beta_{18} \gtrless 0 \tag{11.1}$$

Net foreign assets

$$D\log NFA = \alpha_{24}\log(N\hat{F}A/NFA) +$$
$$\alpha_{25}\log(PMGS_f \cdot E \cdot MGS/PXGS \cdot XGS) \qquad \alpha_{25}<0 \tag{12}$$

where

$$N\hat{F}A = \gamma_{11}e^{\beta_{19}[i_f+\log(FR/E)-i_{TIT}]} (PY)^{\beta_{20}}(PF_f \cdot E \cdot YF)^{-\beta_{21}} \tag{12.1}$$

Monetary authorities' reaction function on money supply

$$Dm = \alpha_{26}(\hat{m}-m) + \delta_3 Dh + \delta_4 Dr \tag{13}$$

where

$$\hat{m} = m^* + \{\delta_1[D\log(PY)-(\varrho_P+\varrho_Y)]$$

$$+ \delta_2 Di_{TIT}\}\qquad \delta_1 \gtrless 0,\quad \delta_2 \gtrless 0 \tag{13.1}$$

Taxes

$$D\log T = \alpha_{27}\log(\hat{T}/T) \tag{14}$$

where

$$\hat{T} = \gamma_{14}(PY)^{\beta_{22}} \tag{14.1}$$

Public expenditure

$$D\log G = \alpha_{28}\log(\gamma_{13}Y/G) + \alpha_{29}D\log Y \qquad \alpha_{29} \gtrless 0 \tag{15}$$

Monetary authorities' reaction function on international reserves

$$D\log R = b\delta_5\log(E_c/E) + (1-b)\delta_6\log(\hat{E}/E) - \delta_7 D\log E$$
$$+ \delta_8\log(\hat{R}/R) \tag{16}$$

where

$$\hat{E} = PXGS/\gamma_{14}PF_f, \hat{R} = \gamma_{15}PMGS_f \cdot E \cdot MGS$$

$$b= \begin{cases} 1 \text{ under fixed exchange rates} \\ 0 \text{ under floating exchange rates} \end{cases}$$

Inventories

$$DV = Y + MGS - C - DK - XGS - G \tag{17}$$

Fixed capital stock

$$D\log K = k \tag{18}$$

Rate of growth in money supply

$$m = D\log M \tag{19}$$

Public sector's borrowing requirement

$$DH = PG - T \tag{20}$$

Rate of growth in international reserves

$$r = D\log R \tag{21}$$

Rate of growth in bank advances

$$a = D\log A \tag{22}$$

Rate of growth in H

$$h = D\log H \tag{23}$$

Balance of payments

$$PXGS \cdot XGS - PMGS_f \cdot E \cdot MGS + (UT_a - UT_p) - DNFA - DR = O \tag{24}$$

Table A3.2   Variables of the model

	Endogenous
A	Nominal stock of bank advances
a	Proportional rate of growth of A
C	Private consumption expenditure in real terms
E	Lira–dollar spot exchange rate
G	Public expenditure in real terms
H	Public-sector borrowing requirement
h	Proportional rate of change of H
i_{TIT}	Domestic nominal interest rate
K	Stock of fixed capital in real terms
k	Proportional rate of change of K
M	Nominal stock of money (M2)
m	Proportional rate of change of M
MGS	Imports of goods and services in real terms
NFA	Nominal stock of net foreign assets
P	Domestic price level
$PXGS$	Export price level
R	Nominal stock of international reserves
r	Proportional rate of change of R
T	Nominal taxes
V	Stock of inventories in real terms
W	Money wage rate
XGS	Exports of goods and services in real terms
$\underline{Y}$	Real net domestic product and income
Y	Expected real net domestic product and income

	Exogenous
E_c	Official lira–dollar parity under fixed exchange rates
FR	Forward exchange rate
i_f	Foreign nominal interest rate
PCC	Permanent capital controls
PF_f	Foreign competitors' export price level (in foreign currency)
$PMGS_f$	Import price level (in foreign currency)
$PROD$	Labour productivity
t	Time
$(UT_a - UT_p)$	Net unilateral transfers, in nominal terms
YF	Real world income

Giancarlo Gandolfo and Pier Carlo Padoan 59

Notes

1. Financial support from the University of Rome 'La Sapienza' and the Ministry of the Universities and of Scientific and Technological Research is gratefully acknowledged.
2. This procedure is similar to that followed (though in a different context) by Jonson, McKibbin and Trevor (1982) in their continuous time model of the Australian economy.
3. The introduction of capital control variables in the equation for real imports reflected an attempt to account for clandestine capital movements. An earlier study (Gandolfo, 1977) found significant empirical evidence for this phenomenon in the Italian economy on the import side. Clandestine outflows are presumably positively related to controls in international capital movements.

4. With perfect capital mobility, the relation

$$[(1-\theta)(1+\theta)^{-1}/E](1+i_f)\bar{E} = (1+i_h)$$

should hold. If we multiply both members by

$$(1+i_f)^{-1}(1+\theta)/(1-\theta)$$

and subtract 1, we obtain

$$[(1+\theta)(1+i_h) - (1-\theta)(1+i_f)]/[(1-\theta)(1+i_f)] = (\bar{E}-E)/E$$

By manipulating the left-hand side and neglecting, as is usually done, the denominator, we obtain

$$i_h - [(1-\theta)i_f-2\theta](1+\theta)^{-1} = (\bar{E}-E)/E$$

or, equivalently,

$$[2\theta+(1+\theta)i_h](1-\theta)^{-1} - i_f = (\bar{E}-E)/E$$

In the absence of the tax, the relation would be

$$i_h - i_f = (\bar{E}-E)/E$$

In both cases, the presence of a risk premium explains why the equality does not hold even with perfect capital mobility.
5. The relationship between θ and t is given by

$$[(1-\theta)i_f-2\theta)]/(1+\theta) = (1-t)i_f$$

With a value of i_f around 12 per cent – 13 per cent per annum in the simulation period, this gives a value of θ around 1.6 per cent for $t = 30$ per cent.

60   *Perfect Capital Mobility: the Italian Economy*

References

Basevi, G. and Cavazzuti, F. (1985) 'Regole del gioco o discrezionalità amministrativa? Il caso della libertà di movimento dei capitali in Italia', *Political Economica* (April).
Cutilli, B. and Gandolfo, G. (1963) 'The Role of Commercial Banks in Foreign Exchange Speculation', *Banca Nazionale del Lavoro Quarterly Review* (June).
Cutilli, B. and Gandolfo, G. (1972) 'Wider Band and "Oscillating" Exchange Rates', *Economic Notes* (January–April).
Cutilli, B. and Gandolfo, G. (1973) *Un contributo alla teoria della speculazione in regime di cambi oscillanti* (Rome: Ente per gli studi monetari bancari e finanziari Luigi Einaudi, Quaderno di Ricerche, no. 10).
Driffill, J. (1988) 'The Stability and Sustainability of the European Monetary System with Perfect Capital Markets', in Giavazzi, F., Micossi, S. and Miller, M. (eds), *The European Monetary System*, Cambridge: Cambridge University Press.
Frankel, J.A. (1988) 'International Capital Mobility and Exchange Rate Volatility', in Fieleke, N.S. (ed.), *International Payments Imbalances in the 1980s*, Boston: Federal Reserve Bank of Boston Conference Series, no. 32, pp. 162–88.
Gandolfo, G. (1977) 'Esportazioni clandestine di capitali e sovrafatturazione delle importazioni', *Rassegna Economica* (November–December)
Gandolfo, G. (1981) *Qualitative Analysis and Econometric Estimation of Continuous Time Dynamic Models*, Amsterdam, North-Holland.
Gandolfo, G. (1987) *International Economics II*, Berlin: Springer-Verlag.
Gandolfo, G. and Padoan, Pier Carlo (1987) *The Mark V Version of the Italian Continuous Time Model*, Siena, Quaderni dell'Istituto di Economia, no. 70, Università di Siena.
Gandolfo, G. and Padoan, Pier Carlo (1989) 'Continuous Time Econometric Modelling and the Issue of Capital Liberalization', in Phillips, P.C.B. and Hall, V.B. (eds), *Models, Methods and Applications of Econometrics*, London: Basil Blackwell.
Gandolfo, G. and Padoan, Pier Carlo (1990) 'The Italian Continuous Time Model: Theory and Empirical Results', *Economic Modelling* (April).
Gros, D. (1987) 'The Effectiveness of Capital Controls', *IMF Staff Papers* (June).
Jonson, P.D., McKibbin, W.J. and Trevor, R.G. (1982) 'Exchange Rates and Capital Flows: A Sensitivity Analysis', *Canadian Journal of Economics* (November).
Khan, M. and Zahler, R. (1983) 'The Macroeconomic Effects of Changes in Barriers to Trade and Capital Flows: A Simulation Analysis', *IMF Staff Papers* (June).
Khan, M. and Zahler, R. (1985) 'Trade and Financial Liberalization Given External Shocks and Inconsistent Domestic Policies', *IMF Staff Papers* (March).
Mundell, R.A. (1963) 'Capital Mobility and Stabilization Policy Under Fixed and Flexible Exchange Rates', *Canadian Journal of Economics and Political Science* (November).

Obstfeld, M. (1988)   'Competitiveness, Realignments and Speculation: The Role of Financial Markets', in Giavazzi, F., Micossi, S. and Miller, M. (eds), *The European Monetary System*, Cambridge: Cambridge University Press.

Palmisani, F. and Rossi, S. (1988)   'Aspetti macroeconomici dei controlli valutari. Il caso italiano', *Note Economiche*, no. 3.

Papadia, F. and Rossi, S. (1990)   'Are Asymmetric Exchange Controls Effective?', Banca d'Italia, *Temi di discussione del Servizio Studi*, no. 131.

Papadia, F. and Vona, S. (1988)   'Exchange Rate Management and Monetary Policy: Issues Raised by the Italian Experience', in Bank for International Settlements, *Exchange Market Intervention and Monetary Policy*, Basel.

Tobin, J. (1978)   'A Proposal for International Monetary Reform, *Eastern Economic Journal* (July–October).

Wymer, C.R. (various dates) TRANSF, RESIMUL, CONTINEST, PREDIC, APREDIC computer programs and relative manuals; supplement no. 3 on solution of non-linear differential equation systems (mimeo).

Wyplosz, Charles (1986)   'Capital controls and balance of payments crises', *Journal of International Money and Finance* (June).

Discussion

John S. Flemming

Gandolfo and Padoan present a model in which the private sector's net wealth is subject to partial adjustment towards a desired position which is related to the economy's relative size (despite the implication of global accounting identities, both desired and actual private net financial asset positions appear to have always to be positive, or at least of the same sign). The effects of financial liberalisation are simulated by raising the speed of this adjustment to a very high level.

I agree with the authors that the macro-economic effects of liberalisation need to be assessed in the context of a fully-specified model, and I agree that a continuous time specification has considerable merits. My disagreements are, however, probably more important.

I am not convinced that capital controls are generally best represented as slowing portfolio adjustment. I am not convinced that in the absence of controls portfolio adjustment will become virtually instantaneous. The adjustment of net asset positions in particular must reflect factors other than the speed of adjustment of a financial portfolio.

On the first point the authors acknowledge that interest (equalisation) and transaction taxes may have permanent effects and cite Gros's (1987) work on controls in EMS countries, which is probably specific to that context, although Italy's controls are of much longer standing. Certainly the UK's exchange controls between 1939 and 1979 had effects which showed no signs of being purely transitory.

Even if controls did have such an effect, it does not follow that their removal would render adjustment instantaneous. The persistence of portfolios overweighted in national assets is evidence of this, as is the composition and adjustment of portfolios in countries where controls have been absent for many years. At the Conference Giancarlo Gandolfo said that stability problems would arise even if the quarterly adjustment coefficient were only doubled from a fitted 0.1 to 0.2 rather than raised to 90.

Were it not for the buffer-stock role of the foreign-exchange reserves instantaneous adjustment of the net foreign-asset position would simply be impossible, as it would require an infinite rate of flow in the balance of payments. This problem is mitigated in the present model by its buffer-stock structure, with inventories, money, and reserves each playing that role. Note, however, that this must threaten the non-negativity of the reserves which, if breached, would invalidate the logarithmic specification of the intervention equation (16). It would also be disturbing if private-sector behaviour were such as to make a clean float impossible. An appropriate change in the real exchange rate would also reduce this problem, but if that were fixed at PPP by perfect goods arbitrage only big swings in real output could save the day.

Given this (design) feature of the model, many of the authors' results, as to both the effect of freer capital movements and the compensating effect of goods arbitrage and intervention policy, are unsurprising.

To model financial liberalisation satisfactorily as raising adjustment speeds would require a model with a much richer set of assets so that portfolios had composition (which might adjust much more or less rapidly) as well as scale (whose speed of adjustment must be dominated by real considerations). In a model extended in that way I suspect that financial liberalisation reflected in more rapid portfolio equilibration would not have the dramatic effects found here and viewed as supporting foreign-exchange transaction taxes.

Reference

Gros, D. (1987)   'The Effectiveness of Capital Controls', *IMF Staff Papers* (June).

4 Floating Exchange Rates and Capital Mobility

Esko Aurikko

4.1 INTRODUCTION

Since the breakdown of the Bretton Woods fixed exchange-rate system in the early 1970s, Finland, like Sweden and Norway and some other small countries, has pursued a policy of pegging the exchange rate by means of a currency index.[1] Lately, however, adherence to this policy has clearly diminished the scope for conducting monetary policies independently from the rest of the world because of the increased mobility and sensitivity of foreign-capital flows. As financial integration increases, a fixed exchange-rate regime in which the exchange rate is pegged to the currency index or to the EMS currencies is an obvious choice for exchange-rate policy as part of the integration process. However, the reduction of autonomy in domestic monetary policy could be especially severe if there were a loss of confidence in the fixed exchange-rate policy and consequent inflation target because of insufficient flexibility in the labour market and fiscal policy. In these circumstances, domestic monetary policy becomes tightly constrained by the need to safeguard external liquidity.

Autonomy in domestic monetary policy could be desirable if economic gains could be expected. This might be the case when insulation from different shocks impinging on the economy is sought, or when economic structures and economic policy targets differ across countries. Differences in economic developments and in requirements for the conduct of successful economic policies might also call for an independent monetary policy.

Autonomy of monetary policy could be supported in the short run by isolating domestic and foreign financial markets, either by increasing controls on foreign-capital movements or by flexible exchange rates. As the former is clearly not a realistic alternative under increased worldwide financial integration, introducing exchange-rate flexibility is the only way to increase monetary autonomy.[2]

The choice between alternative exchange-rate regimes by a small open economy seeking to insulate the economy from domestic and foreign shocks or from the point of view of policy effectiveness has been treated extensively in the literature, and seems to depend on a range of structural factors.[3] These include the openness of the economy and the degree of capital mobility, the rigidity of wage and price adjustment and the interest-rate elasticity of domestic demand.

On the other hand, insulation and policy effectiveness properties of flexible exchange rates also depend on similar factors. Normally this issue is studied assuming perfect capital mobility (i.e., uncovered interest-rate parity). However, for many small open economies, such as Finland, perfect capital mobility cannot be assumed. The degree of capital mobility as well as wage and price rigidity thus become important. To study this issue a theoretical model is first constructed in Section 4.2. In Section 4.3 simulations with an econometric macro-model for Finland incorporating varying capital mobility is conducted. In Section 4.5 some concluding comments are given.

4.2 THEORETICAL CONSIDERATIONS

The model

In Section 4.2 the significance of capital mobility and wage indexation under a flexible or floating exchange-rate regime in the adjustment of the economy to various kinds of shocks is examined with a simple rational expectations equilibrium model. The equations of the model are:

$$-a_1\Delta r_t + a_2\Delta y_t = \Delta H_t/P_t + \Delta R_t/P_t \tag{1}$$

$$e_t - e_{t-1} = \beta\Delta R_t/P_t = \beta\{b_2(p_t^* + e_t - p_t) - b_3y_t + b_4y_t^* + f\Delta[r_t - r_t^* - (E_te_{t+1} - e_t)]\} + \Delta T_t^{cb}/P_t\}, \beta \leqslant 0 \tag{2}$$

$$P_t = \gamma(p_t^* + e_t) + (1 - \gamma)w_t, 0 \leqslant \gamma \leqslant 1 \tag{3}$$

$$w_t = E_{t-1}p_t + \theta(p_t - E_{t-1}p_t), 0 \leqslant \theta \leqslant 1 \tag{4}$$

$$y_t = b_1y_t + CA_t/P_t = b_1y_t + b_2(p_t^* + e_t - p_t) - b_3y_t + b_4y_t^* \tag{5}$$

In the model lower-case variables (except interest rates and production) are expressed as logarithms and r is the domestic interest rate, y production, H banks' Central Bank financing, R the foreign-exchange reserves of the Central Bank, CA the current account, e the exchange rate, r^* the foreign interest rate, p^* the foreign price level, y^* a stochastic foreign demand shock, p the domestic price level and w wages. The expectations operator is denoted by E, with the subscript showing the period when expectations are formed for the endogenous variable in the next period.

Equation (1) is the equilibrium condition for the demand for and supply of real money balances. The foreign component of the supply of money is the change in the foreign-exchange reserves, consisting of the current account and capital account:

$$\Delta R_t/P_t = CA_t/P_t + \Delta F_t/P_t - \Delta F_t^b/P_t \qquad (6)$$

where F is the net stock of foreign liabilities of the public and F^b banks' forward cover in the form of deposits with foreign banks.

The open foreign-exchange position of the public is:

$$A_t^p/P_t = (F_t - T_t)/P_t = f[r_t - r_t^* - (E_t e_{t+1} - e_t)] \qquad (7)$$

where T is forward-exchange purchases.

It is assumed that the banks' foreign-exchange position is closed, i.e.:

$$A_t^b/P_t = T_t/P_t - F_t^b/P_t - I_t^{cb}/P_t = 0 \qquad (8)$$

where T^{cb} is forward-exchange sales by the Central Bank.

According to equations (7) and (8)

$$F_t/P_t - F_t^b/P_t = A_t^p/P_t + T_t^{cb}/P_t \qquad (9)$$
$$= f[r_t - r_t^* - (E_t e_{t+1} - e_t)] + T_t^{cb}/P_t$$

Equation (2) shows the exchange policy rule and the Central Bank is assumed to lean against the wind. If $\beta = 0$, the exchange rate is completely fixed and if $\beta = -\infty$, it is floating. Domestic prices are determined according to equation (3) as a weighted average of foreign prices and wages. Wages are set in equation (4) to be equal to expected prices in the previous period, corrected for wage indexation. The indexation parameter θ varies between 0 (no indexation) and 1 (complete indexation). In equation (5) the demand for the domestic commodity depends on relative prices and exogenous demand shocks. When b_2 approaches infinity domestic and foreign commodities become perfect substitutes, implying PPP. For simplicity, it is assumed that domestic demand is not affected by the interest rate.

In the model the important parameters which are related to the economic policy or to the adjustment of the economy are β, describing the degree of exchange policy activity; f, financial openness, so that as f increases towards infinity the uncovered interest-rate parity (perfect capital mobility) obtains; b_2, commodity-market openness, and θ wage indexation.

The model can be reduced by inserting equations (3)–(5) into equations (1)–(2). The endogenous variables r_t and e_t depend on the exogenous variables H_t, T_t^{cb}, p_t^*, r_t^*, y_t^*, and expectations $E_t e_{t-1}$, $E_{t-1} e_t$ and $E_{t-1} p_t$. To close the model it is assumed that expectations are formed rationally. As the model is simultaneous and dynamic with respect to the exchange rate, prices and expectations concerning them, the model cannot be solved explicitly. The model can, however, easily be solved in some special cases. In the following the effects of unanticipated, temporary shocks in the short run and the effects of unanticipated, permanent disturbances in the long run are examined.

Short-run effects

In the case of an unanticipated and temporary shock in period t it can be assumed without loss of generality that

$$E_t h_{t+1} = E_t p_{t+1}^* = E_t r_{t+1}^* = E_t y_{t+1}^* = 0$$

so that also

$$E_t e_{t+1} = 0$$

Correspondingly,

$$E_{t-1} h_t = E_{t-1} p_t = E_{t-1} r_t^* = E_{t-1} y_t^* = 0$$

implying

$$E_{t-1} e_t = E_{t-1} p_t = 0$$

Under these assumptions and using approximations

$$H_t/P_t \simeq \omega_1(h_t - p_t)$$

and

$$T_t^{cb}/P_t \simeq \omega_2(t_t^{cb} - p_t)$$

the reduced form of the model is

$$Ar_t + Be_t = -\omega_1 h_t - \omega_2 t_t^{cb} + Cp_t^* + fr_t^* + Dy_t^* \tag{10}$$

$$Er_t + Fe_t = \beta t_t^{cb} + Gp_t^* - \beta fr_t^* + Hy_t^* \tag{11}$$

where

$$A = a_1 + f > 0$$

$$B = (b_2 - a_2 b_2' - b_3 b_2')(1 - \gamma') + f - (\omega_1 + \omega_2)\gamma' > 0$$

$$C = -(b_2 - a_2 b_2' - b_3 b_2')(1 - \gamma') + (\omega_1 + \omega_2)\gamma' \gtreqless 0$$

$$D = (a_2 + b_3)b_4' - b_4 \gtreqless 0$$

$$E = -\beta f > 0$$

$$F = 1 - \beta(b_2 - b_3 b_2')(1 - \gamma') - \beta(f - \omega_2\gamma') > 0$$

$$G = \beta(1 - \gamma')(b_2 - b_3 b_2') - \beta\omega_2\gamma' < 0$$

$$H = -\beta(b_3 b_4' - b_4) < 0$$

$$\gamma' = \gamma/[1 - (1 - \gamma)\theta] > 0$$

$$b_2' = b_2/(1 - b_1 + b_3) > 0$$

$$b_4' = b_4/(1 - b_1 + b_3) > 0$$

The slopes of the *SS* curve in Figure 4.1 determined by the equilibrium in the money market, and the *EE* curve determined by the exchange policy rule are both negative. It can be shown that the latter is steeper.

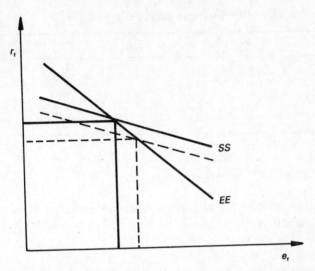

Figure 4.1 Effects of an anticipated, temporary increase in banks' central bank financing

According to the model an unanticipated, temporary increase in banks' Central Bank financing lowers the interest rate and depreciates the exchange rate. In the model, forward-market intervention by the Central Bank is similar to sterilised intervention in the spot market. This is due to the banks' closed foreign-exchange position together with endogenous interest-rate and flexible exchange-rate determination. A forward sale by the Central Bank appreciates the exchange rate, while the effect on the interest rate is ambiguous. Effects of a foreign price level and demand shock are also ambiguous. A rise in the foreign interest rate raises the domestic interest rate and the exchange rate. The impact effects are as shown in Table 4.1.

With increased indexation of wages the exchange rate also adjusts more sharply. But, according to equation (5), there is no exchange-rate effect on production when indexation is complete. This is due to the absence of any lag between changes in wages and prices (i.e., the real wage is constant). On the other hand, changes in exchange rates are transmitted in full to domestic prices.

Next, short-run effects of the shocks are examined when the exchange rate is flexible and capital mobility increases. First it is assumed that the exchange rate is completely flexible, thus $\beta = -\infty$. If we write

Table 4.1   Short-run effects, $\beta > -\infty, f < \infty$

	de_t	dr_t	dp_t	dw_t	dy_t
dh_t	+	−	+	+	+
dt_t^{cb}	−	?	−	−	−
dp_t^*	?	?	?	?	?
dr_t^*	+	+	+	+	+
dy_t^*	?	?	?	?	?

$$\Delta R_t/P_t = \Delta V_t^{cb}/P_t \simeq \omega_3(v_t^{cb} - p_t)$$

intervention by the Central Bank in the spot exchange market can also be studied. With a floating exchange rate, equations (10) and (11) are of the form:

$$a_1 r_t - [a_2 b_2'(1 - \gamma') + (\omega_1 + \omega_3)\gamma'] \, e_t = - \, \omega_1 h_t - \omega_3 v_t^{cb} \qquad (12)$$
$$+ \, [a_2 b_2'(1 - \gamma') + (\omega_1 + \omega_3)\gamma'] \, p_t^* + a_2 b_4' y_t^*$$

$$fr_t + [f + (b_2 - b_3 b_2')(1 - \gamma') - (\omega_2 - \omega_3)\gamma'] \, e_t = \omega_3 v_t^{cb}$$
$$- \, \omega_2 t_t^{cb} + [(1 - \gamma')(b_3 b_2' - b_2) + (\omega_2 - \omega_3)\gamma'] \, p_t^*$$
$$+ \, fr_t^* + (b_3 b_4' - b_4)y_t^* \qquad (13)$$

where v^{cb} is the purchase of foreign exchange by the Central Bank.

In this case, the *SS* curve is upward-sloping. However, the impact effects of unanticipated and temporary shocks are qualitatively similar, as in Table 4.1. Intervention in the foreign-exchange market depreciates the exchange rate, while the interest rate effect is ambiguous.

Next, perfect capital mobility is assumed with parameter f approaching infinity. In this case, the *SS* curve is unchanged while the *EE* curve is determined by simple interest-rate parity: $r_t^* = r_t + e_t$.

With a floating exchange rate and perfect capital mobility, the effects of changes in the exogenous variables are as shown in Table 4.2.

When domestic and foreign assets are perfect substitutes, domestic money-market and foreign-exchange interventions are equivalent while sterilised intervention, being now identical to forward-market intervention, has no effect. An increase in foreign prices has an ambiguous effect on domestic prices, wages and production because

Table 4.2   Short-run effects, $\beta \to - \infty, f \to \infty$

	de_t	dr_t	dp_t	dw_t	dy_t
$dh_t \simeq dv_t^{cb}$	+	−	+	+	+
dt_t^{cb}	0	0	0	0	0
dp_t^*	−	+	?	?	?
dr_t^*	+	+	+	+	+
dy_t^*	−	+	−	−	?

domestic prices are determined in the model by foreign prices and the exchange rate, when $\gamma > 0$.

Long-run effects

As the above disturbances were unanticipated and transitory, their effects on the economy were also transitory. In order to analyse long-run effects of unanticipated and permanent changes in the exogenous variables of the model it can be assumed that expectations are realised, i.e.:

$$E_t e_{t+1} = E_{t-1} e_t = e_t = \bar{e} \text{ and } E_{t-1} p_t = p_t = \bar{p}$$

This implies that in the steady-state solution wage indexation is irrelevant and also that is obtained: $\bar{p} = \bar{p}^* + \bar{e}$.

In the long-run equilibrium solution of the model unanticipated and permanent shocks change domestic interest rate and exchange rate qualitatively, in the same way as unanticipated and temporary shocks in the short run. As in the long-run, PPP applies and relative prices (real exchange rate) are constant, only commodity market disturbances affect production. This result is analogous in the short run if wage indexation is complete.

Equations (10) and (11) are now of the form

$$(a_1 + f)\bar{r} + (f - \omega_1 - \omega_2)\bar{e} = - \omega_1 \bar{h} - \omega_2 \bar{i}^{cb} + f\bar{r}^* + D\bar{y}^*$$
$$+ (\omega_1 + \omega_2)\bar{p}^* \tag{14}$$

$$- \beta f\bar{r} + (1 - \beta f + \beta \omega_2)\bar{e} = \beta \omega_2 \bar{i}^{cb} - \beta f\bar{r}^* + H\bar{y}_t^* - \beta \omega_2 \bar{p}^* \tag{15}$$

The *SS* and *EE* curves are downward-sloping.

The effects of the shocks with a flexible exchange rate and imper-

Table 4.3   Long-run effects, $\beta > -\infty, f < \infty$

	$d\bar{e}$	$d\bar{r}$	$d\bar{p}$	$d\bar{w}$	$d\bar{y}$
$d\bar{h}$	+	−	+	+	0
$d\bar{\imath}^{cb}$	−	?	−	−	0
$d\bar{p}^{*}$	?	+	?	?	0
$d\bar{r}^{*}$	?	+	?	?	0
$d\bar{y}^{*}$	?	?	?	?	?

Table 4.4   Long-run effects, $\beta \to -\infty, f \to \infty$

	$d\bar{e}$	$d\bar{r}$	$d\bar{p}$	$d\bar{w}$	$d\bar{y}$
$d\bar{h} \simeq d\bar{v}^{cb}$	+	−	+	+	0
$d\bar{\imath}^{cb}$	0	0	0	0	0
$d\bar{p}^{*}$	−	+	?	?	0
$d\bar{r}^{*}$	+	+	+	+	0
$d\bar{y}^{*}$	−	+	−	−	+

fect capital mobility are as shown in Table 4.3.

The long-run effects also are rather ambiguous with imperfect capital mobility and a floating exchange rate. When perfect capital mobility prevails the effects are as shown in Table 4.4.

4.3   SIMULATIONS

Introduction

In the framework of the theoretical model in Section 4.2 it was seen in a qualitative fashion that with flexible and floating exchange rates monetary policy retained its effectiveness in both the short and the long run. However, with increasing capital mobility, sterilised interventions are ineffective, as interventions in the domestic money market and foreign-exchange market are equivalent. With various shocks impinging on the economy, monetary policy could thus be used effectively to isolate the economy from disturbances.

To assess quantitatively and dynamically how much capital mobility matters for insulation and the effectiveness of monetary policy under floating exchange rates, we study simulations with the BOF4 model.[4]

BOF4 is an econometric model of the Finnish economy constructed at the Bank of Finland.[5] It is quarterly model of about 300 equations. In the short run the model is Keynesian with production determined by demand and prices by costs while the long-run properties are classical, with wages equilibrating the labour market, production adjusting according to capacity and domestic prices determined by foreign prices and the exchange rate.

Specification of the financial market in the BOF4 model is characterised by assuming that all non-money assets which are denominated in domestic currency are close substitutes, so that there is a single market rate of interest sufficient to measure the intertemporal opportunity costs of investment, consumption and money-holding. Moreover, money is treated like a durable good for which a stable demand function exists. Assets denominated in foreign currency are assumed to be imperfect substitutes for domestic assets (Tarkka and Willman, 1990).

The version of the model in which the domestic interest rate is flexible and the exchange rate floating is used below. In the model, exchange-rate expectations are restrictedly rational in the sense that agents know the structure of the model only with respect to the foreign-exchange market and also all future changes in the exogenous variables are unexpected.[6]

The results

In the following the effects of unanticipated and permanent changes in the exogenous variables in the floating-rate version of the model are examined when capital mobility is increasing. As noted above, this has occurred in Finland during recent years and is expected to continue as international financial integration proceeds.[7]

In the equation for the net import of foreign capital in the basic version of the BOF4 model (version A), capital imports increase by FIM 3 billion as the difference between the domestic and foreign interest rate increases by 1 percentage point. To examine the significance of increasing capital mobility for the adjustment of the economy, capital mobility was increased 2, 10 and 50 times (versions B, C and D). These four versions of the model are used to run the following simulations for the period 1988Q1–1933Q4:

1. Money market intervention: a FIM 100 million purchase of FIM-denominated CDs on the interbank market by the Central Bank.

2. Unsterilised foreign-exchange intervention: a purchase of foreign currency in the amount of FIM 100 million by the Central Bank.
3. Sterilised foreign-exchange intervention: a FIM 1000 million forward-exchange purchase by the Central Bank.
4. A foreign price shock: an increase of 1 per cent in foreign prices.
5. A foreign interest-rate shock: an increase of 1 percentage point in the foreign interest rate.
6. A foreign demand shock: an increase of 1 per cent in foreign export demand.

The effects of these changes in the four versions of the model are summarised in Tables 4.5–4.10.

According to Tables 4.5 and 4.6, money-market intervention and unsterilised foreign-exchange intervention have roughly identical effects, regardless of capital mobility. This is due to the fact that even in the basic version A of the model domestic and foreign assets are fairly close substitutes for each other so that interventions are indifferent. Immediately after the intervention, the domestic interest rate decreases and the exchange rate depreciates because of capital exports. Soon, as a counter-effect, there occurs a reversal with the interest rate rising and the exchange rate appreciating.

When capital mobility is increasing the exchange rate depreciates more sharply because the immediate interest-rate effect of the intervention does not depend much on the degree of capital mobility. The effectiveness of monetary policy for stabilisation purposes thus increases.

In the model, sterilised foreign-exchange intervention (i.e., a simultaneous sale of spot foreign exchange and an increase of an equivalent amount in the Central Bank financing of the banks) corresponds to a forward-market intervention. This follows from the fact that in the model the interest rate is flexible and the foreign-exchange position of the banks is closed. According to Tables 4.5 and 4.6, the effects of a sterilised foreign-exchange intervention are minor. In Table 4.7 a 10-fold intervention compared with the above interventions displays visible effects. In particular, the conventional result emerges that when capital mobility is increasing the effects of a sterilised intervention are reduced and only minor and short-run exchange rate changes can be effected.

According to Table 4.8, a permanent increase in foreign prices in the different versions of the model is reflected only in an immediate and permanent appreciation of the exchange rate, regardless of

Table 4.5 Money-market intervention: a FIM 100 million purchase of FIM-denominated CDs on the interbank market by the Central Bank

Model	Quarter				Year					
version	I	II	III	IV	1	2	3	4	5	6
Exchange rate (%)										
A	1.6	0.3	0.9	0.2	0.7	−0.1	0.1	0.2	0.1	0.1
B	2.0	0.1	0.9	0.0	0.7	−0.1	0.2	0.2	0.2	0.2
C	3.1	−1.2	1.7	−1.2	0.5	0.1	0.2	0.2	0.2	0.2
D	4.1	−3.4	4.4	−4.9	0.0	−0.2	0.2	0.9	1.4	1.4
Domestic interest rate (percentage points)										
A	−3.8	0.7	0.6	1.0	−0.4	0.2	−0.1	−0.0	−0.1	−0.1
B	−3.7	0.8	0.6	0.8	−0.3	0.2	−0.1	−0.0	−0.1	−0.1
C	−3.7	1.1	0.7	0.6	−0.3	0.1	−0.0	−0.0	−0.0	−0.0
D	−3.6	1.3	0.5	0.6	−0.3	0.1	−0.1	−0.1	−0.2	−0.1
GDP (%)										
A	0.1	0.4	0.4	0.4	0.3	0.1	−0.0	−0.0	−0.1	−0.1
B	0.1	0.5	0.4	0.4	0.3	0.1	0.0	−0.0	−0.1	−0.1
C	0.2	0.5	0.3	0.3	0.3	0.1	0.0	−0.0	−0.1	−0.1
D	0.2	0.5	0.2	0.4	0.3	0.1	−0.0	−0.1	−0.2	−0.2
Consumption prices (%)										
A	0.2	0.2	0.3	0.3	0.2	0.2	0.2	0.2	0.2	0.2
B	0.3	0.2	0.2	0.3	0.2	0.2	0.2	0.2	0.2	0.2
C	0.4	0.2	0.3	0.2	0.3	0.2	0.2	0.2	0.3	0.2
D	0.5	−0.0	0.4	−0.0	0.2	0.2	0.3	0.3	0.4	0.4
Current account (billion FIM)										
A	0.2	−0.0	−0.0	−0.1	−0.0	−0.1	0.1	0.1	0.1	0.1
B	0.2	−0.1	−0.1	−0.1	−0.1	−0.1	0.1	0.1	0.1	0.1
C	0.3	−0.2	−0.0	−0.2	−0.2	−0.0	0.0	0.1	0.1	0.2
D	0.4	−0.4	0.1	−0.5	−0.4	−0.4	0.1	0.4	0.7	0.7

Table 4.6   Unsterilised foreign-exchange intervention: a purchase of foreign currency in the amount of FIM 100 million by the Central Bank

Model	Quarter				Year					
version	I	II	III	IV	1	2	3	4	5	6
Exchange rate (%)										
A	1.6	0.3	0.9	0.2	0.7	−0.1	0.1	0.2	0.1	0.1
B	2.0	0.1	0.9	0.0	0.7	−0.1	0.2	0.2	0.2	0.2
C	3.1	−1.2	1.7	−1.2	0.5	0.1	0.2	0.2	0.2	0.2
D	4.1	−3.4	4.4	−4.9	0.0	−0.2	0.2	0.9	1.4	1.4
Domestic interest rate (percentage points)										
A	−3.8	0.7	0.6	1.0	−0.4	0.2	−0.1	−0.0	−0.1	−0.1
B	−3.7	0.8	0.6	0.8	−0.3	0.2	−0.1	−0.0	−0.1	−0.1
C	−3.7	1.1	0.7	0.6	−0.3	0.1	−0.0	−0.0	−0.0	−0.0
D	−3.6	1.3	0.5	0.6	−0.3	−0.1	−0.1	−0.1	−0.2	−0.1
GDP (%)										
A	0.1	0.4	0.4	0.4	0.3	0.1	−0.0	−0.0	−0.1	−0.1
B	0.1	0.5	0.4	0.4	0.3	0.1	0.0	−0.0	−0.1	−0.1
C	0.2	0.5	0.3	0.3	0.3	0.1	0.0	−0.0	−0.1	−0.1
D	0.2	0.5	0.2	0.4	0.3	0.1	−0.0	−0.1	−0.2	−0.2
Consumption prices (%)										
A	0.2	0.2	0.3	0.3	0.2	0.2	0.2	0.2	0.2	0.2
B	0.3	0.2	0.2	0.3	0.2	0.2	0.2	0.2	0.2	0.2
C	0.4	0.2	0.3	0.2	0.3	0.2	0.2	0.2	0.3	0.2
D	0.5	−0.0	0.4	−0.0	0.2	0.2	0.3	0.3	0.4	0.4
Current account (billion FIM)										
A	0.2	−0.0	−0.0	−0.1	−0.0	−0.1	0.1	0.1	0.1	0.1
B	0.2	−0.1	−0.1	−0.1	−0.1	−0.1	0.1	0.1	0.1	0.1
C	0.3	−0.2	−0.0	−0.2	−0.2	−0.0	0.0	0.1	0.1	0.2
D	0.4	−0.4	0.1	−0.5	−0.4	−0.4	0.1	0.4	0.7	0.7

Table 4.7 Sterilised foreign-exchange intervention: a FIM 1000 million forward-exchange purchase by the Central Bank

Model	Quarter				Year					
version	I	II	III	IV	1	2	3	4	5	6
Exchange rate (%)										
A	0.7	0.3	0.4	0.2	0.4	0.1	0.1	0.1	0.1	0.0
B	0.5	0.1	0.2	0.1	0.2	0.1	0.1	0.1	0.1	0.1
C	0.2	0.0	0.1	−0.0	0.1	0.0	0.0	0.0	0.0	0.0
D	0.0	−0.0	0.0	−0.0	0.0	0.0	0.0	0.0	0.0	0.0
Domestic interest (percentage points)										
A	0.1	0.1	0.3	0.4	0.2	0.2	0.1	0.1	0.0	0.0
B	0.0	0.1	0.2	0.2	0.1	0.1	0.1	0.1	0.0	0.0
C	0.0	0.0	0.0	0.1	0.0	0.0	0.0	0.0	0.0	0.0
D	0.0	0.0	0.0	0.0	0.0	0.0	0.0	0.0	0.0	0.0
GDP (%)										
A	0.0	0.1	0.1	0.1	0.1	0.0	−0.0	−0.1	−0.1	−0.1
B	0.0	0.1	0.1	0.1	0.1	0.0	−0.0	−0.0	−0.0	−0.1
C	0.0	0.0	0.0	0.0	0.0	0.0	0.0	−0.0	−0.0	−0.0
D	0.0	0.0	0.0	0.0	0.0	0.0	0.0	−0.0	−0.0	−0.0
Consumption prices (%)										
A	0.1	0.1	0.1	0.1	0.1	0.1	0.1	0.1	0.1	0.1
B	0.1	0.1	0.1	0.1	0.1	0.1	0.1	0.1	0.1	0.1
C	0.0	0.0	0.0	0.0	0.0	0.0	0.0	0.0	0.0	0.0
D	0.0	0.0	0.0	0.0	0.0	0.0	0.0	0.0	0.0	0.0
Current account (billion FIM)										
A	0.1	0.0	0.0	0.0	0.1	0.1	0.2	0.2	0.2	0.2
B	0.0	0.0	0.0	0.0	0.1	0.0	0.1	0.1	0.1	0.1
C	0.0	0.0	0.0	0.0	0.0	0.0	0.0	0.0	0.0	0.0
D	0.0	0.0	0.0	0.0	0.0	0.0	0.0	0.0	0.0	0.0

Table 4.8   Foreign price shock: an increase of 1 % in foreign prices

Model version	Quarter				Year					
	I	II	III	IV	1	2	3	4	5	6
Exchange rate (%)										
A	−0.7	−1.0	−1.0	−1.0	−1.0	−1.0	−1.0	−1.0	−1.0	−1.0
B	−0.8	−1.0	−1.0	−1.0	−1.0	−1.0	−1.0	−1.0	−1.0	−1.0
C	−0.8	−1.1	−1.0	−1.1	−1.0	−1.0	−1.0	−1.0	−1.0	−1.0
D	−0.8	−1.1	−0.9	−1.1	−1.0	−1.0	−1.0	−1.0	−1.0	−0.9
Domestic interest rate (percentage points)										
A	0.0	0.0	0.0	0.0	0.0	−0.0	−0.0	−0.0	−0.0	−0.0
B	0.0	0.0	0.1	−0.0	0.0	−0.0	−0.0	−0.0	−0.0	−0.0
C	0.0	0.0	0.1	−0.0	0.0	−0.0	−0.0	−0.0	−0.0	0.0
D	0.0	0.0	0.0	0.0	0.0	−0.0	−0.0	−0.0	−0.0	−0.0
GDP (%)										
A	0.0	0.0	0.0	−0.0	0.0	−0.0	−0.0	−0.0	−0.0	0.0
B	0.0	0.0	0.0	−0.0	0.0	−0.0	0.0	0.0	0.0	0.0
C	0.0	0.0	−0.0	0.0	0.0	−0.0	0.0	0.0	−0.0	−0.0
D	0.0	0.0	−0.0	0.0	0.0	−0.0	0.0	0.0	−0.0	−0.0
Consumption prices (%)										
A	0.0	0.0	0.0	0.0	0.0	−0.0	−0.0	−0.0	−0.0	0.0
B	0.0	0.0	0.0	0.0	0.0	−0.0	−0.0	−0.0	0.0	0.0
C	0.0	0.0	0.0	0.0	0.0	−0.0	−0.0	−0.0	−0.0	−0.0
D	0.0	0.0	0.0	0.0	0.0	0.0	0.0	0.0	0.0	0.0
Current account (billion FIM)										
A	0.0	−0.0	0.0	0.0	−0.0	0.0	0.0	0.0	0.0	−0.0
B	0.0	−0.0	0.0	0.0	−0.0	0.1	0.0	0.0	0.0	0.0
C	−0.0	−0.0	0.0	0.0	−0.0	0.0	0.0	0.0	0.0	0.0
D	−0.0	−0.0	0.0	−0.0	−0.0	0.0	0.0	0.0	0.0	0.0

capital mobility. Thus, with relative prices (real exchange rate) unchanged the effects on the domestic interest rate, prices and production are small.

In Table 4.9 a permanent rise in the foreign interest rate leads to capital exports which depreciate the exchange rate. This has a positive GDP effect, with both the demand for money and the domestic interest rate increasing.

The greater is capital mobility the more the exchange rate depreciates in the short run. This is because changes in the domestic interest rate bring the money market into equilibrium only after a lag, causing fluctuations in the exchange rate. In the long run the exchange rate and the interest rate change more with increasing capital mobility.

As a result of the rise in foreign demand the exchange rate immediately appreciates because of an improvement in the current account (Table 4.10). The domestic interest rate has to decline because in the short run the exchange-rate appreciation has a negative effect on production and the demand for money. In the longer run, these effects are weaker. Again, when capital mobility increases, adjustment of the domestic interest rate and the exchange rate is smaller and thus insulation from the demand disturbance is more complete.[8]

4.4 CONCLUDING COMMENTS

As economic and financial integration in Europe is advancing rapidly and, moreover, exchange-rate cooperation is intensifying, a natural choice for a small European country participating in the economic dimension of integration is to peg its currency to the EMS currencies. However, this would entail loss of independence in both monetary and fiscal policy. If this is deemed undesirable a policy option to support economic policy autonomy is to let the currency float.

In this paper floating exchange rates are studied in Finland in the circumstances of increasing financial integration and capital mobility. The effects of various shocks and the effectiveness of monetary policy in the framework of a theoretical model and the BOF4 econometric macro-model of the Finnish economy are examined. The results of this paper suggest that, with increasing capital mobility, the economy is better insulated from all the shocks studied except the foreign interest-rate shock.

Policy implications from the results are quite conventional. As

Table 4.9   Foreign interest-rate shock: an increase of 1 percentage point in the foreign interest rate

Model version	Quarter				Year					
	I	II	III	IV	1	2	3	4	5	6
Exchange rate (%)										
A	1.9	0.8	1.1	0.5	1.1	0.3	0.2	0.3	0.2	0.2
B	2.5	0.8	1.3	0.5	1.3	0.4	0.4	0.5	0.4	0.4
C	4.2	0.0	2.1	−0.2	1.5	0.7	0.8	0.9	0.9	0.9
D	6.0	−2.2	4.7	−3.6	1.1	0.5	0.9	1.5	2.0	2.1
Domestic interest rate (percentage points)										
A	0.1	0.5	0.8	1.1	0.7	0.7	0.3	0.2	0.1	0.0
B	0.2	0.6	1.1	1.2	0.8	0.8	0.4	0.4	0.3	0.2
C	0.3	1.0	1.4	1.2	1.0	0.9	0.6	0.6	0.6	0.6
D	0.4	1.4	1.5	1.3	1.1	1.0	0.7	0.7	0.7	0.7
GDP (%)										
A	0.1	0.3	0.3	0.3	0.3	0.1	−0.1	−0.2	−0.3	−0.3
B	0.1	0.4	0.4	0.4	0.3	0.1	−0.1	−0.2	−0.3	−0.3
C	0.2	0.5	0.4	0.4	0.4	0.1	−0.1	−0.2	−0.3	−0.4
D	0.3	0.6	0.4	0.5	0.4	0.1	−0.1	−0.3	−0.4	−0.5
Consumption prices (%)										
A	0.3	0.3	0.3	0.4	0.3	0.4	0.4	0.4	0.3	0.2
B	0.3	0.4	0.4	0.4	0.4	0.5	0.5	0.5	0.5	0.4
C	0.5	0.5	0.4	0.4	0.5	0.6	0.7	0.8	0.8	0.8
D	0.8	0.3	0.7	0.4	0.5	0.7	0.8	0.9	1.1	1.1
Current account (billion FIM)										
A	0.2	0.1	0.0	0.0	0.3	0.2	0.5	0.5	0.5	0.5
B	0.2	0.1	0.0	0.0	0.4	0.3	0.5	0.6	0.7	0.8
C	0.4	0.0	0.1	−0.0	0.4	0.4	0.7	0.9	1.1	1.3
D	0.5	−0.2	0.2	−0.3	0.2	0.2	0.8	1.2	1.7	2.0

Table 4.10   Foreign demand shock: an increase of 1 % in
foreign export demand

Model	Quarter				Year					
version	I	II	III	IV	1	2	3	4	5	6
Exchange rate (%)										
A	–1.7	–0.8	–0.9	–0.7	–1.0	–0.6	–0.5	–0.5	–0.5	–0.4
B	–1.6	–0.6	–0.7	–0.6	–0.9	–0.5	–0.5	–0.5	–0.5	–0.4
C	–1.4	–0.1	–0.7	–0.2	–0.6	–0.4	–0.4	–0.4	–0.4	–0.4
D	–1.2	0.2	–0.9	0.4	–0.4	–0.2	–0.2	–0.3	–0.3	–0.4
Domestic interest rate (percentage points)										
A	–0.0	–0.2	–0.6	–0.5	–0.3	–0.4	–0.2	–0.2	–0.1	–0.1
B	–0.0	–0.2	–0.4	–0.5	–0.3	–0.3	–0.1	–0.1	–0.1	–0.1
C	–0.0	–0.1	–0.3	–0.2	–0.2	–0.1	–0.1	–0.1	–0.1	–0.1
D	–0.0	–0.1	–0.1	–0.1	–0.1	–0.0	–0.0	–0.0	–0.0	–0.0
GDP (%)										
A	0.0	–0.1	–0.1	–0.1	–0.1	0.0	0.2	0.3	0.3	0.3
B	0.0	–0.1	–0.1	–0.1	–0.1	0.1	0.2	0.2	0.2	0.2
C	–0.0	–0.1	–0.1	–0.0	0.0	0.1	0.2	0.2	0.2	0.1
D	0.0	0.0	0.1	0.0	0.0	0.1	0.1	0.1	0.1	0.1
Consumption prices (%)										
A	–0.2	–0.3	–0.3	–0.4	–0.3	–0.4	–0.4	–0.4	–0.3	–0.3
B	–0.2	–0.3	–0.2	–0.3	–0.2	–0.3	–0.3	–0.3	–0.3	–0.3
C	–0.2	–0.2	–0.2	–0.2	–0.2	–0.2	–0.2	–0.2	–0.2	–0.2
D	–0.2	–0.1	–0.2	–0.1	–0.1	–0.2	–0.2	–0.2	–0.1	–0.1
Current account (billion FIM)										
A	0.0	0.1	0.1	0.1	0.3	0.3	0.1	–0.0	–0.1	–0.1
B	0.0	0.1	0.1	0.1	0.3	0.3	0.1	0.0	–0.0	–0.1
C	0.0	0.1	0.1	0.1	0.4	0.4	0.3	0.2	0.1	0.1
D	0.1	0.2	0.1	0.2	0.5	0.4	0.3	0.3	0.2	0.2

capital becomes more mobile the effectiveness of monetary policy in the form of intervention in the money market or unsterilised foreign-exchange interventions increases while sterilised foreign-exchange interventions become ineffective. However, this increase in the effectiveness of monetary policy is achieved at a cost of a loss in the effectiveness of fiscal policy.

Notes

1. The Finnish exchange-rate basket is constructed using bilateral trade weights, the effective weight of the EMS currencies being more than 60 per cent. The Central Bank can allow for fluctuations within the 6 per cent band. Realignments of the band are made by the government on the proposal of the Parliamentary Supervisory Board.
2. Exchange-rate flexibility would also serve directly to decrease capital mobility, which is inversely related to exchange risk; see Aurikko (1985).
3. For recent surveys, see Marston (1985) and Argy (1989).
4. In the simulations cooperation with Alpo Willman is gratefully acknowledged.
5. See BOF4 (1987) and Willman (1989).
6. This assumption seems not to be overly restrictive as simulations with a model in which expectations are strictly rational are similar; see Aurikko (1989).
7. In countries with a floating exchange rate, it is normally the case that capital movements are also free and uncovered interest-rate parity is assumed. Experiences gained in Australia and New Zealand after letting the exchange rate float and abolishing exchange controls indicate that uncovered interest-rate parity also obtains (see Argy, 1987; 1989 Murphy, 1986).
8. This result, as well as simulations with a fiscal shock, indicate that as capital mobility increases effectiveness of fiscal policy diminishes.

References

Argy, V. (1987) 'International Financial Liberalization – The Australian and Japanese Experiences Compared', *Bank of Japan Monetary and Economic Studies* (May).

Argy, V. (1989) 'Choice of Exchange Rate Regime for a Smaller Economy – A Survey of Some Key Issues', IMF Conference on Exchange Rate Policy in Selected Industrial Countries, Brussels.

Aurikko, E. (1985) 'Active Pegging, Rational Expectations, and Auton-

omy of Monetary Policy', *Economic Letters* (November).
Aurikko, E. (1989) 'Rational Exchange Rate and Price Expectations Under
   Different Exchange Rate Regimes in Finland', *Finnish Economic Papers*
   (Spring).
BOF4 (1987) 'The BOF4 Quarterly Model of the Finnish Economy: Equa-
   tions', *Bank of Finland Research Papers*, TU 6/87.
Marston, R. (1985) 'Stabilization Policies in Open Economies', in Jones,
   R. and Kenen, P. (eds), *Handbook of International Economics*, vol. II,
   Amsterdam, North-Holland.
Murphy, C.W. (1986) 'Exchange Rate Policy in the AMPS Model', in D.T.
   Nguyen and Gregory, R.G. (eds), *Exchange Rates and the Economy*,
   Supplement to the Economic Record, Melbourne.
Tarkka, J. and Willman, A. (1990) 'Financial Markets in the BOF4 Model
   of the Finnish Economy', *Bank of Finland Discussion Papers*, 1/90.
Willman, A. (1989) 'If the Markka Floated: Simulating the BOF4 Model
   with Fixed and Floating Exchange Rates', *Finnish Economic Papers*
   (Spring).

Discussion

Jürgen Siebke

Both models presented in Aurikko's paper – the theoretical and the econometric model – have in common that capital mobility between countries is imperfect. The assumption of finite capital mobility is important in two respects: first, even in the highly integrated world capital market of today uncovered interest-rate parity does not prevail; second, the theoretical analysis becomes interesting because the balance of payments influences the exchange rate in the short run.

In Section 4.2 a rational expectations equilibrium model is formulated, and the author states: 'As the model is simultaneous and dynamic with respect to the exchange rate, prices and expectations concerning them, the model cannot be solved explicitly'. Aurikko therefore solves his model for two special cases: (1) unanticipated temporary shocks, termed short-run effects, and (2) anticipated permanent disturbances, termed long-run effects. In the first case the change of the expectations compared with their former equilibrium levels is zero, so that all expectation operators cancel out. In the other case all expectations equal their realised values (according to Aurikko this is valid for all periods; hence the permanent shock is anticipated, not *un*anticipated). In neither case is an explicit solution for the expectations necessary. But the feature of the model being 'simultaneous and dynamic' in two variables and their expectations seems not to be a sufficient argument that a rational expectations model cannot be solved explicitly (Schneider, 1990). The calculations of the expectations and of the changes of the variables may be complicated and tedious, but in general (or very often) an explicit solution is possible.

The way both models are presented is somewhat technical. The author reports only the analytical results of the theoretical model and the results of the simulations with the econometric model. Nothing at all is said about how these models work, how exogenous shocks are transmitted to the endogenous variables. Of course, this is not possible for a large-scale econometric model. But when modelling the open economy as in Section 4.2 we are especially interested how

84

the international transmission channels do their work. For instance, an unanticipated increase in the foreign interest rate has well-known effects (Table 4.1), whereas changes in the foreign price level and in the foreign real activity have ambiguous effects on all variables of the small economy. In the case of unanticipated shocks the domestic price level is proportional to the exchange rate $p = \gamma'e$ with $0 < \gamma' < 1$, hence given the foreign price level p^* nominal and real exchange rates move in the same direction. Now the interest-rate shock can easily be explained: according to equation (2) an increase of r^* leads to a depreciation and hence to an increase of p. The real depreciation improves the current account and raises economic activity y, according to equation (5). On the money market, equation (1), this implies an increase of the domestic interest rate. But how can it be explained that an increase of the foreign economic activity is negatively transmitted to the economic activity of the small country? According to equation (5), this transmission requires a strong real appreciation. How does this happen?

Reference

Schneider, Ch. (1990) 'An Explicit Solution of a Simultaneous and Dynamic Rational Expectations Model', *Discussion Paper*, no. 147, Department of Economics, University of Heidelberg.

5 Monetary Integration of Eastern Europe Into the World Economy

Christoph Buchheim

5.1 INTRODUCTION

There is a widespread feeling in all Eastern European countries belonging to the Council for Mutual Economic Assistance (CMEA, Russian acronym Comecon) that an essential element of their market-oriented reforms has to be a closer integration into the world economy. For only then will the internal price structure of non-autarkic countries be right – i.e., permanently adapting to true scarcities. That, however, is an indispensable prerequisite for efficient production and the disappearance of immisering trade. In addition such integration would – through imports – increase competition on the domestic market and thus put firms under pressure to enhance their own competitiveness, which would benefit demand. And attraction of much-needed foreign capital and know-how can also not be secured unless a greater degree of openness is achieved in the Eastern European economies.

A necessary element of this is convertibility of currencies, which in fact constitutes monetary integration in the sense used in this paper; it is considered an important target of economic policy in all European Comecon countries. Full convertibility means that every person, firm or organisation can for the current rate exchange any amount of its own money into foreign money, in order freely to import goods and services or to invest abroad. Full convertibility therefore necessitates liberalisation of international trade and capital movements. This can safely be undertaken by a country strong enough to support its currency by always having sufficient foreign-exchange reserves at its disposal, which excludes a permanent balance of payments deficit. To a large part such strength depends on the ability of enterprises to produce goods and services which are competitive in the world market, thus earning the foreign exchange needed for imports and investment abroad. Otherwise a devaluation can be expected, and the competitive framework of the country will thereby in principle be eased. However, this is true only if structural rigidities do not prevent quick adaptation of the economy to the new situation. But if that is the case, establishing full convertibility too early will lead to an accelerating decline of the exchange rate, high inflation and destruction of the currency by a loss of confidence. Because of their history of central planning Eastern European economies do suffer from very high structural rigidities. Almost all observers therefore agree that full convertibility of East European currencies cannot be adopted at once without incurring very high costs. Although the Soviet rouble might constitute an exception from a purely economic point of view, there are, as will be shown, political reasons for postponing full convertibility even for the rouble. On the other hand, the governments of Eastern European countries are trying immediately to establish restricted forms of currency transferability and to design possibilities of reaching full convertibility, at least for current transactions, in the near future.

The first part of the paper deals with the structural rigidities of Eastern European economies which exclude an immediate adoption of full convertibility for most of them. Then the steps towards this aim undertaken in Hungary, Poland and the Soviet Union will be described, and the contribution various forms of convertibility can make in tackling the inevitable problem of inflation connected with price reform. Finally, the possibilities and advantages of full convertibility being gradually established by the Comecon countries as a group are considered, using the example of the postwar (Western) European Payments Union (EPU).

5.2 STRUCTURAL RIGIDITIES IN EASTERN EUROPEAN ECONOMIES

János Kornai (1980) explicitly called the socialist economies of Eastern Europe 'shortage economies'. This expression points to the fact that shortages can be considered the predominant feature of these economies. Indeed queues, empty shops and production holdups because of missing inputs demonstrate the appropriateness of this characterisation; demand for many specific products outstrips available supply. The reasons are well-known and need only brief discussion here:

- Prices are administratively fixed and held stable, even if economic conditions change; so an important mechanism which normally works to balance supply and demand in individual markets is paralysed. In the course of time the whole price structure gets more and more distorted, transmitting wrong information to firms.
- The main target for enterprises is not profitability but fulfilment of the central plan; consequently there is no danger of bankruptcy. Financial losses, which may occur even with economically efficient and valuable production because of the distorted price structure, are covered by the state. This fact seriously further changes incentives to firms; they use their weak-budget constraint to get ever more inputs and means for investment, and shortages occur.
- The experience of shortages greatly strengthens the hoarding tendency, thus aggravating the problem. Typically, in centrally-planned economies the stocks of inputs at firms are much larger than in capitalist countries.
- Because of widespread shortages almost everything which is produced finds its demand. Therefore enterprises need not react flexibly to altered demand conditions, and the stimulus for innovation is not high. This results in very slow structural change, and great production rigidities are endemic.

The foreign-trade sector does not constitute an exception from the general picture. The insatiable demand of firms for inputs which also leads to a limitless desire for imports makes foreign exchange permanently scarce. The supply of foreign exchange through exports, however, suffers from a lack of competitiveness on the world market. This is clearly shown by the recent export performance of Eastern European countries in the industrialised market economies. Whereas their share of manufactured imports of OECD countries in the 1960s and 1970s fluctuated around 2 per cent, it fell to 1.3 per cent in the middle of the 1980s. So-called research-intensive goods like chemicals and machines in 1965 were 10 per cent of all OECD imports from European Comecon countries; in 1986 this had risen to 13 per cent. In comparison, the share of such products in OECD imports from the Asian newly-industrialised countries (NICs) was about 4 per cent in 1965, but 35 per cent in 1986.[1] This shows that Eastern Europe has been falling more and more behind. An additional indication is the prices obtained by East European countries for their engineering products. In 1965 the price per kilogram weight was still half the average price of all such exports to the EC market; in 1985, however, it had been reduced to little more than a quarter (Winiecki, 1989). So the statement of a high (East) German official in 1990 that the former GDR received for its machinery exports on the world market only 15 pfennig for every Mark internal value seems credible.[2] Indeed, production in Eastern Europe, valued at world market prices, frequently seems to result in negative value-added. Prices for CMEA manufactures exported do not recover real costs in many instances, making trade an immisering activity. Imports and foreign credits, on the other hand, have often also been wasted in inefficient production and projects, because a reliable measure of scarcity is missing (Wass von Czege, 1989). This fact lies at the root of the convertible-currency debt problem of some Eastern European countries.

The tendencies just described were hardened by the existence of the CMEA. Founded in 1949 as a Soviet response to the Marshall Plan it aimed at economic integration of the socialist countries. Thorough specialisation of production in individual countries and close coordination of national plans, however, was not attained.[3] On the other hand, the transferability of the so-called 'transferable rouble', the common currency for clearing purposes, largely remained on paper, for trade balances cannot normally be transferred to other Comecon countries. Even additional deliveries from a debtor country itself, if possible at all, frequently necessitate protracted bargaining, because central planning means that exportable product reserves are not readily available, a problem which is accentuated by the widespread shortages. All East European countries therefore try to avoid export surpluses with any other Comecon member by negotiating rather strict bilateral agreements. They aim to strike a balance not only between the amount of bilateral exports and imports as a whole, but also between so-called 'hard products' (which can be sold on Western markets) and 'weak products' (which cannot), or even between individual categories of goods. The reasons for this phenomenon are to be found in the lack of a reliable price system. Prices in intra-Comecon trade are calculated in transferable roubles on the basis of lagged world market prices. This may be possible for agricultural goods or raw materials, but for manufactures there often does not exist 'the' world market price. As a result, prices for the same goods sometimes display wide discrepancies in different bilateral relations. The dollar exchange rate of the transferable rouble, on the other hand, is artificially held constant, which has lead to rising overvaluation in course of time. Exports of hard products or of weak products containing convertible currency inputs thus entail losses to the exporter if they are not reciprocated by similar imports (Clement, 1988). Both factors contribute to the rigidity of bilateral agreements between the Comecon countries.

About 60 per cent of the total trade of Eastern Europe remains within the region, of which the Soviet Union alone accounted for 45 per cent in the middle of the 1980s.[4] The trade of the smaller Eastern European countries with the Soviet Union therefore almost equals the whole trade among themselves. The Soviet Union clearly is the dominant economy of Eastern Europe, and while the trade between the smaller Eastern European countries mainly consists of an exchange of machinery and transport equipment, their trade with the Soviet Union reveals a different pattern. In the 1980s about half of their imports from the Soviet Union were fuels. In 1982 the Soviet share of all energy imports of the smaller Eastern European countries amounted to 80 per cent, representing almost 30 per cent of their total energy consumption (Ostkolleg der Bundeszentrale für politische Bildung, 1987). The Soviet Union itself bought in exchange machinery and vehicles from its East European partners which accounted for 60 per cent of its imports from them. For example, Czechoslovakia in 1987 sold half of its machinery exports to the Soviet Union and another third to the rest of Eastern Europe; the proportions for Poland in 1988 were 37 and 25 per cent.[5] The problem with these machinery exports of the smaller East European countries is that, as has been shown, they are hardly competitive on Western markets. The Soviet energy exports, however, in principle are. Intra-Comecon trade therefore is characterised by a highly one-sided structural dependence of the smaller East European countries on the Soviet Union which until 1990 supplemented their political and ideological dependence.

The differing structure of trade of the smaller Eastern European countries between that to the CMEA (where they appear highly industrialised) and that to the West (where their exports and imports are rather similar to those of a less-industrialised country) cannot easily be overcome,[6] for prices of manufactures exported to other Comecon countries are difficult to raise in bilateral negotiations. As a result, it does not pay to apply innovations to these products, nor to increase their content of Western inputs. Manufactured exports to the Comecon have therefore also become increasingly less competitive on Western markets, which is why Gorbachev once called the CMEA a 'dustbin'. On the other hand, manufactures which are especially produced for Western countries and are competitive there cannot profitably be sold in the East. The compartmentalisation of trade has thus been hardened over time; and since the biggest enterprises are most heavily involved in the intra-CMEA trade, because handling them is much easier for the planning authorities than coordinating a multitude of smaller firms, a powerful lobby favouring the existing situation has thereby also been created.[7]

In order to become wholly competitive on Western markets again, it is necessary for the Comecon countries to get rid of the division of foreign trade into two separated sub-sections. But that is possible only if the state monopoly to conduct foreign trade, administrative prices and bilateralism is replaced by firms independently engaging in export and import activities, a free price system and multilateralism. These are conditions for full convertibility, too, and they can quickly be introduced, at least partially. However, convertibility means still more: it includes liberalisation of trade. But the deeply entrenched structural rigidities of foreign trade in the smaller East European countries exclude immediate liberalisation, in the same way it was excluded after 1945 in Western Europe in view of the large dollar gap. For liberalisation would at once substitute manufactures imported from the West for intra-Comecon trade, especially in investment goods; the majority of markets of the smaller Eastern European countries (which now take more than 60 per cent of all their manufactured exports) would rapidly shrink. The development of alternative export outlets for the amount required would take far longer, even if demand was sharply restricted and currencies were devalued, particularly because the flexibility of Eastern European economies was hitherto rather low, and they were thus unable to finance a large share of their vital import needs in energy, raw materials and food. To avoid a deadly blow to the already very weak economies of Eastern Europe the West would have to spend dozens of billions of dollars per year for some time in order to fill the gap by foreign aid.

Incidentally, for the same reasons the heads of the smaller East European states at the CMEA Conference of January 1990 did not accept the Soviet proposal for using Western currencies and actual world market prices for the intra-Comecon clearing from 1991 onwards, although some of them urgently demanded the quick beginning of far-reaching reforms within the CMEA. A Czechoslovakian delegate explained that the immediate adoption of the Soviet proposal would mean a catastrophe for the CSSR which had been forced to remain in the Eastern Bloc for forty years; it was therefore the duty of the Soviet Union to share the costs of any reform with its partner countries. Moscow apparently agreed with this position.[8]

5.3   FIRST STEPS TOWARDS CONVERTIBILITY IN EASTERN EUROPE

As has been said already, there are various conditions for convertibility – or, better, adopting convertibility and introducing a market economy is a comprehensive process in which the steps undertaken are mutually interdependent. Convertibility is, for example, unthinkable without price reform abolishing price distortion and instituting flexible prices that can adapt to scarcities. Only then it is possible also to have a meaningful unified exchange rate. On the other hand, convertibility would enhance the decontrol of hitherto regulated prices. Convertibility requires competitiveness of firms on the world market and therefore the abolition of monopolistic structures. That in turn, however, would be greatly aided by liberalisation of imports, which is a further ingredient of convertibility. Convertibility necessitates firms autonomously taking decisions regarding foreign trade, and therefore is not compatible with central planning; but if convertibility is established, there will be much-desired foreign investment. Joint ventures and foreign-owned firms are generally excluded from the plan; they will therefore undermine the planning system from within. It is thus clear that convertibility cannot be treated in isolation from reform of the economic process as a whole; it even seems impossible to say which is more important. It depends on circumstances whether one should first institute convertibility as fully as possible, hoping that this will ease economic reforms or whether economic reforms are needed to raise competitiveness thus making convertibility feasible. The first steps towards convertibility and the problems connected with them in Hungary, Poland and the Soviet Union will now be analysed.

Hungary

Hungary has slowly advanced quite a long way in the direction of a market economy. Important institutional reforms – of the tax and banking system, of the regulative framework for firms and of the planning process, have already been undertaken. There have been repeated devaluations of the Forint, as well as a start of the liberalis-

ation of foreign economic relations. The state monopoly to conduct
foreign trade has been abolished, and since 1988 every firm can
engage in exports and imports. Excepted from this, however, is trade
in strategic products like energy, some raw materials and agricultural
products as well as the whole trade in transferable roubles. In 1989
about 40 per cent of imports in convertible currencies, mainly investment goods, were freed from quotas with the intention of increasing
this proportion to 60 per cent in 1990 and to 80 per cent by 1995. In
addition, the conditions for direct foreign investment were much
improved (Wass von Czege, 1989).

Despite all these reforms Hungary still is far from full convertibility
of the Forint. The greater part of its foreign trade is as yet not
liberalised, enterprises are not allowed to keep the foreign exchange
earned, Hungarians who travel abroad have to be content with a
rather small allowance of convertible currencies (even reduced in
1990). Nevertheless problems are mounting. The current-account
deficit in convertible currencies was unexpectedly high in 1989; the
fact that the Hungarian tourist balance became substantially negative
and high interest payments for the hard currency debt were blamed
for this result.[9] However, a current-account deficit is no new phenomenon in Hungary, and its indebtedness climbed from 9 billion to 20
billion dollars in the 1980s. The government, urged by the IMF, took
decisive measures to restrict demand at the beginning of 1990,
reducing subsidies and deregulating food prices. These are important
actions, but they probably cannot cure the balance of payments
deficits, especially since social unrest is increasing.[10] The basic problem is that Hungarian exports sold for hard currency stagnated
around 5 billion dollars per year throughout the 1980s. On the other
hand, a huge surplus of transferable roubles has developed, to which
the liberalisation of convertible currency imports contributed because of the substitution of Comecon products by those from Western countries (Wass von Czege, 1989). Both factors again point to the
low competitiveness of Hungarian and Comecon manufactures as the
deepest reason for the economic difficulties. With additional steps
towards full convertibility these difficulties will probably even increase, if the compartmentalisation between trade to the Comecon
and to the West is not reduced. For further liberalisation of convertible currency imports will, *ceteris paribus*, augment the tendency to
show a hard currency deficit and a transferable rouble surplus at the
same time. Whereas the latter can be diminished only by a reduction
of exports to the CMEA which would result in great strain for the

biggest enterprises as well as in unemployment, the former makes necessary even more foreign aid or further demand restriction.

Poland

Under the Solidarity government Poland has recently undertaken radical reforms, in order quickly to establish a full market economy.[11] At the beginning of 1990 almost all prices were freed, most subsidies abolished and a tight monetary policy adopted. The result was a push upwards in inflation which was already running at about 1000 per cent. High unemployment is expected, as the budget constraints of state enterprises are now hard. Living standards have appreciably dropped, the first strikes have occurred. A big privatisation and demonopolisation programme of firms is under way.

Regulations concerning foreign exchange were altered in the spring of 1989. The black foreign-exchange market was legalised, and foreign-exchange auctions were extended. At these auctions, firms can purchase convertible currencies from the state or from exporting firms which are generally allowed to keep a part of their foreign-exchange earnings; the exchange rate freely adapts to demand and supply. With the foreign money thus bought enterprises can import production inputs and investment goods, but not consumer goods. Some strategic products like mineral oil or grain, however, continue to be centrally imported (Kostrzewa, 1989b). Since September 1989 the official exchange rate of the Zloty has repeatedly and substantially been devalued from less than 1500 to 9500 Zloty to the dollar. The aim was to unify the official and the free-market rate and to establish so-called 'domestic convertibility'. After the last drastic devaluation of more than 50 per cent at the beginning of 1990, that was more or less attained. According to an agreement with the IMF the new rate, which is supported by a stabilisation loan from Western countries of 1 billion dollars, should be held stable for at least three months. In this way limited convertibility of the Zloty at a fixed rate was to be guaranteed to foreign investors at least.[12]

At first sight it seems quite unnecessary and even dangerous to equate official and free-market exchange rates by devaluations of the former. After the currency reform of 1948 in West Germany the free-market exchange rate of the Deutsche Mark was far lower than the official rate for a long time.[13] With increasing international competitiveness of the German economy, however, the free-market rate climbed up, and in 1958 convertibility was introduced at the official rate. If, on the other hand, the official rate had continuously been lowered, in order to close the gap between official and free-market rates, high inflation would have resulted. It therefore seems probable that the development of hyperinflation in Poland in the second half of 1989 owed much to the big devaluations of the Zloty.

However, the situation of West Germany after 1948 was quite different in other respects from that in Poland today. In West Germany, the internal price level was basically stable, whereas in Poland the monetary surplus, a typical characteristic of all centrally-planned economies, resulted not only in great shortages, but also, during the 1980s, in accelerating inflation. Because of that, the dollar has become the second currency in Poland, with ever-increasing importance. The pervasiveness of the dollar economy and of the foreign-exchange free market apparently doomed to failure any effort to stabilise the Zloty at an exchange rate substantially lower than the free-market rate; a tight monetary policy alone could not have restored confidence into the Zloty quickly enough, thus reversing the trend to the dollar economy and stopping inflation. The government had to take the risk of hyperinflation in order to equate official and free-market exchange rates through devaluation of the former and by doing so stabilise the Zloty.

'Domestic convertibility' is therefore a concept of achieving price stability by bringing the official and the free-market exchange rate of indigenous money close together in a situation where, because of inflation, internal money has largely been substituted by a foreign currency. For this strategy to be successful it will be necessary to avoid the development of another gap between the two rates, until the Zloty has again undertaken its role of being the principal medium of exchange in Poland. Fiscal discipline, monetary restriction and the stabilisation loan, all serve this purpose. For 'domestic convertibility' to work satisfactorily, however, it is not necessary to liberalise most imports; in fact that has not been done, therefore full convertibility will not automatically be established if the Zloty is stabilised (i.e., if 'domestic convertibility' has reached its aim). In principle, Poland experiences the same obstacles on its path to full convertibility as does Hungary, obstacles which originate in the compartmentalisation of foreign trade.

Soviet Union

The situation in the Soviet Union is quite different. The steps towards introduction of a market economy have until now been far more restricted than in Hungary or Poland.[14] Since 1988 most enterprises have formally had the right to plan their production and the obligation fully to finance themselves. In 1989 all firms were allowed to engage in foreign trade, if they were centrally registered and competitive on international markets; they can keep a part of their foreign-exchange earnings, and either use if for their own imports or sell it to other firms. As in Poland foreign-exchange auctions are organised for this purpose, the first of which resulted in an average exchange rate of 1 dollar for 9 roubles, which is fourteen times the official rate.[15] Nevertheless the bureaucrats have as yet hardly retreated. The independence of firms is undermined by mandatory production orders which take up a great part of their capacity; there are many goods the export and import of which continues to be possible only with a special licence. There are no products which firms can freely import, paying with roubles exchanged at the official rate, which means that there are no truly liberalised imports. And – the biggest drawback of all – no price reform has so far been undertaken. The government is afraid of deregulating prices, because in view of the great monetary surplus this would lead to inflation rates and social unrest possibly getting out of control.

But for the Soviet Union there could be a way of solving the problem without accepting high inflation. It seems feasible in its case simultaneously to introduce price reform and convertibility of the rouble at a much lower rate than the current free-market exchange rate.[16] As the Soviet economist Nikolai Petrakow explained: 'I think that our rouble must become convertible immediately. In this respect we are not permitted to wait any longer'.[17] To do that one could either think of backing the rouble by the Soviet gold reserves (i.e., making it convertible against gold at a rate which would result in an exchange rate of 1 or 2 roubles to the dollar). Or a limited amount of special roubles, possibly called '*Czervonez*' like a similar money in the 1920s (Kostrzewa, 1989a), could be introduced with a fixed parity *vis-à-vis* the dollar supported by gold and raw materials certificates. The '*Czervonez*' could be put into circulation through government expenditures, as was done with the '*Rentenmark*' at the end of the great German inflation in 1923. Some additional means would thus be available to the government for balancing its budget despite the adoption of strict monetary discipline with regard to the old rouble. By such action a stable free-market exchange rate between the '*Czervonez*' and the rouble would soon develop, and in fact make the rouble convertible, too. At the same time the price distortion could more safely be cured by thoroughly freeing prices.

As has been said earlier in their section, it depends on the country's circumstances whether price reform is essential long before convertibility can be adopted, or whether convertibility can be established more or less simultaneously with price reform. Poland and the Soviet Union furnish good examples of this difference. The reason has again to do with the international competitiveness of economies. Whereas in Poland price reform is a necessary condition slowly to improve the competitiveness of manufactured exports on the world market which hitherto has not been strong, about 70 per cent of the Soviet exports today consist of fuels, raw materials and gold, which are competitive on the world market. In addition, the Soviet Union appears to be capable of raising the amount of these goods sold for convertible currencies at short notice, either out of its reserves or by diminishing the share of such exports paid by their recipients in transferable roubles. In this way, therefore, the Soviet Union can guarantee the convertibility of the rouble at a fixed exhange rate, even if market-oriented reforms of its economy are lagging behind.

5.4 A WAY TO FULL CONVERTIBILITY OF THE COMECON COUNTRIES AS A GROUP

The rouble could thus be made fully convertible at once, which would greatly increase the chances for a successful transformation of the Soviet economy. However, at the same time it would lead to the economic collapse of the smaller Eastern European economies because of their structural dependence on the Soviet market for their manufactured exports, with which they finance vital imports of raw materials. To prevent that, massive Western aid for each individual country would be required. In this situation the model of the postwar EPU provides a way out of the dilemma[18] According to the example of the EPU, the Comecon can be reorganised into an area within which trade is liberalised and multilateralised, and currencies made transferable. At the same time, imports from the Western industrialised countries would continue to be discriminated against, as was done by EPU countries against the dollar area. As did the EPU (with the colonies and overseas sterling countries) the Comecon includes, with the Soviet Union, a big supplier of raw materials as well as regions capable of developing a large potential for efficient production and export of investment goods. Therefore intra-Comecon trade, if restructured along lines of economic rationality, could – as did intra-EPU trade – greatly reduce the need for Western imports, which is presently felt so greatly in all East European countries, and by doing so make it ultimately easier to achieve full convertibility of currencies. It is therefore no wonder that some East European economists also argue for establishing convertibility within the Comecon first.[19]

The necessary prerequisites for intra-bloc convertibility are in principle the same as for full convertibility (i.e., the abolition of the state monopoly to conduct foreign trade and price reform in order to establish a meaningful exchange rate). It seems that all Eastern European countries are actively engaged in fulfilling these conditions.[20] In the Soviet Union, however, great problems are seen regarding the price reform. But they can be reduced, if convertibility of the rouble is adopted simultaneously. In order not to endanger the closer integration of the Comecon according to economic principles, the rouble convertibility has only to be somewhat restricted for the time being; the rouble can be made fully convertible for foreigners and for Soviet private citizens. This will certainly suffice to increase the confidence of the public in its stability, and enable the government to undertake the price reform without provoking accelerating inflation. On the other hand, for enterprises within the Soviet Union, including joint ventures and foreign-owned firms, the rouble will not be fully convertible in the sense that imports from the West will be liberalised, too. Instead, restrictive quotas will at first have to remain in force for this part of Soviet trade. The economic losses which the Soviet Union incurs by further discriminating against Western industrial countries will be considered as the Soviet contribution towards making its Eastern European partner countries economically viable. The OECD countries, for their part, should help in the process by a moratorium on convertible-currency debts. In addition, the EC could support the development of multilateral trade within the Comecon, if its members made available capital for a central reserve fund to the CMEA as a whole, as well as financial aid to individual CMEA countries in case their full participation in the liberalisation experiment otherwise seemed impossible. The new European Bank could be used for the purpose, and the EC would thus fulfil the same role *vis-à-vis* Eastern Europe which the USA fulfilled towards the EPU.

Technically speaking the Comecon would need to be restructured in the following way, much in line with the example of the EPU:

- Trade within the area has to be liberalised by greatly reducing commerce conducted through the state, as well as by abolishing quotas on private imports from other CMEA members. To begin with, 50 per cent of all such imports in each of the three categories food, raw materials and manufactures could be liberalised, with an agreement to raise this percentage every six months to 60, 75 and 90 per cent.
- All discrimination against imports from individual partner countries should be forbidden.
- Each country would be required to fix a unified rouble exchange rate; then multilateral clearing among the Comecon as a whole would replace bilateral clearing between pairs of Eastern European countries. For each member only the net balance *vis-à-vis* the group of participating countries would thus constitute an important policy parameter. The already existing International Bank for Economic Cooperation in Moscow could function as clearing agent, using the rouble for accountancy purposes.
- Net balances up to a certain limit are to be covered partly by payment of a fully-convertible currency including the rouble, partly by credit. At the beginning the respective percentages could be 50:50; the share of payment should then be raised step by step. Net deficits accumulating over the prescribed limit should be fully paid in convertible currencies.
- Each of the smaller countries is permitted to liberalise its imports from the West as it sees fit. Only the Soviet Union would from the outset agree to a limit of such liberalisation, especially with regard to manufactures; but this limit should be widened, in order to include (say) 20 per cent more of its imports every year.

On the one hand, a Comecon reorganised along these lines would give the smaller Eastern European countries the shelter needed for some time against immediate full Western competition in the Comecon, especially the Soviet market. On the other hand, it would nevertheless appreciably increase competition for the industries of each individual member by the free access of products from other members. Monopoly profits would be wiped out, rationalisation of production and innovative activity stimulated. Some pressure for liberalisation of certain productive imports from the West could also be expected, because such high-quality inputs would increase competitiveness within the Comecon. In addition, the whole process would probably be aided by Western firms investing large amounts of capital in Comecon countries, as prospects of profitability for them became better as convertibility approached. All this would obviously be very advantageous for the Soviet Union, the biggest importer of manufactures from the smaller East European countries, and effectively reduce the costs of being hampered from immediately switching to Western supplies. However, the new Comecon would also display two built-in mechanisms favouring the ultimate achievement of full convertibility by its members. The first is the agreement to raise the share of net balances which has to be covered by convertible currency payment. That provision not only increases more and more greatly the incentive of individual countries to have export surpluses within the Comecon, thus reversing the current situation; it also diminishes step by step the difference between a net balance in intra-Comecon trade and in trade for convertible currencies, and by doing so lowers the gains to be reaped from that distinction for debtor countries. The second – possibly even more powerful – factor strictly limiting the transition period is the interest of the Soviet Union fully to liberalise its imports from the West. The prospect that such liberalisation would increase year by year according to the agreed schedule would put the smaller East European countries under pressure to raise their international competitiveness as quickly as possible.

In this way the intra-Comecon exchange of products would be based more and more on purely economic criteria, the compartmentalisation of the trade of Comecon members would disappear, and with it the principal obstacle to adopting full convertibility. By this approach convertibility will be reached only after four or five years; but that delay will prove very beneficial; for through initially protecting them from full competition from Western industrialised countries the structural rigidities of Eastern European economies can be more gradually overcome. Many enterprises presently producing (measured at world market prices) too small or even negative value-added can thus be saved from the bankruptcy which would occur if convertibility were immediately established. Another way to achieve the same result would be the levy of a temporary tax on the efficient firms, in order to subsidise the inefficient; however, by doing that incentives facing the efficient producers would appreciably be lowered. The stimulus for dynamic growth would be restricted for the sake of allocative efficiency, probably leading to poorer prospects of quickly rising living standards.

Notes

1. Without intra-German trade; see Kostrzewa (1988).
2. 'DDR-Exportschwäche verschärft Nachteile der Mark', *Süddeutsche Zeitung (SZ)* (24 October 1989).
3. Compare, for the following as well, Fink and Levcik (1989); Hedtkamp (1988).
4. For the trade figures, see Vienna Institute (1988).
5. Statistická rocenka Ceskoslovenské socialistické republiky (1988); Maly Rocznik Statystyczny (1989).
6. See, for Hungary as an example, Rácz and Richter (1989).
7. For instance, the firm of Skoda in Czechoslovakia, see, 'Auch in Prag nehmen Wirtschaftssorgen zu', *SZ* (23 November 1989).
8. 'Vorsichtige Annäherung des COMECON an ein neues Handelssystem', *Neue Zürcher Zeitung (NZZ)* (12 January 1990).
9. 'Hungary's Growing Shortage of Convertible Currency', *Radio Free Europe* (14 November 1989).
10. 'Ungarn steht kurz vor der Zahlungsunfähigkeit', *Frankfurter Allgemeine Zeitung (FAZ)* (16 December 1989); 'Ungarns steiniger Weg zur Marktwirtschaft', *SZ* (13–14 January 1990).
11. See Quaisser (1989); 'Statement by Leszek Balcerowicz, Deputy Prime Minister and Minister of Finance of Poland, at the Annual Meeting of the IMF and the World Bank', Deutsche Bundesbank, *Auszüge aus Presseartikeln* (2 October 1989); 'Die Pioniere des neuen Ostens', *SZ* (21 December 1989); 'Jahresauftakt beschert Polen drastisch höhere Preise', *Frankfurter Rundschau* (2 January 1990).
12. *Reuter* (20 November 1989); 'Entwicklungsfonds der Industriestaaten für Polen', *NZZ* (5 January 1990).
13. *Fünfter und Sechster Bericht der Deutschen Bundesregierung über die Durchführung des Marshallplans*, Bonn, 1951, p. 149.
14. See Weißenburger (1989); 'Sowjetische Außenwirtschaft: Devisenknappheit behindert Außenwirtschaftsreform', Deutsches Institut für Wirtschaftsforschung, *Wochenbericht* (24 August 1989).
15. *AP* (11 November 1989).
16. See for the following, 'Put the Soviet Economy on Golden Rails', *Wall Street Journal* (5 October 1989); 'Die Sowjetunion auf dem Weg zur Marktwirtschaft?', *FAZ* (28 March 1989); 'In Moskau wird über die Einführung einer harten Parallelwährung diskutiert', *Handelsblatt* (25 September 1989); *Reuter* (29 October 1989).
17. 'Ohne konvertierbaren Rubel ist die Ökonomie chancenlos', *Handelsblatt* (19 December 1989).
18. Of the same opinion is Günter Schleiminger, former General Director of the Bank for International Settlement which has been the clearing agent of the EPU; see 'Ost-Reformern wird Studium der EZU empfohlen', *Handelsblatt* (8 January 1990). Compare also Nötzold (1989).
19. 'Soviet Banker Says East Bloc Currency Convertibility Possible', *Reuter* (17 October 1989); Nikolow (1989).
20. Besides the countries already dealt with, see for Bulgaria, 'Marktwirtschaft zieht auch in Bulgarien ein', *SZ* (20 November 1989); for the

102	*Eastern Europe and the World Economy*

CSSR; 'Die Zukunft des COMECON', *NZZ* (18 January 1990); for the GDR, 'DDR-Mark bis 1992 voll konvertierbar', *SZ* (25 January 1990).

References**References**

Clement, H. (1988)Clement, H. (1988) *Funktionsprobleme der gemeinsamen Währung des RGW (Transferabler Rubel)*, Arbeiten aus dem Osteuropa-Institut München, no. 129, Munich.

Fink, G. and Levcik, F. (1989) *Integrationsbestrebungen osteuropäischer Staaten*, Wiener Institut für Internationale Wirtschaftsvergleiche, Reprint-Serie no. 117, Vienna

Hedtkamp, G. (1988) 'Neuere Entwicklungen im Rat für Gegenseitige Wirtschaftshilfe (RGW)', *Osteuropa*, vol. 33, no. 7/8.

Kornai, J. (1980) *Economics of Shortage*, Amsterdam.

Kostrzewa, W. (1988) *Verpaßt Osteuropa den Anschluß auf den Weltmärkten?*, Kieler Diskussionsbeiträge, no. 144, Kiel.

Kostrzewa, W. (1989a) 'Zur Diskussion der Währungskonvertibilität in Osteuropa – die sowjetischen Erfahrungen in den zwanziger Jahren', *Die Weltwirtschaft*. no. 1.

Kostrzewa, W. (1989b) 'Polens neue Währungsordnung: Vom Devisenschwarzmarkt zur beschränkten Währungskonvertibilität', *Außenwirtschaft*, vol. III/IV.

Nikolow, T. (1989) 'Zur Konvertierbarkeit der sozialistischen Währungen', *RGW. Wirtschaftliche Zusammenarbeit*, no. 1/2.

Nötzold, J. (1989) *Die Ordnung des europäischen Wirtschaftsraumes und die außenwirtschaftliche Orientierung Osteuropas*, Stiftung Wissenschaft und Politik Ebenhausen.

Ostkolleg der Bundeszentrale für politische Bildung (1987) *Rat für Gegenseitige Wirtschaftshilfe: Strukturen und Probleme* Bonn.

Quaisser, W. (1989) *Die Wirtschaftsentwicklung Polens im 1. Halbjahr 1989 – Schwerpunkt: Die Bankenreform sowie Möglichkeiten und Probleme einer restrictiven Geldpolitik*, Arbeiten aus dem Osteuropa-Institut München, no. 133, Munich.

Rácz, M. and Richter, S. (1989) *Some Aspects of the Hungarian–Soviet Economic Relations in 1971–1985*, Wiener Institut für Internationale Wirtschaftsvergleiche Forschungsberichte, no. 153.

Vienna Institute for Comparative Economic Studies (1988) *COMECON Foreign Trade Data 1986*, London.

Wass von Czege, A. (1989) 'Ungarns Integration in die Weltwirtschaft: Vision oder Alptraum?', *Außenwirtschaft* vol. III/IV.

Weißenburger, U. (1989) 'Wirtschaftsreformen in der Sowjetunion: Eine Zwischenbilanz', *Vierteljahrshefte zur Wirtschaftsforschung* vol. 1.

Winiecki, J. (1989) 'Eastern Europe: Challenge of 1992 Dwarfed by Pressures of System's Decline', *Außenwirtschaft* vol. III/IV.

Discussion

Pierre Maillet

We must be grateful to Christoph Buchheim for providing us with an opportunity to discuss a problem of the utmost importance for the evolution of Europe. At present, trade inside the Comecon is unevenly distributed: the Soviet Union sells energy and raw materials, products which could be sold everywhere if the prices were attractive; Eastern European countries (Eastern ECs) sell manufactured goods of rather low quality which, therefore, can be sold only to the Soviet Union.

Eastern ECs cannot, at least for some time to come, pay for their imports from the West by selling their own products to the West and two alternative solutions are open to them:

- Huge financial help given by the West for equilibrating their balance of payments.
- A reorganisation of the Comecon, introducing multilateral clearing and providing Eastern ECs with transferrable currencies, especially roubles, thus permitting them to buy Western products – in other words, creating a triangular system of balances and payments between Eastern ECs, the USSR and the West.

Buchheim favours a solution of the second type. I disagree with this attractive proposition on two important points, the first concerning its economic feasibility and the second its political framework.

The first point concerns the aspect of time. Some countries' needs are urgent and the system elaborated by Buchheim would take months if not years to yield full results. It follows that the West cannot avoid helping these countries immediately.

Second, it is obvious that, for political reasons, important circles in Eastern European countries are very much in favour of a close association with the EC. For economic – and also political – reasons, entry into the EC of those countries, even individually, seems impossible today (with the exception of the former GDR). But if it is our intention that, in ten or fifteen years' time, these countries will become full members of the EC (which, by that time, will have moved towards much closer economic integration and real political union), it is important that the Eastern ECs immediately start preparing themselves to produce goods exportable to the West (i.e., suitable in nature and quality), instead of concentrating on equipment goods sold to the Soviet Union; a strong reorientation of trade flows is, however, necessary to achieve this goal.

From this point of view the solution suggested by Buchheim has to be carefully revised: if some of the main basic ideas on economic mechanisms are to remain valid, especially on the liberalisation of external trade, the institutional and practical implementation has to be adapted, in particular by a dissolution of the present Comecon (but maintaining some important economic relations between Eastern Europe and the Soviet Union).

By providing substantial aid to the Eastern ECs we have, at the same time, a powerful tool for stimulating some reorganisation of the economies in these countries, on the lines of the USA's Marshall Plan which, at the time, obliged Europeans to cooperate with each other; in this case, however, on the way towards some integration between the donor countries (EC) and the recipient countries. Pursuing this kind of strategy would enable these Eastern ECs to prepare efficiently for their eventual membership of the EC.

The comparison between both scenarios, Buchheim's and mine, is summarised in Table 5.1.

Table 5.1 Effects of Eastern Europe's monetary integration in alternative scenarios

Countries	Scenario Buchheim	Scenario Maillet
Eastern ECs		
• Liberalised trade	Mostly multilateral inside Comecom	Rapidly reoriented towards EEC
• Imports from the West		
Rate of increase	Low	High
Payment	Transferable roubles	Western aid
• Increase of investment	Rather slow	Fast
• Integration into EEC	No	Progressive

Table 5.1   continued

Countries	Scenario Buchheim	Scenario Maillet
USSR		
Import of equipment goods	Mainly from Eastern ECs	More and more from West
Payment by sales of	Energy to Eastern ECs	Energy and gold to the West
EC		
Aid to Eastern ECs	Small	High (or very high)

Part II
Flexible Exchange Rates and Central Bank Policy

6 Non-Sterilised Intervention and the Floating Exchange Rate

Slobodan Djajić

6.1 INTRODUCTION

The collapse of the Bretton Woods system has released Central Banks from the commitment to maintain fixed parities. Nonetheless, monetary authorities of all countries continue to play an active role in the foreign-exchange market. While official participation has been particularly extensive in the case of the EMS countries, it has also been a factor in the currency markets outside of the EMS. The movements in the value of the US dollar in 1990, for example, were frequently interrupted by waves of official intervention.

Whatever the specific motive behind any given intervention measure may be, provided the measure is not sterilised it exerts an important influence on the time path of the exchange rate.[1] The purpose of the present paper is to investigate the nature of this influence within the framework of a simple model of a small open economy operating under the conditions of perfect international capital mobility.

Throughout much of the analysis it is assumed that the country's monetary authority maintains a certain rate of domestic credit creation. In the absence of current or anticipated future intervention, this policy of credit creation gives rise to a corresponding rate of decline in the value of domestic currency. It is further assumed that the Central Bank holds a stock $\bar{s}$ of foreign-exchange reserves, which it plans to use at some point in an attempt to slow down the pace of depreciation.

There are a number of ways of using any given stock of reserves in an effort to bolster a falling currency. One method is particularly interesting in the light of the actual behaviour of some Central Banks: reserves are sold in exchange for domestic money at certain *levels* of the exchange rate which, sometimes for purely psychological reasons, are regarded to be critical. In an attempt to model this type of intervention as simply as possible, I shall initially assume that the Central Bank has decided to sell s_1 units of reserves when the exchange rate reaches the level e_1, and to use the remaining $\bar{s}$-s_1 units at some higher level of e (say, e_2). Supposing that the intervention programme is credible, how does the announcement of the programme affect the time path of the floating exchange rate?

After addressing this and other related questions, the paper goes on to examine the effects of intervention when the quantity of reserves sold by the central bank at $e = e_1$ is not predetermined, but rather an increasing function of the rate of depreciation recorded just prior to intervention. Also considered are the implications of intervention measures which turn out to be relatively larger (or smaller) than those expected by the public. The analysis of this problem offers some insights as to why Central Banks may not intervene as aggressively as their statements on intervention policy would seem to indicate. Finally, the paper ends with some brief remarks on the problems involved in evaluating the effects of non-sterilised intervention measures.

6.2 THE MODEL

The economy under consideration produces and consumes a single traded commodity. By defining units of this commodity such that each unit's foreign-currency price is equal to 1, the domestic price level at time t is given by the exchange rate, e_t.

The menu of assets available to domestic residents consists of domestic and foreign currencies and short-term securities. Agents are assumed to have perfect foresight and to view securities denominated in terms of domestic and foreign currencies as perfect substitutes. The uncovered interest-parity condition holds at each instant. This condition relates the domestic rate of interest, i_t, to the sum of the (constant) foreign rate of interest, i^*, and the expected (equal to the actual) proportional rate of depreciation of domestic currency, $\dot{e}_t/e_t$.

$$i_t = i^* + \dot{e}_t/e_t \tag{1}$$

where a '·' over a variable indicates differentiation with respect to time. In the event that the path of $\dot{e}_t$ exhibits a discontinuity at time t, $\dot{e}_t$ should be interpreted to be the right-hand derivative of e_t.

Following Flood and Garber (1984), let us assume that the demand for real balances is given by:

$$m_t^d = b - \alpha i_t$$

where both α and b are positive constants.

With the aid of equation (1), we may write the money-market equilibrium condition as

$$M_t/e_t = \beta - \alpha(\dot{e}_t/e_t) \tag{2}$$

where M_t is the nominal supply of domestic currency and $\beta \equiv b - \alpha i^* > 0$.

Implicit in equation (2) is the assumption that foreign residents do not hold domestic money.

In the absence of intervention, the nominal money stock is assumed to grow – due to domestic credit expansion – at a constant rate $dM_t/dt = \mu$.[2] If we define the stock of real balances as $m_t \equiv M_t/e_t$, it follows that

$$\dot{m}_t = m_t[(\mu/M_t) - (\dot{e}_t/e_t)] \tag{3}$$

Since equation (2) implies that

$$\dot{e}_t/e_t = (\beta - m_t)/\alpha \tag{4}$$

we may rewrite equation (3) as

$$\dot{m}_t = \mu/e_t + m_t(m_t - \beta)/\alpha \tag{5}$$

The dynamic system consisting of equations (4) – (5) is illustrated in Figure 6.1. On the basis of equation (4), the $\dot{e}_t = 0$ schedule is depicted as a vertical line at $m_t = \beta$. For values of $m_t \gtrless \beta$, $\dot{e}_t \lessgtr 0$, as shown by the arrows pointing north and south in the Figure 6.1. Turning to equation (5), we note that the $\dot{m}_t = 0$ schedule is negatively-sloped for values of $m_t < \beta/2$ and positively-sloped for $m_t > \beta/2$. This is because $\partial \dot{m}_t/\partial e_t = -\mu/e_t^2 < 0$, while $\partial \dot{m}_t/\partial m_t = (2m_t - \beta)/\alpha \gtrless 0$ as $m_t \gtrless \beta/2$. Moreover, since $\partial \dot{m}_t/\partial e_t < 0$, $\dot{m}_t < 0 \ (>0)$ in the region above (below) the $\dot{m}_t = 0$ locus, as indicated by the arrows pointing east and west.

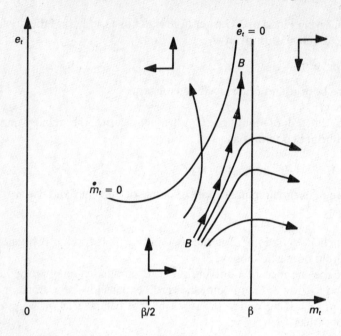

Figure 6.1   The dynamic system of equations (4)–(5)

In the absence of current or anticipated future unsterilised intervention, we shall follow the convention of assuming that the economy's equilibrium path is the unique path *BB* along which the value of *e* reflects exclusively the fundamental determinants of the exchange rate.[3] This path provides an important point of reference in our analysis below. It is the path followed by the economy after all expected intervention measures have been executed. The value of the exchange rate along *BB* at time *t* is[4]

$$e_t = (\alpha\,\mu/\beta^2) + (M_t/\beta) \tag{6}$$

However, the general solution for e_t is given by

$$e_t = K \exp[\beta t/\alpha] + \alpha\,\mu/\beta^2 + M_t/\beta \tag{7}$$

where *K* is an arbitrary constant determined at $t = 0$.

For positive (negative) values of *K*, the economy follows one of the unstable trajectories which lie to the left (right) of *BB*. As we shall

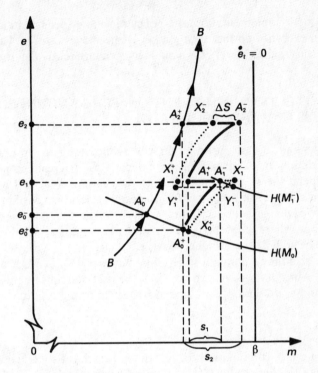

Figure 6.2   Effects of intervention

see below, in anticipation of intervention in *support* of domestic currency, the economy will always be on one of the paths to the right of BB.

For future reference it is also useful to establish that, in the light of equation (4), the value of $\dot{e}_t/e_t$ at any given point in Figure 6.2 is inversely related to m_t. Thus if we consider two paths along which domestic currency depreciates from one level of the exchange rate, e_1, to another, higher, level, e_2, it will take the economy relatively more time to reach the exchange rate e_2 when travelling along the path which is located further to the right. In addition, because in the relevant range (i.e., in the region between the *BB* curve and the $\dot{e}_t = 0$ locus) $\partial \dot{m}_t > 0$ and $\partial \dot{e}_t/\partial m_t < 0$, we note that at each level of e, the slope of a given perfect-foresight path is greater than the slope of another such path which lies to the right of it.

Having described the principal features of the model under a pure float, we shall consider next the effects of an announcement and

114 Non-sterilised Intervention and the Floating Exchange Rate

subsequent implementation of a policy of selling specific amounts of foreign exchange on the open market at specific levels of e. The time when each 'critical' level of e is attained is endogenously determined.[5]

6.3 EFFECTS OF INTERVENTION: PRE-ANNOUNCED LEVELS OF e AND AMOUNTS OF s

Let us suppose that, in an attempt to reduce the pace of currency depreciation, the Central Bank announces at $t = 0$ a plan temporarily to suspend the rules of pure floating by selling a total of $\bar{s}$ units of foreign currency in exchange for domestic currency at certain levels of the exchange rate: s_1 units are scheduled for sale when the exchange rate reaches the level e_1 and the remaining $s_2 = \bar{s} - s_1$ units are to be sold at some higher level, e_2.[6]

The economy's nominal stock of money at $t = 0$, M_0, is predetermined. Since $m_t \equiv M_t/e_t$, we note that the post-announcement values of m and e, m_0^+ and e_0^+, are linked by the following relationship:[7]

$$M_0 = m_0^+ e_0^+ \tag{8}$$

In Figure 6.2, combinations of m_0^+ and e_0^+ which satisfy equation (8) lie along the hyperbola $H(M_0)$. The economy's initial position *after* the announcement is one of the points along this curve. Assuming that the suspension of pure floating was totally unexpected, the economy's position just *before* the announcement is described by point A_0^-.

It is also clear that the execution of a fully-anticipated intervention measure cannot give rise to an exchange-rate jump along the economy's equilibrium perfect-foresight path. A jump in the level of e along a perfect-foresight path would offer speculators a profitable arbitrage opportunity. Because the existence of any such opportunity is inconsistent with the requirement that markets continuously clear, a path which exhibits an anticipated exchange-rate jump cannot be an equilibrium (see Calvo, 1977; Salant and Henderson, 1978; Krugman, 1979).

The requirement that e_t be continuous for all $t > 0$ (and right-continuous at $t = 0$) provides us with an important restriction on the economy's equilibrium path. For instance, when the intervention programme is completed with the sale of s_2 units of official reserves at $e = e_2$, signalling the return to pure floating, the economy must resume its ascent along the BB locus from point A_2^+ in Figure 6.2.

This in turn implies that the economy must reach point A_2^- the instant *before* the Central Bank removes s_2 units of domestic real balances from the market. By backtracking along the unique trajectory which passes through A_2^-, we note that the economy's equilibrium position *after* the first official sale at $e = e_1$ is point A_1^+. Because this first sale reduces m by s_1 units, the economy's position immediately before the sale is described by A_1^-. Tracing now the trajectory which passes through A_1^- back to the $H(M_0)$ locus, we reach A_0^-, the economy's initial post-announcement position.

In comparison with the path that would have been followed by the economy under pure floating, the path followed in anticipation of the announced intervention measures features the following: (a) an instantaneous appreciation of domestic currency, (b) a decline in the *rate* of depreciation at each level of $e < e_2$, (c) a tendency for the rate of depreciation to fall as e approaches a 'critical' level at which intervention is scheduled, and (d) an upward jump in the rate of depreciation immediately after each pre-announced sale of reserves.

These findings are summarised in Figure 6.3, where the dash–dot–dash line (furthest to the left) depicts the path of the exchange rate under pure floating and the solid line describes the path associated with the policy analysed above. The announcement of the intervention programme entails an instantaneous appreciation of domestic currency from e_0^- to e_0^+ at $t = 0$, and a simultaneous drop in the rate of depreciation. The proportional rate of depreciation declines until $t = T_1$, the moment at which e reaches the level e_1, triggering the first official sale of reserves. This sale removes s_1 units of m from the economy, resulting in a fully-anticipated, upward jump in the short-term money rate of interest and a corresponding jump in $\dot{e}_t/e_t$. As e approaches the level e_2, $\dot{e}_t/e_t$ declines once again in anticipation of the second round of intervention. With the completion of the intervention programme at $t = T_2$, $\dot{e}_t/e_t$ undergoes its final upward jump, rising to the rate that would have prevailed at $e = e_2$ under the perfectly flexible exchange-rate regime. This reflects the fact that once the exchange rate passes through the level e_2, it does indeed become perfectly flexible.

6.4 POLICY SHIFT: REALLOCATION OF RESERVE USE

How would the path of the exchange rate differ if the announced intervention programme were to call for a relatively larger sale of reserves at $e = e_1$ and a correspondingly smaller sale at $e = e_2$? In

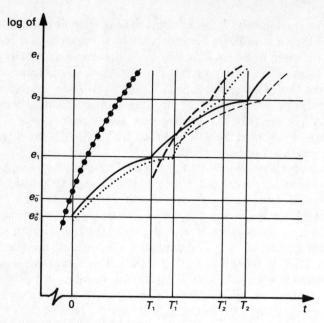

Figure 6.3   Summary of findings

Figure 6.2, let Δs represent the amount by which the quantity of reserves sold at the exchange rate e_2 is smaller (and at e_1 larger) than the quantity sold under the previously-considered policy. As before, by the process of backward induction, we are able to determine that the economy's equilibrium path is the one consisting of dotted curves which connect the points x_0^+, X_1^-, X_1^+, X_2^- and A_2^+ in Figure 6.2.

The path $X_1^+ X_2^-$, which the economy follows in transition from the first to the second round of intervention is shown to be to the left of the path $A_1^+ A_2^-$. This reflects the fact that under the new policy a *smaller* sale of official reserves at e_2 is anticipated to place the economy at A_2^+. Furthermore, because at each level of e the slope of any one trajectory in the relevant range is *greater* than the slope of another trajectory which lies to the right of it, the horizontal distance between X_1^+ is necessarily *smaller* than Δs. As the quantity of reserves sold at e_1 under the new policy exceeds the quantity sold under the old policy by *exactly* Δs units, it follows that X_1^- lies to the right of A_1^- and so the path $X_0^+ X_1^-$ lies to the right of $A_0^+ A_1^-$.

In summary, announcement of an increase in the quantity of reserves scheduled for sale in the first round of intervention at the expense of reserves available for the second round has the following effects on the time path of the exchange rate: it gives rise to an instantaneous appreciation of domestic currency and a fall in the rate of depreciation at each point in time for as long as $e<e_1$. This implies that the policy extends the period over which e remains below e_1. However, the policy also entails an increase in the rate of depreciation at each level of e between e_1 and e_2, and hence a *reduction* in the length of the period between the first and second rounds of intervention.

Because it takes the exchange rate *more* time to reach the level e_1 and *less* time to travel from e_1 to e_2, it appears that the effect of the policy change on the length of the period over which the exchange rate remains below e_2 is ambiguous. It can be shown, however, that under the new policy e reaches e_2 *sooner* than it does under the old policy. Recalling equation (6), which describes the relationship between e_t and M_t along BB, we observe that the value of M_t at point A_2^+ (call it M_2^+) is given by

$$M_2^+ = \text{ß}e_2 - (\alpha \, \mu/\text{ß}) \tag{6'}$$

We also know that if the nominal money stock grows at constant rate μ, it will have increased by μT_2^+ units over the interval from $t = 0$ to $t = T_2^+$, where T_2^+ is the moment when the economy reaches point A_2^+. In addition, the first and second rounds of intervention will have removed, over that same interval, $e_1 s_1$ and $e_2 s_2$ units of domestic currency from the market. Consequently, $M_2^+ = M_0 + \mu T_2^+ - e_1 s_1 - e_2 s_2$. This relationship, along with equation (6'), enables us to solve for T_2^+ as a function of the policy variables and the parameters of the model:

$$T_2^+ = [\text{ß}e_2 - (\alpha\mu/\text{ß}) - M_0 + e_1 s_1 + e_2 s_2]/\mu \tag{9}$$

Because $e_1<e_2$, an increase in s_1 *at the expense of s_2* necessarily lowers T_2^+. This result becomes more transparent if we note that the sale of a unit of official reserves reduces M by a *smaller* amount the lower the value of e at which the sale is conducted. In light of the fact that the underlying rate of growth of nominal balances is constant, it follows that the economy reaches its post-intervention position A_2^+ (and the corresponding nominal money stock M_2^+) sooner, the lower the value of e at which any given unit of foreign-exchange reserves is sold by the Central Bank.

The results of this section are summarised in Figure 6.3, which illustrates the relationship between the dotted exchange-rate path followed under the new policy, and the solid path followed under the old policy. The amount of time that elapses before e reaches e_1 under the new (old) policy is given by T_1' (T_1) and the amount of time that elapses before e reaches e_2 is given by T_2' (T_2). Moreover, the foregoing results are not affected by the timing of the announcement of the policy change during the relevant interval from $t = 0$ to $t = T_1$. Whenever the announcement is made, it will cause the economy to jump from the solid path to the corresponding point on the dotted path.

6.5 ENDOGENOUS ALLOCATION OF RESERVE USE

The quantity of reserves earmarked for sale at each critical level of e has thus far been treated as exogenous. It may be more realistic to assume that the Central Bank follows a policy according to which the amount of reserves offered for sale at $e = e_1$ is an increasing function of the rate of depreciation just prior to the sale. More specifically, let us suppose that the government announces at $t = 0$ that

$$s_1 = \tau(\dot{e}_1^-), \ \tau(0)=0, \ \tau(\dot{e}_1^*)\leqslant \bar{s}, \ \tau'(\cdot)>0 \tag{10}$$

where $\dot{e}_1^-$ denotes the *left* time derivative of the exchange rate at $e = e_1$, and $\dot{e}_1^*$ is the rate of depreciation along the path BB at $e = e_1$.

Moreover, let us assume that any reserves left over following the first round of intervention will be sold at $e = e_2$. That is, $s_2 = \bar{s} - \tau(\dot{e}_1^-)$, where $\bar{s}$ is constant.

In Section 6.4 we established that an increase in reserve use at $e = e_1$, at the expense of reserve use at $e = e_2$, reduces $\dot{e}_1^-$. Thus $\dot{e}_1^- = f(s_1, \cdot)$, where $\partial f(s_1, \cdot)/\partial s_1 < 0$. In conjunction with the pre-announced reaction function (10), this relationship enables us to solve for the value of s_1 (and the corresponding value of $\dot{e}_1^-$) along the economy's equilibrium perfect-foresight path. From that point, the analysis of the path followed by the economy proceeds along the same lines as in Section 6.3.

Finally, it is useful to note that in terms of this new policy-setting described by equation (10), a shift from the solid to the dotted path of the economy in Figure 6.2 and 6.3 may be interpreted to reflect an upward shift of the function $\tau(\cdot)$; that is to say, a shift to a relatively more aggressive intervention policy on the part of the Central Bank.

6.6 AN UNEXPECTED POLICY CHANGE

Let us consider next the path of the economy when the policy shift referred to in the preceding paragraph is not revealed to the market until the exchange rate reaches the level e_1. Unaware of the policy change, the economy follows the solid path $A_o^+ A_1^-$ in Figure 6.2 (and the corresponding solid path in Figure 6.3), for as long as $e < e_1$. Then, instead of auctioning off a stock of reserves amounting to s_1 units (as defined in Figure 6.2), the Central Bank surprises the market by placing an order to sell $s_1 + \Delta s$ units of foreign exchange. How does this unexpected increase in the magnitude of the first official sale affect the spot rate and the whole sequence of forward rates for $t > T_1$?[8]

Clearly, with only $s_2 - \Delta s$ units of foreign exchange remaining to be auctioned off at $e = e_2$, the economy must reach e_2 by travelling along the trajectory coinciding with the path $X_1^+ X_2^-$. Our problem is to determine the point along this trajectory from which the economy will resume its ascent subsequent to the first round of intervention.

A diagrammatic representation of the solution is simplest and probably the most illuminating. The existing nominal stock of domestic currency at $t = T_1^-$, the time when the economy arrives at point A_1^-, is given by $M_1^- = M_o + \mu T_1^-$. In Figure 6.2, combinations of e and m such that $em = M_1^-$ are points on the rectangular hyperbola $H(M_1^-)$. The economy's position at $t = T_1$ (i.e., after the Central Bank reveals its offer to sell $s_1 + \Delta s$ units of foreign exchange, but *before* the sale is actually executed at the market-clearing value of e), is represented by one of the points along the $H(M_1^-)$ locus. Immediately *following* the sale, the economy's position is, as established above, one of the points along the trajectory passing through X_2^-. Furthermore, we know that the sale reduces m by $s_1 + \Delta s$ units. Accordingly, the economy must be at the points Y_1^- and Y_1^+ just before and after the sale, respectively. These are the only points along the two curves such that the stock of real balances before the sale is greater than that after the sale by exactly $s_1 + \Delta s$ units.

We have seen in Sections 6.3 and 6.4 that a fully-anticipated intervention measure gives rise to a jump only in m and $\dot{e}_t / e_t$. By contrast, an *unanticipated sale* of reserves (amounting to Δs units in the present example) entails, in addition, an instantaneous appreciation of domestic currency. Because the stock of real balances at point Y_1^+ is smaller than the stock of real balances at A_1^+, it is also evident that an unanticipated sale of reserves results in an upward jump of $\dot{e}_t/e_t$ (and the short-term money rate of interest) which is larger than anticipated.

These results are illustrated in Figure 6.3, where e follows the solid path from $t = 0$ until $t = T_1$. Then, instead of continuing to rise along the solid path, e exhibits a downward jump to the starting point of the path depicted by the thick, broken line. In the absence of any further change in intervention policy, this latter curve traces the subsequent path of the exchange rate.

An auction which is smaller than expected

The same reasoning may be employed in studying the path of the economy when the quantity of reserves sold at $e = e_1$ turns out to be *smaller* than anticipated. In terms of the magnitudes defined in Figure 6.2, let us suppose that at $t = 0$ agents expect the Central Bank to sell $s_1 + \Delta s$ units of foreign exchange when e reaches the level e_1, and to retain the remaining $s_2 - \Delta s$ units for the second round of intervention at $e = e_2$. Accordingly, the economy follows the path $X_0^+ X_1^-$ up until $t = T_1'$ – the time when e reaches the level e_1. At that point, the Central Bank reveals its intention to sell only s_1, rather than $s_1 + \Delta s$, units of foreign exchange. As this implies in the present setting that s_2 (rather than $s_2 - \Delta s$) units will be sold at $e = e_2$, the economy's equilibrium position immediately after the first reserve auction is one of the points on the trajectory which passes through A_2^-. To determine the exact point, note that just prior to the auction the economy is located somewhere along the rectangular hyperbola (not shown in Figure 6.2) which passes through point X_1^-. The point we seek lies to the left of this hyperbola by exactly s_1 units. Accordingly, it must be a point on the path $A_1^+ A_2^-$ located somewhere above A_1^+.

The time path of e for $e \leq e_1$ is illustrated in Figure 6.3 by the dotted curve over the interval from time 0 to T_1'. The nature of the actual intervention policy is revealed at the end of that interval, precipitating a jump in e to the starting point of the path depicted by the thin, broken curve. In the absence of any further policy change, it is this latter curve which traces the evolution of e following the first round of intervention.

In studying the effects of a larger-than-expected and a smaller-than-expected sale of reserves at $e = e_1$, we have identified an interesting trade-off between the short-run and long-run effects of unanticipated intervention. For example, if the magnitude of the first auction is *larger* than anticipated, the auction entails an instantaneous *appreciation* of domestic currency and a *larger-than-expected increase in the rate of depreciation*. Thus, from the perspective of bolstering the value of domestic currency, the benefits of the instantaneous unanticipated appreciation are only transitory. This is illustrated in Figure 6.3 by the intersection of the solid curve and the thick, broken curve in the range between $e = e_1$ and $e = e_2$, signifying that the exchange rate reaches the level e_2 *sooner* along the broken curve in spite of the instantaneous appreciation at $t = T_1$.[9]

Alternatively, if the size of the first auction happens to be *smaller* than anticipated, we have seen that e exhibits an *upward* jump while the rate of depreciation rises by *less* than it otherwise would. The relationship between the dotted and the thin, broken path in Figure 6.3 shows, however, that the initial weakness of domestic currency subsequent to the first round of intervention is eventually dominated by the favourable effect of a lower rate of depreciation:[10] after the two paths intersect, the Central Bank reaps the benefits of a smaller-than-expected sale of reserves by enjoying a *permanently* lower time path of e.

On the incentive to deviate from the announced policy

Assuming that the Central Bank's objective is to keep domestic currency as strong as possible over its entire path – given the available stock of official reserves and the underlying rate of domestic credit expansion – can we draw any policy implications from the foregoing analysis? One immediate implication is that the Central Bank has an incentive to sell a smaller-than-expected quantity of reserves at the first critical level of e. With reference to Figure 6.3, a comparison of the solid path with the one consisting of the dotted path from $t = 0$ to $t = T_1'$ and the thin, broken path thereafter, reveals that a policy of convincingly threatening to intervene more aggressively at $e = e_1$, without actually doing so, serves to lower the value of e at *each* point in time. The interested reader can easily verify that the lowest path of e is attained by the Central Bank in the present setting – where reserves are sold at either one or the other critical level of e – by persuading market participants that it will sell its entire stock of reserves at $e = e_1$ while in fact planning to sell it at $e = e_2$.

Within our framework of analysis, would the Central Bank ever have an incentive to auction off a greater-than-expected quantity of reserves in the first round of intervention? If the benefits of such a policy are measured by the extent to which it lowers the time path of e, we have already seen that such benefits are confined to a brief period immediately after the policy is executed. Only a Central Bank with a sufficiently short time horizon would be interested in implementing such a policy. However, in a more general setting where $\bar{s}$ is not exogenously given and where the quantities of reserves that market participants expect to be auctioned off at higher levels of e are directly related to the size of the initial auction, the effects of the policy may be considerably more favourable.

On relaxing some of the constraints

The foregoing analysis has been based on the assumption that $\bar{s}$, the total stock of reserves committed to the intervention programme, is exogenously given. While this assumption may be appropriate in studying intervention programmes undertaken by Central Banks which face rigid foreign-exchange constraints, it is less so when the monetary authority has access to additional reserves.[11]

If the Central Bank is in a position to commit additional units of foreign currency to its intervention programme, the simple link between the observed magnitude of the first auction and the expected magnitude of the second auction is broken. A larger-than-expected official sale at the first critical level of e may now be interpreted by market participants to signify an increase, rather than a decline, in the quantity of reserves earmarked for sale at the second critical level. In comparison with the case considered earlier, a greater-than-expected official sale at $e = e_1$ would entail, under the present interpretation, a relatively larger instantaneous appreciation of domestic currency. Moreover, depending upon the magnitude of the perceived increase in the quantity of reserves committed to the second round of intervention, the short-term rate of interest may either increase or decline. As we may recall, the latter possibility does not emerge when $\bar{s}$ is constant.

In a setting where the rate of domestic credit creation is also subject to change, unexpectedly aggressive unsterilised intervention at the first critical level of e may be perceived to signal a possible future reduction in μ.[12] Because a reduction in μ shifts the path BB in Figure 6.2 to the right, the prospect of such a reduction has a similar effect on the time path of the exchange rate as does the prospect of an increase in the quantity of reserves scheduled for sale at the second critical level of *e*. Should a larger-than-expected sale of reserves in the first round of intervention be viewed in this manner, it would result in an instantaneous appreciation of domestic currency and, as in the case considered in the previous paragraph, possibly an un-anticipated decline in the rate of interest.

6.7 CONCLUDING REMARKS

In concluding the paper, it is useful to discuss the problem of measuring the effects of unsterilised intervention. Clearly, if such an act is fully anticipated, one should not expect it to be followed by a jump either in the exchange rate or in the money rate of interest on long-term bonds (in a framework where the market for such bonds is considered explicitly). A jump should be observed only in the time path of the short-term interest rate and the rate of depreciation.

We have also seen that the larger the magnitude of the expected auction, the lower the rate of depreciation prior to the sale. Accordingly, it may be said that the prospect of unsterilised intervention *does* serve to keep the market in check. However, because the auction is fully anticipated, it is not the fear of a capital loss on the part of speculators that maintains the exchange rate on a path characterised by a relatively lower rate of depreciation. What reduces the rate of depreciation is the growth in the demand for real balances in anticipation of intervention and the implied drop in the stock of domestic currency.

In the event that an intervention measure *is* accompanied by a jump in the exchange rate and/or the long rate of interest, at least some aspect of it has not been anticipated. In analysing the implications of unanticipated intervention, it was useful to consider separately two distinct cases. In one case the stock of reserves committed to the entire intervention programme is fixed. Accordingly, any of the reserves remaining after the first round of intervention are expected to be auctioned off at some higher level (or levels) of *e*. In the second case the Central Bank may be in a position to commit additional reserves to its intervention programme so that a larger-than-expected auction at the first critical level of *e* need not signify a reduction in the quantity of reserves committed to the subsequent rounds of intervention.

The first case, to which most of the present paper is devoted, provides a useful framework for the analysis of intervention programmes undertaken by Central Banks operating under tight reserve constraints. In that particular setting, a smaller-than-expected sale of reserves at the first critical level of e gives rise to an instantaneous depreciation of domestic currency and a tendency for the short rate of interest to increase in relation to its level before the auction, but *not by as much as has been anticipated*. Accordingly, one would observe a decline in the long-term money rate of interest (or the average of expected future short-term rates). Alternatively, if an intervention measure gives rise to an instantaneous appreciation of domestic currency and an increase in the long rate of interest, one may infer that the magnitude of the official sale was *larger* than anticipated.

If the Central Bank is in a position to commit additional reserves to its intervention programme or to alter the rate of domestic credit creation, a larger-than-expected official sale at the first critical level of e may be interpreted by market participants in a number of ways. To the extent that the measure is perceived to signal a possible future reduction in the rate of domestic credit creation or an *increase* in the quantity of reserves committed to the subsequent round (or rounds) of intervention, it is possible to observe, along with an instantaneous appreciation of domestic currency, either an increase or a decline in the short- and long-term rates of interest.

Notes

* I wish to thank the participants in seminars at Columbia University and the University of Pennsylvania and the conference on 'Exchange Rates and Currency Unions' at the Bundesbank in February 1990, for helpful comments on an earlier draft of this paper. Any of the remaining errors are my own.

1. Reasons for intervening in the foreign-exchange market are discussed by Argy (1982); Boyer (1978); Buiter (1979); Djajić (1984); Frenkel and Aizenman (1982); and Turnovsky (1983), among others.

2. Proceeding, instead, under the assumption that the *proportional* rate of growth of M_t is constant would not alter any of the main conclusions of the present study.

3. Our analysis of the economy in the absence of intervention does not take into consideration exchange-rate paths which may reflect divergent speculative bubbles. Some of the implications of embarking on such a path within the framework of the present model are discussed by Flood and Garber (1984). See also Obstfeld and Rogoff (1983) who show that, in the context of a maximising model, both implosive and explosive price

paths can be ruled out under reasonable assumptions.

4. Following Flood and Garber (1984), let us conjecture that the solution for e_t is of the form

$$e_t = \gamma_0 + \gamma_1 M_t$$

Noting that $dM_t/dt = \mu$, we then have $\dot{e}_t = \gamma_1 \mu$. In addition, money-market equilibrium implies that

$$\dot{e}_t = (\beta e_t - M_t)/\alpha$$

By setting the two expressions for $\dot{e}_t$ equal to each other, we find that

$$\gamma_1 \mu = (\beta e_t - M_t)/\alpha$$

or

$$e_t = (\gamma_1 \mu \alpha/\beta) + (M_t/\beta)$$

It is now possible to determine the values of coefficients γ_0 and γ_1: $\gamma_0 = \mu\alpha/\beta^2$ and $\gamma_1 = 1/\beta$, as stated in equation (6).

5. Intervention programmes which call for occasional sales of official reserves can take any one of three different forms, depending on which of the following the Central Bank leaves to market forces to determine: (a) the levels of the exchange rate, e_i, at which intervention is to take place, (b) the quantities of foreign-exchange reserves, s_i, sold by the Central Bank when intervening at the exchange rate e_i, or (c) the timing of intervention, T_i. The present study considers intervention programmes which fix e_i and s_i, while allowing T_i to be determined endogenously. However, if one is interested in studying the implications of intervention within regimes of the crawling-peg type, one would assume that the Central Bank sets e_i and T_i, allowing market forces to determine s_i. Similarly, the effects of a series of reserve auctions at specific points in time may be studied by fixing s_i and T_i and allowing e_i to be endogenously determined.

6. This policy is similar in nature to those examined by Salant and Henderson (1978) and Salant (1983) in the context of an exhaustible-resource market. Salant and Henderson (1978) study the price path of a resource in anticipation of a *single* possible auction of a stock held by the government. Salant (1983) briefly discusses how the prospect of such an auction after the collapse of an official pegging policy affects the magnitude and timing of the speculative attack that terminates the price-fixing scheme. Of related interest are the works of Flood and Garber (1983), Obstfeld (1984), Obstfeld and Stockman (1985), and Dyajić (1989), which study the dynamics of a floating exchange rate in anticipation of a pegging policy which is expected to maintain e at *one specific level* for an *extended period* of time.

7. Because m and e will generally jump in response to an announcement of a new policy, it is necessary to distinguish between the left-hand and right-hand limits of those variables which are not predetermined.

Throughout the paper the following convention is adopted: superscripts '−' and '+' signify left-hand and right-hand limits of variables, respectively.

8. From a practical point of view, this question is an interesting one because Central Banks, more often than not, conduct policy measures which are, with respect to their timing and magnitude, not fully anticipated by market participants. From the theoretical perspective, however, the analysis of an unanticipated change in intervention policy raises a number of important questions, including those related to the specification of the Central Bank's objective function and the time consistency of the announced policy measures. No attempt is made to resolve these questions within the limited space available for the present paper. Instead, I treat intervention policy as exogenous and consider policy changes which, within the simple framework of our model, resemble those actually implemented by Central Banks.

9. This can be easily verified by noting that the quantities of foreign exchange auctioned in the first and second rounds of intervention are identical to those which produce the dotted path. The only difference in the present case is that the $s_1 + \Delta s$ units offered in the first round are sold at $e < e_1$. In the light of equation (9), this implies that e reaches the level e_2 sooner when travelling along the thick, broken path than it does when travelling along either the dotted or the solid path.

10. That the thin, broken path intersects the dotted path at some value of $e < e_2$ can be verified by recalling equation (9) and observing that the quantities of foreign exchange auctioned in the first and second rounds of intervention are identical to those which produce the solid path. However, in contrast with the policy followed along the solid path, the s_1 units offered in the first round are sold at $e > e_1$. This guarantees that, when travelling along the thin, broken path, e reaches the level e_2 at $t > T_2$.

11. The problem of borrowing reserves in an effort to maintain a fixed exchange rate has been analysed by Buiter (1986) and Obstfeld (1986).

12. The possibility that intervention may be interpreted as a signal of future changes in monetary policy (or other policies which may affect the time path of the exchange rate) is discussed by Genberg (1981) and Kenen (1987).

References

Argy, Victor E. (1982) 'Exchange Rate Management in Theory and Practice,' Princeton Studies in International Finance, no. 50.

Boyer, Russell S. (1978) 'Optimal Foreign Exchange Market Intervention', *Journal of Political Economy '86* (December) pp. 1045–55.

Buiter, Willem H. (1979) 'Optimal Foreign Exchange Market Intervention with Rational Expectations', in Martin, J. and Smith, A. (eds), *Trade and Payments Adjustment under Flexible Exchange Rates*, London. Macmillan.

Buiter, Willem H. (1986) 'Borrowing to Defend the Exchange Rate and the Timing and Magnitude of Speculative Attacks', NBER Working

Paper, no. 1894 (February).

Calvo, Guillermo A. (1977) 'The Stability of Models of Money and Perfect Foresight: A Comment', *Econometrica*, 45 (October) pp. 1737–9.

Djajić, Slobodan (1984) 'Currency Management and Economic Stability', *Economic Journal*, 94 (June) pp. 324–39.

Djajić, Slobodan (1989) 'Dynamics of the Exchange Rate in Anticipation of Pegging', *Journal of International Money and Finance*, 8 (December) pp. 559–71.

Feldstein, Martin (1986) 'New Evidence on the Effects of Exchange Rate Intervention', NBER Working Paper, no. 2052 (October).

Flood, Rober E. and Garber, Peter M. (1983) 'A Model of Stochastic Process Switching', *Econometrica*, 51 (May) pp. 537–51.

Flood, Robert E. and Garber, Peter M. (1984) 'Collapsing Exchange Rate Regimes: Some Linear Examples', *Journal of International Economics*, 17 (August) pp. 1–13.

Frenkel, Jacob A. and Aizenman, Joshua (1982) 'Aspects of the Optimal Management of Exchange Rates', *Journal of International Economics*, 13 (November) pp. 231–56.

Genberg, Hans (1981) 'Effects of Central Bank Intervention in the Foreign Exchange Market', *International Monetary Fund Staff Papers*, 28 (September) pp. 451–76.

Ito, Takatoshi (1986) 'The Intra-Daily Exchange Rate Dynamics and Monetary Policies after the G5 Agreement', NBER Working Paper, no. 2048 (October).

Kenen, Peter B. (1987) 'Exchange Rate Management: What Role for Intervention?', *American Economic Review*, 77 (May 1987) pp. 194–9.

Krugman, Paul (1979) 'A Model of Balance-of-Payments Crises', *Journal of Money, Credit, and Banking*, 11 (August) pp. 311–25.

Obstfeld, Maurice (1984) 'Balance-of-Payments Crises and Devaluation', *Journal of Money, Credit, and Banking*, 16 (May) pp. 208–17.

Obstfeld, Maurice (1986) 'Speculative Attack and the External Constraint in a Maximizing Model of the Balance of Payments', *Canadian Journal of Economics*, 19 (February) pp. 1–22.

Obstfeld, Maurice and Rogoff, Kenneth (1983) 'Speculative Hyperinflations in Maximizing Models: Can We Rule Them Out?', *Journal of Political Economy*, 91 (August) pp. 675–87.

Obstfeld, Maurice and Stockman, Alan C. (1985) 'Exchange-Rate Dynamics', in Nenan, P.B. and Jones R.W. (eds), *Handbook of International Economics*, vol. 2, Amsterdam, North-Holland.

Salant, Stephen W. (1983) 'The Vulnerability of Price Stabilization Schemes to Speculative Attack', *Journal of Political Economy*, 91 (February) pp. 1–38.

Salant, Stephen W. and Henderson, Dale W. (1978) 'Market Anticipations of Government Policies and the Price of Gold', *Journal of Political Economy*, 86 (August) pp. 627–48.

Turnovsky, Stephen J. (1983) 'Exchange Market Intervention Policies in a Small Open Economy', in Bhandari, J.S., and Putnam, B.H. (eds), *Economic Interdependence and Flexible Exchange Rates*, Cambridge, Mass., MIT Press.

Discussion

André M.M. Kolodziejak

The interesting paper presented by Slobodan Djajić studies the influence exerted on the path of a floating exchange rate by non-sterilised intervention in the foreign-exchange market. This is done within the theoretical mathematical framework of a simple model of a small open economy operating under the conditions of perfect international capital mobility.

The question I want to focus on is: what does the analysis tell us, and what does it fail to tell us – or rather what is it unable to tell us?

1. Djajić supposes that in an attempt to reduce the pace of currency depreciation, the Central Bank announces at $t = 0$ a plan temporarily to suspend the rules of pure floating by selling a total of $\bar{S}$ units of foreign currency in exchange for domestic currency at certain levels of the exchange rate: $S_2 = \bar{S} - S_1$ units are to be sold at some higher level, e_2; when the exchange rate passes through level e_2 it becomes perfectly flexible. The analysis carried out by Djajić shows the picture of the path of the exchange rate under pure floating, and also the one arising from an intervention policy. The intervention is effective: the announcement of the intervention programme entails an instantaneous appreciation of domestic currency from e_0^- to e_0^+ at $t = 0$, and a simultaneous drop in the rate of depreciation.

2. The analysis further shows how the path of the exchange rate would differ if the announced intervention programme were to call for a relatively larger sale of reserves at $e = e_1$ and a correspondingly smaller sale at $e = e_2$ In that case, it takes the exchange rate more time to reach the level e_1 and less time to travel from e_1 to e_2, and under this policy e reaches e_2 sooner than it does under the old policy.

3. Djajić also introduced the possibility of endogenous allocation of reserve use, which means that the Central Bank follows a policy according to which the amount of reserves offered for sale at $e = e_1$ is an increasing function of the rate of depreciation recorded just prior to the intervention.

4. After having analysed the fully-anticipated intervention measure

which gives rise to a jump only in the stock of real balances m and the expected (= actual) proportional rate of depreciation of domestic currency ($\dot{e}_+/e_t$, Djajić goes into an unanticipated sale of reserves which entails, by contrast to the fully-anticipated sale, an instantaneous appreciation of domestic currency. An unanticipated sale of reserves results in an upward jump of the rate of depreciation of the domestic currency $\dot{e}_+/e_t$ and in a short-term money rate of interest larger than expected.

5. Djajić then analyses an auction smaller or larger than expected, and he identifies an interesting trade-off between the short-run and long-run effects of unanticipated intervention. If, for instance, the magnitude of the first auction is larger than anticipated, the auction entails an instantaneous appreciation of domestic currency and a larger-than-expected increase in the rate of depreciation. From the perspective of bolstering the value of domestic currency, the benefits of the instantaneous unanticipated appreciation are only transitory.

6. At the end of the analysis the author moves to policy implications, assuming that the Central Bank's objective is to keep domestic currency as strong as possible over its entire path – given the available stock of official reserves and the underlying rate of domestic credit expansion. An interesting implication is that the Central Bank has an incentive to sell a smaller-than-expected quantity of reserves at the first critical level of the exchange rate e. The lowest path of e is attained by the Central Bank in the present setting – where reserves are sold at either one or the other critical level of the exchange rate e – by persuading market participants that it will sell its entire stock of reserves at $e = e_1$ while in fact planning to sell it at $e = e_2$. Within the framework of Drajić's analysis, only a Central Bank with a sufficiently short time horizon would ever have an incentive to auction off a greater-than-expected quantity of reserves in the first round of intervention.

So far, we have the answer to the question of what this interesting paper tells us. But what does it or can it not, tell us in my opinion the policy implications that follow from this theoretical analysis are rather limited. And when we talk about intervention in the exchange market and floating exchange rate we talk about economic reality, which cannot, I think, be modelled as simply as is done here as long as we as economists intend to produce scientific work that is linked in one way or another to the real world.

We have to take care that we do not fall into the trap of what Whitehead in 1965 called 'The fallacy of misplaced concreteness'. We have to ask ourselves whether our conclusions have to be modified in the light of what we omitted from the analysis, but should have taken into account.

Djajić makes correct and creative use of the model he develops, but the problems are inherent in the model itself and in the far-reaching abstractions needed to build it in the way it has been constructed:

1. Can a small open economy ever cushion a falling currency by selling reserves? Or can it use only the interest instrument, not the money volume instrument?
2. What about imperfect international capital mobility? If there is imperfect international capital mobility, domestic money supply is not the only source of money creation, as empirical research shows.
3. The empirical proof of an important influence exerted by non-sterilised intervention measures is rather weak.
4. The economy under consideration produces and consumes only a single traded commodity. Leaving economic growth out of the analysis, the situation examined shows a trend of currency depreciation.
5. The analysis is rather ambiguous as far as the influence of interventions via the expectations channel is concerned. The question is whether the influence of interventions via the expectations channel and via the monetary channel can be modelled simultaneously.
6. Djajić thinks that his analysis can explain to some extent why Central Banks may not intervene as aggressively as their statements on intervention policy would seem to indicate. I consider the results from the analysis concerning the effectiveness of interventions to be very much influenced by the way the money market is modelled, including the demand for real balances.

7 On the Effectiveness of Daily Intervention by the Deutsche Bundesbank and the Federal Reserve System in the US Dollar – Deutsche Mark Exchange Market*

Sylvester Eijffinger and Noud Gruijters

7.1 INTRODUCTION

The purpose of this paper is to test empirically whether interventions by the Deutsche Bundesbank and the Federal Reserve System in the US dollar–Deutsche Mark spot exchange market were effective during the period from February 1985 until August 1988.

After a short description of some aspects of official interventions in foreign–exchange markets and a description of three mechanisms through which intervention can influence the exchange rate in theory (Section 7.2), an empirical study is carried out with daily data on interventions by the Bundesbank and the Federal Reserve (Section 7.3). With these daily data it is possible to test whether interventions had an immediate impact on the dollar–Deutsche Mark exchange rate by altering the market expectations, whether coordinated interventions were more effective than non-coordinated interventions and whether the effectiveness of interventions was determined solely by their announcement effect.

7.2　SOME ASPECTS OF OFFICIAL INTERVENTION

Definition

Since the breakdown of the Bretton Woods fixed exchange-rate system in the early 1970s, the exchange value of the major currencies in the industrialised world (for instance, the US dollar, the Deutsche Mark and the Japanese Yen) has in principle been determined by market forces. However, in the present system of managed floating the exchange rate is not the outcome of supply and demand by market participants only. The monetary authorities of many countries have tried to influence the relative value of their currencies, frequently by exchange-market interventions.

An official intervention is a sale or purchase of foreign exchange against domestic currency, which monetary authorities undertake in the exchange market.[1] According to the Report of the Working Group on exchange market intervention (1983), interventions in the past have served as a means for different kinds of objectives, related to both short-term and long-term market conditions.

In the short run, monetary authorities intervened to 'counter disorderly market conditions', as indicated by a widening of bid–offer spreads, increasing uncertainty in the market or large intra-day exchange-rate movements. Under such circumstances official interventions were used to influence market psychology and to resist exchange-rate movements that gain a momentum of their own (so-called 'bandwagon' effects). Monetary authorities intervened over longer periods to smooth exchange-rate movements and to bring the exchange rate into line with an equilibrium value based on 'fundamentals' (for example, inflation, money growth and balance of payment accounts).

Beside these 'active' interventions to influence the exchange-rate directly, Central Banks at times intervened for other motives, such as to build up foreign-exchange reserves or to carry out customer transactions.[2] These customer transactions are purchases or sales of foreign currency undertaken by a Central Bank on behalf of (for example) its government. Although their ultimate objectives differ, the effect of these 'passive' interventions and the 'active' interventions on the exchange rate may be the same in practice, if the customer transactions are guided by exchange policy considerations and if these transactions are timed properly.[3]

The monetary authorities can intervene in either the spot or the forward market. A purchase or sale of foreign currency in the forward market will be preferred if the monetary authorities want to postpone the effects of an intervention on the domestic monetary base or money supply. However, an intervention in the forward market will the current spot exchange rate affect only if the opponent of the Central Bank in the forward market transaction immediately offsets the exchange risk on the uncovered forward position in the spot market.[4]

Finally, a distinction can be made between sterilised and non-sterilised interventions. 'Sterilised intervention' refers to purchases and sales of foreign currency whose impact on the home country's money stock is offset through domestic open-market transactions.[5] If, for instance, the Central Bank purchases foreign exchange against domestic currency from commercial banks in order to support the value of foreign currency, the reserve position of the banking sector as a whole increases. As soon as the commercial banks supply more credit facilities to the public based upon their increased liquidity position, the exchange-market intervention results in an increase of the domestic money supply. If such an increase is not consistent with the Central Bank's monetary growth objective, the Central Bank can sterilise the liquidity effect of the intervention by selling domestic currency assets to the banking sector, leaving the monetary base unchanged.

If sterilised interventions have a permanent effect, the monetary authorities are able to realise an exchange-rate target independent of a monetary growth target. If, on the other hand, sterilised interventions are not effective and non-sterilised (or partially sterilised) interventions do affect the exchange rate, the effectiveness of interventions will depend primarily on the influence of a change in the money supply on the exchange rate. In theory both sterilised and non-sterilised interventions may have a permanent influence on the relative value of a currency through different transmission mechanisms.

Three channels of influence[6]

Humpage (1986) mentions three different channels through which exchange-market intervention can influence exchange rates: the monetary channel, the portfolio-adjustment channel and the expectations channel (see Figure 7.1).

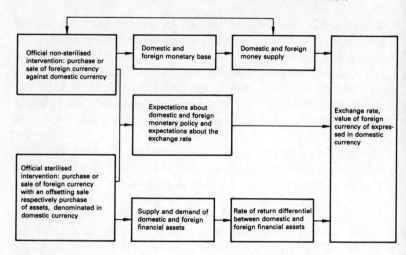

Figure 7.1   Three channels of influence of official intervention

1. In the *monetary channel*, an intervention influences the exchange rate if the effect of the intervention on the relative money supply of both countries is not completely sterilised. Under this condition a purchase of foreign exchange by the monetary authorities will result in an increase of the domestic money supply. According to the classical quantity theory of money, an increase of the money supply will result in a similar increase of the domestic price level. If the exchange rate is determined by trade flows and PPP, the domestic currency will depreciate as a consequence of the rise in the domestic price level. Although this adjustment process takes time, and although PPP may not hold, the relative rates of money growth between different countries are important determinants of nominal exchange rates and, therefore, non-sterilised interventions may be effective in the long run. Moreover, an intervention may be effective through the monetary channel in the short run, under the assumption of rational expectations. If, for instance, a purchase of foreign currency by the domestic Central Bank is interpreted by the market as a sign of a future expansionary monetary policy, the domestic currency will depreciate immediately.[7]

2. A sterilised intervention can be effective through the *portfolio-adjustment channel* under the two assumptions, that (1) the public holds both domestic and foreign financial assets in their portfolios and that (2) these assets are not perfect substitutes. In this situa-

tion investors will not be indifferent about the currency denomina-
tion of the securities in their portfolios, because of (for instance)
differences in exchange-rate risk, political risk and default risk
between domestic and foreign assets. In order to induce the
risk-averse investors to hold the supply of domestic and foreign
assets, equilibrium in the financial markets results in a risk premium on the more risky (foreign) assets. This risk premium equals
the nominal interest differential between foreign and domestic
assets plus the expected rate of depreciation of the domestic
currency against the foreign currency.

A sterilised intervention can influence the exchange rate by
changing the relative supply of domestic and foreign assets. Suppose that the monetary authorities sterilise the expansionary effect
of a purchase of foreign currency on the domestic money supply
by an offsetting sale of domestic securities. This sterilised intervention results in an excess supply of domestic securities and, in
order to rebalance their portfolios, an excess demand for foreign
securities by the investors. Given the supply of foreign assets, the
foreign interest rate and the expected future spot rate, financial-
market equilibrium will be restored by a rise in the domestic
interest rate and a depreciation of the domestic currency (a rise in
the current spot rate) both leading to a drop in the risk premium
on foreign assets. Thus, in theory, monetary authorities can realise both a monetary growth objective and an exchange-rate objective by sterilising interventions.

In practice, the empirical evidence on the effectiveness of sterilised intervention is weak,[8] and monetary policy-makers themselves have expressed their doubts on the possibility of exerting a
significant effect on exchange rates in the face of persistent market
pressures by sterilised intervention.[9] Furthermore, in reality the
distinction between sterilised and non-sterilised intervention becomes fuzzy in the short run, as Central Banks do not automatically compensate an intervention by an offsetting open-market
operation.[10]

3. Finally, monetary authorities can try to influence the exchange
   rate through the *expectations channel*.

   If foreign-exchange markets were perfectly efficient, all the
relevant information on exchange-rate determinants would be
aggregated, correctly interpreted and finally processed by the
market participants into a rational expectation for the future spot
rate. If no market imperfections such as transaction costs and

capital restrictions existed, the current spot rate would be consistent with this expectation for the future spot rate at any moment because of the positions taken by profit-maximising speculators and arbitragers in the market. In such a world Central Banks would not be able to influence the exchange rate through interventions, without changing their monetary policies but, on the other hand, there would be no need for interventions. Nevertheless, in the real world of uncertainty, excessive exchange-rate movements, 'bandwagon' effects, speculative bubbles and market imperfections, there is a case for official intervention. As soon as the market does not take account of all the relevant information of 'fundamentals' or of changes in these exchange-rate determinants, Central Banks can try to give the market a signal by an intervention. This supposes, however, that the monetary authorities have a better insight in economic developments or possess better information than the market. But if the monetary authorities are able to emphasise neglected information or to provide new information by intervening, the exchange rate will be affected immediately in a highly (although not perfectly) efficient market.

It is thus possible that interventions, whether sterilised or non-sterilised, affect the exchange rate through the expectations channel. Although it can be very difficult to change market expectations, the monetary authorities have intervened frequently on a large scale to remove perceived market inefficiencies.[11] The effectiveness of these interventions will, however, depend on the specific circumstances, the timing and scale of the intervention, the opinion and determination of the market as well as on the credibility of the monetary authorities.[12]

3.   INTERVENTIONS BY THE DEUTSCHE BUNDESBANK AND THE FEDERAL RESERVE SYSTEM IN THE DOLLAR–DEUTSCHE MARK MARKET

Specification of the regression equations

In this section, an empirical study is undertaken, using daily intervention data and intra-day exchange-rate data, into the question whether the Deutsche Bundesbank and the Federal Reserve System have been able to influence the dollar–Deutsche Mark exchange rate systematically through the expectations channel from February 1985 until August 1988. Although the effectiveness of interventions depends (as mentioned above) on the specific circumstances at the moment of the intervention, it makes sense to test for the systematical effectiveness of interventions, under the assumption that the Bundesbank and the Federal Reserve will intervene only when the circumstances are favourable for attaining their exchange-rate objective in the short run.

This empirical analysis is limited to the spot interventions of the Bundesbank and the Federal Reserve in the US dollar–Deutsche Mark market.[13] Officially, both the Bundesbank and the Federal Reserve intervene in the first place to 'counter disorderly market conditions'. However, the criterion of 'disorderly market conditions' is open to discussion, and therefore compatible with different strategies for intervention. For example, if 'disorder' is associated with erratic short-term exchange-rate fluctuations a policy of 'leaning against the wind' would seem to be appropriate for intervention. A 'leaning against the wind' policy is oriented towards the actual path of the exchange rate; as soon as the current exchange rate rises or falls the Central Bank will sell or purchase foreign exchange in order to smooth excessive exchange-rate swings in both directions.

If, on the contrary, 'disorder' is associated with an under- or overvaluation of a currency regarding 'fundamentals', the intervention policy will be oriented towards an equilibrium value of the exchange rate. In this case a Central Bank will sell or purchase foreign currency as long as it is believed to be over- or undervalued.

Ex post, it can be inferred from the change in the foreign-currency reserves of a Central Bank during a long period, which policy has been followed. If a 'leaning against the wind' policy is carried out the Central Bank reserves will not have changed significantly: the sales of foreign currency will in general equal the purchases. If, however, a Central Bank has tried to guide the exchange rate to an equilibrium level by interventions, the foreign currency reserves will change noticeably in one direction through either sales or purchases of foreign exchange.[14]

The daily data on interventions of the Bundesbank and the Federal Reserve in the dollar–Deutsche Mark exchange market from February 1985 until September 1988 show that interventions were concentrated in specific months, and thus that periods of interventions alternated with longer periods of non-intervention. Moreover, the interventions in these relatively short periods were one-sided (either purchases or sales) with the expectations of September 1986 and

August 1987. In these two months the Bundesbank first sold dollars and later purchased dollars. It may thus be concluded that neither the Bundesbank (although intervening more frequently and for larger amounts), nor the Federal Reserve intervened only to smooth exchange rate movements, but tried also to influence the exchange rate (or market sentiment) in a specific direction towards an equilibrium value.[15]

Therefore, whatever the ultimate objective and the precise strategy followed by the Bundesbank and the Federal Reserve, interventions are considered to be effective in this study as soon as a purchase (sale) of dollars results in (1) a rise (fall) of the dollar–Deutsche Mark exchange rate, or (2) a deceleration of a downward (upward) movement in the exchange rate. In the first case the Central Banks reverse the exchange-rate movement and in the second they slow down the exchange-rate movement by intervening.

Under the assumption of highly efficient markets, effective interventions will influence the exchange-rate movement immediately (i.e., within the same day) by altering the expectations of market participants. The intra-day change of the dollar–Deutsche Mark exchange rate can thus be written as a function of (*inter alia*) interventions by the Bundesbank and the Federal Reserve:

$$S_t^u - S_t^p = f[\overset{(-)}{\Delta (i^{DM} - i^\$)_t}, \overset{(+)}{INV_t^{DBB}}, \overset{(+)}{INV_t^{FED}}] \tag{1}$$

where S_t^u = the dollar–Deutsche Mark closing rate (ultimo) in Frankfurt on day t defined as the Deutsche Mark price of one dollar

S_t^p = the dollar–Deutsche Mark opening rate (primo) in Frankfurt on the same day t

$\Delta(i^{DM} - i^\$)_t$ = the change in the interest differential between one-month Euro–Deutsche Mark and Euro-dollar-deposits in London during day t

INV_t^{DBB} = spot market interventions by the Bundesbank during day t, defined as purchases of dollars and expressed in billions of Deutsche Mark

INV_t^{FED} = spot market interventions by the Federal Reserve during day t defined as purchases of dollars and expressed in billions of Deutsche Mark[16]

Assuming that trade flows adjust slowly and that other 'fundamentals' do not change in the short term, the intra-day exchange-rate movement is explained primarily by short-term capital flows. Supposing that investors balance their portfolios at every moment, a change in the interest rate differential will cause imbalances, and thus immediately induce an adjustment process in the highly efficient financial markets. A relative rise in the Deutsche Mark interest rate will bring about a demand surplus for Deutsche Mark assets. Given the supply of Deutsche Mark assets in the short run, portfolio equilibrium will be restored by a fall in the exchange rate (i.e., an appreciation of the Deutsche Mark and a depreciation of the dollar). If the Bundesbank and the Federal Reserve are able to influence the market sentiment, the exchange rate will rise after the news of dollar purchases by the Central Banks.

Reasoning along the same lines, a smoothing of exchange-rate movements by interventions of the Bundesbank and the Federal Reserve can be formalised as follows:

$$(S_t^u - S_t^p) - (S_t^p - S_{t-1}^u) = f[\overset{(-)}{\Delta(i^{DM} - i^\$)_t}, \ \overset{(+)}{INV_t^{DBB}} \overset{(+)}{INV_t^{FED}}] \quad (2)$$

By purchasing dollars during the day the Central Banks may try to retard a depreciation of the dollar, started during the preceding night

$$(S_t^p - S_{t-1}^u) < (S_t^u - S_t^p) < 0^{17}$$

In order to capture both elements of effective interventions, reversing and slowing down exchange-rate movements, the empirically estimated equation is chosen to be of an unrestricted form:

$$S_t^u = a_0 + \overset{(+)}{a_1 S_t^p} + \overset{(-)}{a_2 S_{t-1}^u} + \overset{(-)}{a_3 \Delta(i^{DM} - i^\$)_t}$$
$$+ \overset{(+)}{a_4 INV_t^{DBB}} + \overset{(+)}{a_5 INV_t^{FED}} \quad (3)$$

According to the discussion above, the estimates are expected to yield positive values for the opening-rate coefficient (a_1) and the intervention coefficients (a_4, a_5) and negative values for the lagged closing-rate coefficient (a_2) and the interest coefficient (a_3). Because the effectiveness of interventions does not only depend on the volume of dollar purchases or sales,[18] but also on other circumstances, the empirical analysis is extended with two other equations.

In the first place it is generally supposed that coordinated interventions of both Central Banks are more effective than non-coordinated interventions by either the Bundesbank or the Federal Reserve.[19] The reason for a difference in their effectiveness is that coordinated interventions are interpreted by the market as a strong signal that both monetary authorities have adopted the same exchange-rate objective and are determined to reach this objective even if it means adjusting their policies.

If the Bundesbank and the Federal Reserve intervene on the same day, these interventions are closely coordinated by a concerted procedure. The daily data can therefore be divided in three non-overlapping categories: coordinated interventions by both central banks ($CINV_t$), non-coordinated interventions by the Bundesbank ($NCINV_t^{DBB}$) and non-coordinated intervention by the Federal Reserve ($NCINV_t^{FED}$). The resulting regression equation can be written as:

$$
\overset{(+)}{S_t^u} = a_0 + \overset{(+)}{a_1 S_t^p} + \overset{(-)}{a_2 S_{t-1}^u} + \overset{(-)}{a_3 \Delta(i^{DM} - i^\$)_t} + \overset{(+)}{a_4 CINV_t}
$$
$$
+ \overset{(+)}{a_5 NCINV_t^{DBB}} + \overset{(+)}{a_6 NCINV_t^{FED}} \tag{4}
$$

If the hypothesis that coordinated interventions are more effective is correct, the coordination coefficient (a_4) will come out positive and more significant than the non-coordination coefficients (a_5, a_6).

The second adaptation of the original regression equation (3) is based on Humpage (1988). In an highly efficient market the effectiveness of an intervention through the expectations channel depends primarily on the information content of the intervention for the market participants. Humpage (1988) distinguishes 'initial' and 'subsequent' interventions. An 'initial' intervention is defined as an official transaction after a period of a few days without interventions. Humpage (1988) argues that the announcement effect, and thus the news content of initial interventions, is larger than the news content of the subsequent interventions, falling within a few days after the initial interventions. The effectiveness of initial interventions is thus expected to be higher than the effectiveness of subsequent interventions.[20]

If initial interventions are defined arbitrarily as an official transaction after three business days without interventions,[21] the daily intervention data can be split up into initial and subsequent interventions by the Bundesbank ($IINV_t^{DBB}$ and $SINV_t^{DBB}$) and initial and subsequent interventions by the Federal Reserve ($IINV_t^{FED}$ and $SINV_t^{FED}$):

$$S_t^u = a_0 + \overset{(+)}{a_1 S_t^p} + \overset{(-)}{a_2 S_{t-1}^u} + \overset{(-)}{a_3 \Delta(i^{DM} - i^\$)_t} + \overset{(+)}{a_4 IINV_t^{DBB}}$$
$$+ \overset{(+)}{a_5 SINV_t^{DBB}} + \overset{(+)}{a_6 IINV_t^{FED}} + \overset{(+)}{a_7 SINV_t^{FED}} \tag{5}$$

If initial interventions are more effective than subsequent interventions through their announcement effect, the initial coefficients (a_4, a_6) will be positive and more significant than the subsequent coefficients (a_5, a_7).

Empirical results

The regression equations are estimated due to the availability of intra-day data for the dollar–Deutsche Mark exchange rate for the period February 1985 until August 1988. During this period the dollar fell with interruptions from its maximum level of DM 3.4720 on 26 February 1985 to its minimum level of DM 1.5785 on 31 December 1987 and recovered later to DM 1.8792 on 31 August 1988. These exchange-rate movements indicate many important developments during these years, for instance the growing instability of financial markets, the persistent balance of payments disequilibria between the USA, Japan and Europe, a changing attitude of the US government from 'benign neglect' towards a more 'active' exchange-rate policy and the first efforts towards international coordination of fiscal and monetary policies among the major industrialised countries.[22] As a consequence of the use of daily data, the regressions cannot possibly include these more fundamental developments, because of their stickiness on a daily base. Instead, the estimates are performed for eight sub-periods of (in principle) six months,[23] under the assumption that changes in fundamentals proceed slowly and not within a few days.[24] The influence of 'fundamentals' may therefore be reflected in a positive or negative constant (a_0).

Table 7.1 gives the results for the first regression equation (3), including the amounts of intervention by the Bundesbank and the Federal Reserve. As can be seen, the constant (a_0) is positive and

Table 7.1 The effectiveness of official interventions in the dollar–Deutsche Mark exchange market

Equation (OLS) $S_t^u = a_0 + a_1 S_t^p + a_2 S_{t-1}^u + a_3 \Delta(i^{DM} - i^\$)_t + a_4 INV_t^{DBB} + a_5 INV_t^{FED}$

Period	a_0	a_1	a_2	a_3	a_4	a_5	R^2	$\bar{R}^2$	DW	LM
Feb.–Jun. 1985	-0.0063 (-0.089)	0.9037 (8.650)*	0.0988 (0.948)	-2.0196 (-0.678)	0.0196 (2.741)*	-0.0606 (-1.188)	0.9610	0.9589	2.0786	0.2560
Jul.–Dec. 1985	0.0234 (0.928)	1.0812 (13.378)*	-0.0901 (-1.120)	-1.1928 (-0.841)	0.0079 (0.398)	—	0.9901	0.9897	2.1570	0.8232
Jan.–Jun. 1986	0.0472 (1.573)	1.0189 (14.279)*	-0.0400 (-0.560)	-1.5660 (-1.286)	0.0769 (1.278)	—	0.9806	0.9799	1.8404	0.8099
Jul.–Dec. 1986	0.0030 (0.108)	0.9340 (11.244)*	0.0639 (0.782)	0.1061 (0.164)	0.0022 (0.385)	—	0.9778	0.9770	1.8286	0.8570
Jan.–Jun. 1987	0.2308 (3.724)*	1.0101 (13.381)*	-0.1327 (-1.702)*	0.2672 (1.462)	-0.0057 (-0.556)	0.0142 (0.636)	0.9302	0.9271	1.7659	1.6013
Jul.–Dec. 1987	0.0281 (2.277)*	1.0433 (14.681)*	-0.0591 (-0.823)	0.6620 (2.335)	-0.0090 (-1.390)	-0.0077 (-1.443)	0.9952	0.9950	2.2274	1.7333
Jan.–Jun. 1988	0.0520 (1.177)	0.8605 (7.522)*	0.1096 (0.901)	0.6745 (0.839)	-0.0135 (-1.507)	0.0196 (1.543)	0.9585	0.9567	1.7928	0.5869
Jul.–Aug. 1988	0.2449 (2.364)*	1.1519 (6.910)*	-0.2821 (-1.607)	-0.7297 (-0.531)	-0.0004 (-0.065)	0.0062 (0.918)	0.9024	0.8892	2.2392	1.0305

Note: t-values within brackets.
* = statistically significant at a 5% level.
$\bar{R}^2$ = squared multiple correlation coefficient, adjusted for degrees of freedom.
LM = Lagrange multiplier test of residual serial correlation; critical value test statistic $x^2(1)$ = 3.84 ($\alpha = 0.05$).

significant in three periods. The opening rate coefficient (a_1) is in all cases significantly positive and close to 1, as expected. On the contrary, the lagged closing rate does not contribute significantly to the explanation of the current closing rate in seven cases. In addition, the four positive values (of which one is significant) for the interest-rate coefficient (a_3) are a rather counter-intuitive result; apparently capital flows are influenced by other factors, and cannot be captured by a change in the short-term interest differential between both countries on a daily base.

The results on the effectiveness of intervention by the Bundesbank and the Federal Reserve in Table 7.1 are somewhat disappointing. Only in the first half of 1985 is the intervention coefficient (a_4) significantly positive and thus the interventions of the Bundesbank effective. By selling dollars in sometimes very large amounts during February and the beginning of March the Bundesbank was able to cause a sharp decline in the value of the dollar. As soon as a more negative market sentiment towards the dollar was established in March 1985, as a result of troubles in the Ohio thrift industry and of the slowing US economic growth, the Bundesbank and the Federal Reserve did not intervene despite considerable uncertainty in the dollar–Deutsche Mark exchange market, reflected by sharp daily exchange-rate movements and wider bid–offer spreads. Nor did they intervene when the dollar firmed late in April and was traded relatively steadily until the end of June.[25]

According to our data, the Federal Reserve did not actively intervene in the dollar–Deutsche Mark market from the second half of 1985 until the first half of 1987. There is some evidence for effective interventions by the Bundesbank in the first half of 1986 and by the Federal Reserve in the first half of 1988. However, in the last four periods the intervention coefficients, although not significantly different from 0, sometimes have a negative sign suggesting that interventions may have been counter-productive. In these four periods, the Bundesbank and the Federal Reserve both purchased dollars (especially during the last three months of 1987, after the stock market crash of October 1987) and sold dollars (especially during June, July and August 1988) in order to stabilise the dollar after the Louvre agreement of 22 February 1987.[26] Despite frequent reaffirmations of their commitment to exchange-rate stability and despite frequent interventions, both Central Banks do not appear to have been able to counter the downward pressure on the dollar in the last months of 1987 and the upward pressure on the dollar in the summer of 1988.

An explanation for the ineffectiveness of the interventions in these periods may be that the exchange-rate path implied by the official interventions was the opposite of the market expectations on the future course of the exchange rate, based on the market interpretation of changing 'fundamentals' and on perceived policy changes.[27]

The frequently changing market sentiment in these last four periods indicates a high degree of uncertainty among the market participants. In such an environment public statements by policymakers and the announcement of specific economic indicators (for instance, the monthly announcements of the US trade balance and the US economic growth figures) can cause sharp exchange-rate movements. Because these extreme exchange-rate fluctuations could influence the estimation results, the regression equation (3) is extended with dummy variables $(TD_1–TD_6)$ for the monthly announcements of the US trade balance figure:

$$S_t^u = a_0 + \overset{(+)}{a_1 S_t^p} + \overset{(-)}{a_2 S_{t-1}^u} + \overset{(-)}{a_3 \Delta(i^{DM} - i^{\$})_t} + \overset{(+)}{a_4 INV_t^{DBB}}$$

$$+ \overset{(+)}{a_5 INV_t^{FED}} + b_1 TD_1 + b_2 TD_2 + b_3 TD_3 + b_4 TD_4$$

$$+ b_5 TD_5 + b_6 TD_6 \tag{6}$$

The signs of the trade dummy coefficients $(b_1–b_6)$ will depend on the news content of the announcements: if the US trade deficit is smaller or larger than expected, the announcement will result in an appreciation or a depreciation of the dollar.[28]

Table 7.2 presents the estimates for the modified regression equation (6), including the effects of the monthly announcements of the US trade balance. Two conclusions can be drawn from Table 7.2. First, the news on the US trade balance had a more significant impact on the exchange rate in the last two years, as the attention of the market participants focused on the worldwide balance of payments disequilibria. Secondly, the interventions by the Federal Reserve turn out to have had a significant influence on the exchange rate in the first half of 1988 and the intervention coefficient of the Bundesbank (a_4), although not statistically significant, changes from a negative sign (in Table 7.1) to an expected positive sign in both sub-periods of 1988. A closer inspection of the data reveals that dollar purchases by both Central Banks after disappointing news on the US trade deficit in April 1988 were not effective – that is, the

Table 7.2 The effectiveness of official intervention in the dollar–Deutsche Mark exchange market, adjusted for exchange-rate shocks after news on the US trade balance

Equation $S_t^\mu = a_0 + a_1 S_t^p + a_2 S_{t-1}^\mu + a_3\Delta(i^{DM} - i^\$)_t + a_4 INV_t^{DBB} + a_5 INV_t^{FED} + b_1 TD_1 + b_2 TD_2 + b_3 TD_3 + b_4 TD_4 + b_5 TD_5 + b_6 TD_6$

(OLS)

Period	a_0	a_1	a_2	a_3	a_4	a_5	b_1	b_2	b_3	b_4	b_5	b_6	R^2	$\bar{R}^2$	DW	LM
Feb.–Jun. 1985	-0.0069 (-0.097)	0.8753 (8.393)*	0.1278 (1.222)	-2.8200 (-0.941)	0.0201 (2.855)*	-0.0552 (-1.096)	-0.0542 (-2.041)*	-0.0133 (-0.517)	0.0198 (0.765)	-0.0181 (-0.700)	-0.0328 (-1.272)	-0.0306 (-1.185)	0.9645	0.9600	2.0417	0.0587
Jul.–Dec. 1985	0.0272 (1.039)	1.1169 (12.981)*	-0.1272 (-1.481)	-1.143 (-0.777)	-0.0078 (-0.382)	—	0.0193 (1.184)	0.0071 (0.453)	-0.0118 (0.746)	-0.0147 (-0.939)	0.0138 (0.009)	0.0046 (0.290)	0.9903	0.9895	2.1616	0.8686
Jan.–Jun. 1986	0.0502 (1.597)	1.0138 (13.529)*	-0.0361 (-0.481)	-1.4200 (-1.123)	0.0746 (1.212)	—	-0.0105 (-0.798)	-0.0038 (-0.290)	0.0029 (0.222)	-0.0101 (-0.766)	0.0111 (0.832)	-0.0062 (-0.475)	0.9810	0.9791	1.8365	0.8705
Jul.–Dec. 1986	-0.0011 (-0.039)	0.9704 (12.028)*	0.0295 (0.373)	0.2918 (0.446)	0.0023 (0.418)	—	-0.0062 (-0.720)	-0.0193 (-2.193)*	0.0023 (0.268)	0.0276 (3.186)*	0.0018 (0.203)	-0.0072 (-0.802)	0.9805	0.9788	1.8955	0.3053
Jan.–Jun. 1987	0.1437 (3.769)*	0.9672 (13.736)*	-0.0461 (-0.645)	1.6300 (2.325)*	-0.0015 (-0.174)	0.0015 (0.777)	0.0462 (6.301)*	0.0024 (0.332)		0.0035 (0.458)	-0.0105 (-1.433)	0.0089 (1.206)	0.9513	0.9468	1.6187	4.2338
Jul.–Dec. 1987	0.0199 (1.824)*	1.0584 (17.627)*	-0.0694 (-1.141)	0.6134 (2.500)*	-0.0076 (-1.402)	-0.0060 (-1.328)	-0.0195 (-3.719)*	-0.0189 (-3.583)*	-0.0067 (-1.256)	-0.0123 (-2.350)*	0.0126 (2.389)*	-0.0220 (-4.169)*	0.9968	0.9965	2.0742	0.2141
Jan.–Jun. 1988	-0.0058 (-0.179)	0.9106 (10.931)*	0.0935 (1.058)	0.7556 (1.303)	0.0019 (0.281)	0.0179 (1.944)*	0.0455 (8.036)*	0.0152 (2.708)*	0.0081 (1.450)	-0.0272 (-4.647)*	0.0144 (2.580)*	0.0217 (3.842)*	0.9797	0.9776	1.4834	4.1347
Jul.–Aug. 1988	0.2096 (2.192)*	1.1328 (7.402)*	-0.2438 (-1.510)	-0.7736 (-0.607)	0.0017 (0.330)	0.0071 (1.130)	0.0205 (2.412)*	-0.0152 (-1.787)	—	—	—	—	0.9225	0.9070	1.9875	0.0063

Note: See Table 7.1: *t*-values within brackets.
 * = statistically significant at a 5% level (one-sided test).

dollar dropped 1.6 per cent in Frankfurt the day of the announce-ment. The reverse case held in June and July of 1988; dollar sales of the Bundesbank and the Federal Reserve were accompanied by a rise in the value of the dollar as a result of the announcement of a smaller-than-expected US trade deficit. This result may suggest that interventions are less effective in countering sharp exchange-rate movements after announcements of economic indicators, which are important determinants for market expectations.[29]

Table 7.3 comprises the estimates for the regression equation (4), where a distinction was made between coordinated and non-coordinated intervention.

The results give some support to the hypothesis that coordinated interventions are more effective in influencing the exchange rate. In all periods under review non-coordinated intervention by either the Bundesbank or the Federal Reserve did not have an immediate significant positive impact on the exchange rate. In contrast, coor-dinated interventions influenced the exchange rate immediately, as expected, in the first half of 1985 and 1988.

Although the volume of intervention by the Bundesbank exceeded the volume of intervention by the Federal Reserve more than five times in February and March 1985, a comparison between the coordi-nation coefficient (a_4) and the non-coordination coefficient of the Bundesbank (a_5) suggests that, above all, the coordinated interven-tions with the Federal Reserve were effective in changing the rise of the dollar in the last week of February into a decline.[30] The same conclusion can be drawn for the coordinated dollar purchases of both Central Banks in January 1988, which provided a clear signal to the market that the monetary authorities were committed to the G7 statement of 22 December 1987 (the so-called Telephone Accord), that a further decline of the dollar could be counter-productive by damaging growth prospects in the world economy.[31] In contrast, the significant negative coordination coefficient (a_4) in the second half of 1987 presents a rather counter-intuitive result; although the Bundes-bank and the Federal Reserve coordinated interventions frequently, they were apparently not able to counter the dollar's decline after the stock market crash in October 1987 up to December 1987.

Finally, Table 7.4 presents the estimates for regression equation (5) with the distinction between initial and subsequent interventions by the Bundesbank and the Federal Reserve.

The results indicate the existence of an important announcement effect of initial interventions by the Bundesbank in the first half of

Table 7.3   The effectiveness of coordinated interventions and non-coordinated interventions in the dollar–Deutsche Mark exchange market

$$S_t^u = a_0 + a_1 S_t^p + a_2 S_{t-1}^u + a_3 \Delta(i^{DM} - i^\$)_t + a_4 CINV_t + a_5 NCINV_t^{DBB} + a_6 NCINV_t^{FED}$$

Equation (OLS) Period	a_0	a_1	a_2	a_3	a_4	a_5	a_6	R^2	$\bar{R}^2$	DW	LM
Feb.–Jun. 1985	−0.0183 (−0.265)	0.8926 (8.695)*	0.1139 (1.111)	−3.4800 (−1.188)	0.0219 (3.268)	−0.0068 (−0.665)	—	0.9625	0.9605	2.1083	0.5315
Jul.–Dec. 1985	See Table 7.1, no interventions by the Federal Reserve										
Jan.–Jun. 1986	See Table 7.1, no interventions by the Federal Reserve										
Jul.–Dec. 1986	See Table 7.1, no interventions by the Federal Reserve										
Jan.–Jun. 1987	0.1656 (3.763)*	0.9445 (11.582)*	−0.0352 (−0.424)	1.7800 (2.264)*	0.0066 (0.516)	−0.0022 (−0.218)	0.0077 (0.500)	0.9320	0.9283	1.7791	1.2570
Jul.–Dec. 1987	0.0260 (1.997)*	1.0293 (14.540)*	−0.0440 (−0.614)	0.6698 (2.376)*	−0.0081 (−2.851)	−0.0012 (−1.267)	0.0016 (0.577)	0.9952	0.9950	2.2411	1.9765
Jan.–Jun. 1988	0.0550 (1.353)	0.8437 (7.565)*	0.1246 (1.064)	0.3212 (0.401)	0.0023 (2.754)*	−0.0032 (−2.817)*	−0.0044 (−0.188)	0.9604	0.9584	1.8466	0.1807
Jul.–Aug. 1988	0.2939 (2.877)*	1.1341 (6.406)*	−0.2904 (−1.564)	−0.4982 (−0.332)	0.0026 (0.877)	0.0083 (0.797)	−0.0013 (−0.093)	0.9026	0.8864	2.3616	2.2340

Note: See Table 7.1: t-values within brackets.
       * = statistically significant at a 5% level.

Table 7.4 The announcement effects of official interventions in the dollar–Deutsche Mark exchange market

Equation (OLS) $S_t^u = a_0 + a_1 S_t^p + a_2 S_{t-1}^u + a_3 \Delta(i^{DM} - i^{\$})_t + a_4 IINV_t^{DBB} + a_5 SINV_t^{DBB} + a_6 INVV_t^{FED} + a_7 SINV_t^{FED}$

Period	a_0	a_1	a_2	a_3	a_4	a_5	a_6	a_7	R^2	$\bar{R}^2$	DW	LM
Feb.–Jun. 1985	-0.0123 (-0.190)	0.8481 (8.732)*	0.1560 (1.611)	-3.1142 (-1.140)	0.0424 (4.736)*	-0.0074 (-0.805)	-0.0491 (-0.697)	-0.0101 (-0.124)	0.9678	0.9653	2.0174	0.0337
Jul.–Dec. 1985	0.0252 (1.002)	1.0995 (13.460)*	-0.1090 (-1.339)	-1.1886 (-0.841)	0.0793 (1.402)	-0.0004 (-0.021)	—	—	0.9902	0.9898	2.1439	0.6888
Jan.–Jun. 1986	See Table 7.1, the Deutsche Bundesbank intervenes just once; the Federal Reserve does not intervene in this period											
Jul.–Dec. 1986	-0.0028 (-0.100)	0.9739 (11.755)*	0.0268 (0.330)	0.0779 (0.123)	0.2994 (2.529)*	0.0017 (0.297)	—	—	0.9789	0.9780	1.7843	1.4145
Jan.–Jun. 1987	0.2318 (3.708)*	1.0099 (13.322)*	-0.1331 (-1.700)*	0.2658 (1.447)	-0.0075 (0.518)	-0.0040 (-0.273)	0.0153 (0.656)	—	0.9302	0.9265	1.7621	1.6486
Jul.–Dec. 1987	0.0292 (2.285)*	1.0400 (14.394)*	-0.0565 (-0.774)	0.6338 (2.211)*	-0.0138 (-1.211)	-0.0052 (-0.682)	-0.0170 (-1.201)	-0.0087 (-1.535)	0.9952	0.9950	2.2154	1.5691
Jan.–Jun. 1988	0.0373 (0.838)	0.8591 (7.816)*	0.1199 (1.019)	0.4361 (0.564)	-0.1088 (-3.836)*	-0.0040 (-0.393)	0.0145 (0.7000)	0.0168 (1.229)	0.9626	0.9603	1.8340	0.1935
Jul.–Aug. 1988	0.2273 (2.169)*	1.1355 (6.078)*	-0.257 (-1.351)	-0.898 (-0.648)	-0.0441 (-1.136)	-0.0018 (-0.305)	0.0217 (1.358)	0.0047 (0.686)	0.9102	0.8923	2.0326	0.0781

Note: See Table 7.1: t-values within brackets.
        * = statistically significant at a 5% level.

1985 and the second half of 1986. Besides, there is some evidence for effective initial interventions by the Bundesbank in the second half of 1985 and by the Federal Reserve in July and August 1988. The unexpected negative sign of the initial coefficient (a_4) for the Bundesbank in the first half of 1988 is due to an intervention after disappointing news on the US trade deficit in April 1988. This suggests that even the announcement effect of an initial intervention does not outweigh news on more fundamental economic developments for the market. The estimates provide no evidence for a difference in effectiveness between initial and subsequent interventions by the Federal Reserve; this result may be explained by the fact that the Federal Reserve intervenes in all sub-periods less than the Bundesbank. As the Federal Reserve does not intervene frequently, the difference in the announcement effect between initial and subsequent intervention for the market may be small.

7.4 CONCLUSION

Officially, the Deutsche Bundesbank and the Federal Reserve System intervene in the foreign-exchange market actively to counter disorderly market conditions. In the period between February 1985 and August 1988 daily interventions may, however, have served other purposes, for instance lowering the dollar after the Plaza summit and stabilising the dollar after the Louvre summit. Whatever their precise objective, exchange-market interventions can in theory affect the exchange rate through the expectations channel. If an intervention provides the market with new information or a signal about the future course of the exchange rate or of monetary policy and if the market is highly efficient, the exchange rate will immediately change after the intervention.

Our empirical analysis, on the contrary, suggests that in practice the effectiveness of exchange-market intervention is limited, in the sense that much depends on the specific circumstances under which the monetary authorities intervene. Our results suggests that interventions to counter market pressures, which resulted through changes in market expectations based on 'fundamentals', were not effective. However, this conclusion has to be handled carefully, because of the unresolved methodological problem that the exchange-rate movements might have been more pronounced without the interventions.

Part of the ineffectiveness of interventions may reflect the difficulty for the Bundesbank and the Federal Reserve in countering sharp exchange-rate changes following important news for the market, such as the monthly announcements of the US trade balance figure. The effect of unexpected changes in these economic indicators on market expectations apparently exceeds the effect of news on interventions by both Central Banks. Nevertheless, intervention can have an important effect on the exchange rate, especially when the Bundesbank and the Federal Reserve undertake a concerted action. Our results indicate that coordinated were more effective than non-coordinated interventions. It thus appears that the market interprets a coordinated intervention as an important signal that both monetary authorities are determined to change the exchange rate.

Finally, interventions may have an important announcement effect after a period of no intervention. According to our results initial interventions by the Bundesbank were more effective than subsequent interventions. In order to attain an important announcement effect, a selective intervention strategy and a careful timing of the interventions seems therefore to be very important.

Appendix: Data Description

The opening and closing exchange rates are rates in Frankfurt and were taken from the Statistische Beihefte zu den Monatsberichten der Deutschen Bundesbank, Reihe 5, Tabelle 6: Kassakurse des US-dollar in Tagesverlauf. The opening and closing rates are published from February 1985. The rates are the DM price of 1 dollar. The interest rates are 1–month Euro-dollar and Euro-Deutsche Mark closing rates in London. Euro-rates were preferred to domestic rates because Euro-deposits are close substitutes.

The daily intervention data were kindly provided by the Deutsche Bundesbank and concern active interventions in the US dollar-Deutsche Mark market by the Bundesbank and the Federal Reserve System, expressed in billion Deutsche Mark. However, interventions by the Federal Reserve were listed only as far as these interventions resulted in a change of the net foreign currency reserves of the Bundesbank. The data were available until September 1988. The dummy variables for the announcement effect of the monthly publication of the US trade balance figure have been constructed carefully using the Dutch financial newspaper *Het Financieele Dagblad*. Table A7.1 indicates the news content of the announcements and thus their expected effect on the exchange rate:

A comparison of Table A7.1 and Table 7.2 leads to the conclusion that whenever the US trade balance figure announcement had a significant impact on the exchange rate, the sign corresponds to the expected sign in Table A7.1.

Table A7.1   Announcement of US trade balance figures: expected exchange-rate effects

Year	Month											
	1	2	3	4	5	6	7	8	9	10	11	12
1985[1]		−	−	−	−	−	−	−	+	+	−	−	−
1986	−	+	−	−	−	−	−	−	+	+	+	−
1987	+	−	NA[2]	−	0	+	−	−	−	−	+	−
1988	+	+	+	−	+	+	+	−				

Notes: The US trade deficit figure was smaller-than-expected (+) or larger-than-expected (−) or as expected (0).
   1. In 1985 the pattern of US trade deficit announcements differs somewhat from the more regular monthly pattern in the other periods.

151

2. In March 1987 there was no announcement as the US Commerce Department decided to release the monthly reports about two weeks later in mid-April.

A comparison of Table A7.1 and Table 7.2 leads to the conclusion that whenever the US trade balance figure announcement had a significant impact on the exchange rate, the sign corresponds to the expected sign in Table A7.1.

Notes

* Sylvester Eijffinger was during the summer of 1988 Visiting Scholar at the Deutsche Bundesbank in Frankfurt-am-Main. He wishes to acknowledge Professors Helmut Schlesinger and Leonhard Gleske, Mr Franz Scholl and other employees of the Hauptabteilung Ausland for valuable discussions and for kindly providing daily data of official intervention on a confidential base. It should be noted that this article does not reflect the views of the Deutsche Bundesbank or members of its staff.
1. This definition is taken from the Report of the Working Group on Exchange Market Intervention, under the direction of Ph. Jurgensen (March 1983, p. 4). The Working Group was established at the G7 summit in Versailles (June 1982), to carry out an international study of experience with intervention among these countries.
2. See the Report of the Working Group (1983, p. 4).
3. In reality, this is the case for the Central Bank of West Germany, the Deutsche Bundesbank. See Gleske (1982, p. 269) and Scholl (1983, p. 121).
4. As far as the Central Bank deals with a commercial bank in the forward market, this condition is met because commercial banks are not allowed by regulation to hold large uncovered positions in exchange markets. See Gleske (1982, p. 266) and Scholl (1983, p. 121).
5. The definition is quoted from Humpage (1986, p. 2).
6. This section is based on the more extensive discussion on channels of influence for interventions by Humpage (1986). Genberg (1981): Loopeskoo (1984); and Müller (1984) also discuss transmission mechanisms of interventions by monetary authorities.
7. See Genberg (1981, p. 454). However it is very risky for the monetary authorities to count on this expectations effect of an intervention because this purchase of foreign currency could also be interpreted as a temporary easing of monetary conditions, and hence could generate expectations of future monetary contraction. In the last case, the intervention would result in an undesired appreciation of the domestic currency.
8. See for example Rogoff (1981) and Loopeskoo (1984).
9. See the Report of the Working Group (1983, p. 20). According to the Working Group an intervention is more effective if it is accompanied by domestic policy adjustments. By sterilising an intervention, however, the domestic monetary policy remains unchanged.
10. See Schlesinger (1984, p. 81).
11. See the Report of the Working Group (1983, p. 21): 'The authorities in each of the Summit countries at times undertook large-scale intervention when they judged that market participants had not taken full account of fundamental factors'.
12. See Mayer and Taguchi (1983, p. 8).
13. The Bundesbank does not undertake *dollar* interventions within the EMS. See Scholl (1983, p. 121). For an empirical analysis of interventions within the EMS, see Eijffinger (1988).
14. See Lehment (1980, p. 140).
15. As an example, reference can be made to the weeks immediately after

the G5 Plaza Agreement of 22 September 1985. Although the dollar fell almost without interruption from 26 February 1985, the Bundesbank and the Federal Reserve sold dollars, because they felt that the dollar was overvalued and did not reflect changes in economic conditions. See Cross (Winter 1985–6, p. 46).

16. For a description of the data see the Appendix, p. 000.

17. By choosing the US dollar–Deutsche Mark opening and closing rates in Frankfurt, a 24-hour day can be divided in two segments: the European segment (the day) and the non-European segment (the night). The assumption has been made that Federal Reserve interventions in the dollar–Deutsche Mark market took place during the European segment of the day.

18. See Scholl (1983, p. 121): 'In some situations even small intervention amounts may suffice to slow down or even reverse an undesirable exchange rate movement. In other situations even large intervention amounts may have the opposite effect'.

19. See for instance Ohr (1987, p. 211) and the Report of the Working Group (1983, p. 26): 'closely coordinated action had at times been more effective than intervention by only one central bank'. Loopeskoo (1984, pp. 268–70) finds some empirical evidence that active coordinated German–US intervention had a *different* impact on exchange rates than non-coordinated interventions, but she cannot confirm whether coordinated interventions had a stronger impact than non-coordinated interventions.

20. Humpage (1988) tests this hypothesis for three short periods of intervention by the Federal Reserve. The results are mixed, and he concludes, *inter alia*, that intervention can have a temporary announcement effect, but then this effect is not universal in all periods and is short-lived.

21. Humpage's investigation (1988) differs from this study in some respects: (1) he does not dispose of the amounts of official interventions, but constructs dummy variables for Federal Reserve interventions; (2) he does not include interventions by the Bundesbank in the dollar–Deutsche Mark market; (3) he chooses relatively short periods and defines 'initial intervention' as official transactions after five business days with no intervention. In order to dispose of more observations for initial interventions, we have chosen longer periods and defined 'initial intervention' as official transactions after three business days with no intervention.

22. For a discussion of the origins, the historical background and possible solutions for these worldwide imbalances, see Sijben (1989).

23. With the exception of the first sub-period of five months and the last sub-period of two months. See Appendix, p. 000.

24. Besides, the purpose of this paper is not so much to explain the exchange-rate developments, as to test whether official interventions had an immediate impact on the exchange rate.

25. See Cross (Summer 1985, p. 59) and Cross (Autumn 1985, p. 53).

26. On 22 February 1987 the monetary authorities of the G7 countries (except Italy) agreed on closer cooperation to foster stability of exchange

rates around the levels at the time of the Louvre summit. See Funabashi
(1988, pp. 181–2).

27. The bearish market sentiment after the stock market crash was caused by
doubts in the markets whether the monetary authorities of the G7
countries would maintain exchange-rate stability and international coordination as important policy objectives, by disappointing outcomes of
the US budget reduction negotiations and by pessimistic growth perspectives after the crash. See Cross (Winter 1987–8, pp. 54–6). The
bullish market sentiment on the dollar during the summer of 1988 was a
result of the buoyant US economic growth, market expectations of a
tighter US monetary policy and the announcement of a much smaller-
than-expected US trade deficit in June and July. See Cross (Summer
1988).

28. The news content of the US trade-deficit announcements in the period
February 1985–August 1988 is summarised in the Appendix, p. 151.

29. Such a conclusion is, however, hard to prove, because of the methodological issue that the *ex post* exchange-rate change includes the effect of
interventions. Without the interventions, the exchange-rate change
might have been larger as a result of the announcement.

30. In this respect, the positive and significant intervention coefficient for the
Bundesbank and the negative but insignificant intervention coefficient
for the Federal Reserve during the first half of 1985 in Table 7.1 may lead
to wrong conclusions.

31. See Cross (Winter 1987–8, p. 57).

References

Argy, V. (1981) *The Postwar International Money Crisis – An Analysis*,
London, George Allen & Unwin.

Cross, S.Y. (various issues) 'Treasury and Federal Reserve Foreign Exchange Operations – Report to the Congress', *Quarterly Review*, Federal Reserve Bank of New York.

Eijffinger, S.C.W. (1988) 'The relative positions of the currencies within
the EMS band of fluctuation: an empirical study', in Fair, D.E. and de
Boissieu, C. (eds), *International Monetary and Financial Integration –
The European Dimension*, Dordrecht, Martinus Nijhoff.

Eijffinger, S.C.W. and Gruijters, A.P.D. (1989) *On the short term object-
ives of daily intervention by the Deutsche Bundesbank and the Federal
Reserve System in the U.S. dollar–DM exchange market*, Research
Memorandum, FEW 393, Tilburg University.

Funabashi, Y. (1988) *Managing the dollar: From the Plaza to the Louvre*,
Institute for International Economics, Washington, D.C.

Genberg, H. (1981) 'Effects of Central Bank Intervention in the Foreign
Exchange Market', *IMF Staff Papers*, vol. 28, no. 3, pp. 451–76.

Gleske, L. (1982) 'Die Devisenpolitik der Deutschen Bundesbank, Interventionen am DM–$-Markt und im Europäischen Währungssystem sowie geldmarktorientierte Devisentransaktionen', *Kredit und Kapital*, vol. 15, pp. 259–74.

Humpage, O.F. (1986) 'Exchange Market Intervention: The Channels of Influence', *Economic Review*, no. 3, Federal Reserve Bank of Cleveland, pp. 2–13.

Humpage, O.F. (1988) 'Intervention and the Dollar's Decline', *Economic Review*, no. 2, Federal Reserve Bank of Cleveland, pp. 2–16.

Lehment, H. (1980) *Devisenmarktinterventionen bei flexiblen Wechselkursen, Die Politik des Managed Floating*, Kieler Studien, 162, Tübingen, J.C.B. Mohr (P. Siebeck).

Loopeskoo, B. (1984) 'Relationships Among Exchange Rates, Intervention and Interest Rates: An Empirical Investigation', *Journal of International Money and Finance*, no. 3, pp. 257–77.

Mayer, H. and Taguchi, H. (1983) 'Official intervention in the exchange markets: Stabilising or destabilising?', *BIS Economic Papers*, no. 6 (March).

Müller, B. (1984) 'Der Jurgensen-Bericht: Eine Stellungnahme', in Ehrlicher, W. and Richter, R. (eds), *Devisenmarktinterventionen der Zentralbanken*, Schriften des Vereins für Socialpolitik, no. 139 Berlin.

Ohr, R. (1987) 'Notenbankinterventionen und Effizienz der Devisenmärkte', Ueberlegungen zur Dollarkursentwicklung', *Kredit und Kapital*, vol. 20, no. 2, pp. 200–14.

Report of the Working Group (1983), Working Group on Exchange Market Intervention (Chairman: Philippe Jurgensen).

Rieke, W. (1984) 'Die Rolle von Interventionen als Bestimmungsfaktor der Wechselkurse beim "Floating": Ergebnisse des von einer internationalen Arbeitsgruppe erstellten Erfahrungsberichts', in Ehrlicher, W. and Richter, R. (eds), *Devisenmarktinterventionen der Zentralbanken*, Schriften des Vereins für Socialpolitik, no. 139, Berlin.

Rogoff, K. (1984) 'On the effects of sterilized intervention', *Journal of Monetary Economics*, vol. 14, pp. 133–50.

Schlesinger, H. (1984) 'Stellungnahme zum Thema "Sterilisation"' in Ehrlicher, W. and Richter, R. (eds), *Devisenmarktinterventionen der Zentralbanken*, Schriften des Vereins für Socialpolitik, no. 139, Berlin.

Scholl, F. (1983) 'Implications of Monetary Targeting for Exchange-Rate Policy', in Meer, P. (ed.), *Central Bank Views on Monetary Targeting*, Federal Reserve Bank of New York.

Sijben, J.J. (1989) 'External disequilibria and the burden of economic adjustment in the world economy, in Sijben, J.J. (ed.), *Financing the World Economy in the Nineties*, Tilburg Institute of Advanced Studies, Dordrecht, Kluwer Academic Publishers.

Discussion

Georg Winckler

The paper by Eijffinger and Gruijters is an interesting one. After a survey of the various aspects of official exchange-market interventions, it undertakes an empirical study into the question whether the monetary authorities in Germany or in the USA have been able to influence the dollar–Deutsche Mark exchange rate systematically from 1985 to 1988. What makes this study interesting is the use of daily data for the empirical testing.

The main conclusion of the paper is disappointing for monetary authorities: the interventions to counter market pressures were not effective. Only in the case of concerted actions was some effectiveness found by Eijffinger and Gruijters. These negative results serve to disillusion those who believe in easily manageable exchange rates in the world.

There are several reasons why – on *a priori* grounds – the effectiveness of exchange-market interventions is difficult to assess. For me, two reasons not mentioned in the paper are decisive: (a) the question of the *reputation* of monetary authorities when intervening in the market and (b) the existence of *noise traders*. Both reasons have been dealt in the literature during the past few years.[1]

- Exchange-market interventions form a repeated game when the private sector is unsure of the central banks' objectives and abilities. Hence reputational considerations become important – for example, the interventions in the dollar–Deutsche Mark exchange market may be ineffective because the private sector does not see the monetary authorities as really 'committed' to specific goals. However, if such commitments exist, as in Europe, small interventions may be sufficient to stabilise exchange rates.
- The 'noise trader approach to finance' explains why positive feedback strategies exist (buy when prices rise and sell when prices fall) and why it may be individually rational even for arbitragers to jump on the bandwagon themselves. The path of prices may thus give rise to bubble-like patterns. Given this price dynamics, it is not yet clear what effect market interventions may have. In some circumstances they may be very effective, in some not at all.

157

Some scepticism can be raised about the empirical findings in the paper, especially about the specification of the time structure and about the estimation how it is carried out.

Concerning the time structure, the model assumes that interventions of *both* monetary authorities take place *when the market in Frankfurt is open* and that these interventions are aimed at influencing the *closing rate in Frankfurt* only. Both assumptions seem not to be true, since the Fed may use other market places for interventions, too, and since interventions usually occur in order to counter market pressures *during* a day. Perhaps a model with continuous trading would be preferable, in which the exact time of interventions were recorded. Then the effectiveness of interventions could perhaps more easily be detected.

With regard to the estimation procedure, it would be interesting to have the parameter a_1 in equation (3) forced to be 1, and a_2 forced to be 0 (or $a_1 = 2$ and $a_2 = -1$), since there may be a downward bias. That fixing of parameters would fit to the idea of equation (1); in addition, one might analyse the joint endogeneity of the exchange rate and the interest rate differential in more details.

Note

1. See, for example, K. Rogoff, 'Reputation, Coordination, and Monetary Policy', in Barro, R.J. (ed.), *Modern Business Cycle Theory*, Oxford, Oxford University Press, 1989, p. 236 and the Symposium on 'Bubbles' in the Spring 1990 issue of the *Journal of Economic Perspectives*.

8 The Credibility of Central Banks in Controlling Inflation and the Effect on Exchange-rate Volatility, Theory and Evidence

Olivier Davanne and
Vasumathi Vijayraghavan

8.1 INTRODUCTION

Recent developments in international finance have emphasised the non-homogeneous nature of the actors in the exchange-rate market, distinguishing, for instance, between fundamentalists and chartists (Frankel and Froot, 1987b). In a parallel development, the availability of data on exchange-rate expectations has led to an examination of the question of whether long-term expectations are stabilising or destabilising compared to short-term expectations. 'Destabilising' was taken to mean the existence of 'bandwagon' effects, possibly due to the existence of chartists. Frankel and Froot (1987a) found evidence that long-term expectations (of over a year) exhibited a return to a mean, whereas short-term expectations exhibited a 'bandwagon' effect.

At the same time, it is also a well-known fact that exchange rates at different horizons have different statistical properties, probably reflecting different players with different information sets and interests. There have been findings of mean reversion in the exchange rate in the longer term, which would probably reflect a return of the exchange rate to some equilibrium level, whether to PPP or to current-account balance. Jeffrey Sachs estimated the time required for a return to long-term PPP as being approximately 6.5 years.[1] If the true spot process eventually reverts to the mean, then the long-

159

term expectations identified above could be completely rational.[2] The purpose of this paper is to examine the implications of this for a Central Bank concerned with stabilising the real exchange rate.

There is a voluminous literature which attempts to explain the reasons for exchange-rate volatility. This has been an issue ever since Dornbusch's (1976) paper, which shows why the exchange rate will 'overshoot' due to most kinds of shocks to the economy. Since then, the exchange rate has come to be examined as a purely financial variable, behaving in a speculative fashion (see, for instance, the illuminating survey by Frankel and Meese, 1987; they conclude that excessive exchange-rate volatility – i.e., fluctuations not due to real causes – may be consistent with market efficiency, in particular if risk premia are variable). Our paper deals more precisely with the relation between this excess volatility and the reaction function of Central Banks, which may have a strong influence on the stabilising power of long-term investors and also on risk premia.

It will be shown in the context of a portfolio balance model of real exchange-rate determination that stabilising the long-term inflation rate (i.e., lowering the variance of the long-term inflation rate) most probably also stabilises the real exchange rate.

This result is not completely obvious: stabilising the inflation rate, as seems the order of the day for many central banks,[3] today, is not always compatible *a priori* with stabilising the real exchange rate. On the one hand, stabilising the inflation rate reinforces the stabilising aspect of long-term investment by increasing the substitutability between bonds of different countries. On the other hand, stabilising inflation may have a cost in terms of destabilising the nominal (and hence real) interest rates and, consequently, the real exchange rate. But a theoretical approach tends to show that there is no trade-off between stabilising inflation and stabilising the real interest rate. If this is the case, stabilising inflation will no doubt help to stabilise the real exchange rate.

The paper will show also that there may be more than one solution for the determination of the volatility of the real exchange rate. Even with rational expectations, we can find on the one hand an equilibrium with high volatility of the exchange rate, where this high volatility restricts the substitutability between bonds of different countries and thus the stabilising power of long-term investment and, on the other hand, an equilibrium with low volatility and a strong stabilising power of long-term investment. The existence of more than one rational equilibrium may be a reason in favour of interventions of Central Banks on the exchange market, even sterilised. By comforting long-term investors, interventions may limit the risk of the high-volatility equilibrium.

This paper is organised as follows. Section 8.2 presents the portfolio balance model of real exchange-rate determination, in which it is assumed that the real exchange rate eventually returns to its mean. Section 8.3 presents theoretical reasons, as well as some empirical evidence, for there being no trade-off between stabilising inflation and stabilising real interest rates. Section 8.4 concludes the paper.

8.2 A PORTFOLIO BALANCE MODEL OF THE DETERMINATION OF THE REAL EXCHANGE RATE, AND OF ITS VOLATILITY

Let us consider two countries, the domestic (US) and the foreign (German). The standard portfolio balance CAPM model[4] of the determination of the US demand for German bonds (and vice-versa) is:

$$X_t^{us,\ ger} = \frac{(\overline{r}^*_t - r_t)/2 + \theta\ (\sigma^2 r_t - \sigma r_t \overline{r}^*_t)}{\theta \sigma^2}$$

$$X_t^{ger,\ us} = \frac{(\overline{r}_t - r^*_t)/2 + \theta^*\ (\sigma^2 r^*_t - \sigma \overline{r}_t r^*_t)}{\theta^* \sigma^2}$$

where

$X_t^{us,\ ger} =$	US demand for German bonds (in proportion of US total demand for bonds)
$X_t^{ger,\ us} =$	German demand for US bonds (in proportion of German total demand for bonds)
$r_t =$	real yield of an investment in US bonds over 5 years from t to $t + 5$ (i.e. a long-term investment)
$r^*_t =$	real yield of an investment in German bonds over 5 years from t to $t + 5$ (i.e. a long-term investment).
$\overline{r}_t =$	real yield of an investment in US bonds

	over 5 years from a German point of view (i.e., after having taken into account the change in the real exchange rate between the USA and Germany)
$\overline{r}_t^* =$	real yield of an investment in German bonds over 5 years from a US point of view (i.e., after having taken into account the change in the real exchange rate between the USA and Germany)
$r_t, r_t^*, \overline{r}_t, \overline{r}_t^* =$	not known at the date t but anticipated by the investors
$_tr_t, _tr_t^*, _t\overline{r}_t, _t\overline{r}_t^* =$	the values of these anticipations; more generally, the t in front of a variable is the investor's anticipation of the variable at time t
$\sigma^2_{r_t}, \sigma^2_{r_t^*}, \sigma^2_{\overline{r}_t}, \sigma^2_{\overline{r}_t^*} =$	the variances of these variables as they are perceived by the investors ($\sigma_{r_t\overline{r}_t^*}, \sigma_{\overline{r}_t r_t^*}$ are the covariances); in the rest of this paper, we shall suppose that anticipations are rational, so $_tr_t$ and σ^{2r_t} are the objective mean and variance of r_t taking into account the information known at date t.
$\sigma^2 =$	variance of $r_t - \overline{r}_t^*$ (we shall see that $r_t - \overline{r}_t^* = \overline{r}_t - r_t^*$)
$\theta =$	coefficient of American relative risk aversion.
$\theta^* =$	coefficient of German relative risk aversion[5]
$r_t, r_t^*, \overline{r}_t, \overline{r}_t^* =$	determined by the nominal interest rates and the rates of inflation in the two countries, and by the evolution of the real exchange rate
$i_t =$	nominal yield of an investment in US bonds over 5 years
$i_t^* =$	nominal yield of an investment in German bonds over 5 years
$e_t =$	log of the real exchange rate (in DM per \$)
$\pi_t^{us} =$	increase in the US consumer prices between t and $t + 5$
$\pi_t^{ger} =$	increase in the German consumer prices between t and $t + 5$

So:

$$r_t = i_t - \pi_t^{us} \qquad\qquad \bar{r}_t = i_t - \pi_t^{us} + e_{t+5} - e_t$$

$$r_t^* = i_t^* - \pi_t^{ger} \qquad\qquad \bar{r}_t^* = i_t^* - \pi_t^{ger} - e_{t+5} + e_t$$

$r_t - \bar{r}_t^* = \bar{r}_t - r_t^*$: the relative real yield of German and US bonds is the same from a US or a German point of view.

We now assume the following stochastic law for the inflation rates in the two countries and for the future exchange rate (e_{t+5}).

$$\pi_t^{us} \approx N(\bar{\pi}^{us}, \sigma^2\pi^{us})$$

$$\pi_t^{ger} \approx N(\bar{\pi}^{ger}, \sigma^2\pi^{ger})$$

$\bar{\pi}^{us}$ and $\bar{\pi}^{ger}$ =

increases in the consumer prices in the two countries which are assumed to be the target of the central banks of the USA and Germany; those targets are supposed to be constant over time

$\sigma^2\pi^{us}$ and $\sigma^2\pi^{ger}$ =

variances of π_t^{us} and π_t^{ger}: they measure the uncertainty that face the investors; the variance of inflation depends on the reaction function of the Central Bank as well on other shocks, and this variance is thus supposed to be under the control of the Central Bank.

We also assume that the real exchange rate comes back to its long-term mean or equilibrium in 5 years $e_{t+5} \approx N(e^*, \sigma_e)$. We assume anticipations are rational so these laws are known by the investors when they make their choices.

thus:

$$_tr_t \approx i_t - \bar{\pi}^{us} \qquad \bar{r}_t = i_t - \bar{\pi}^{us} + e^* - e_t \qquad \sigma_{r_t}^2 = \sigma_{\pi}^{2us}$$

$$_tr_t^* \approx i_t^* - \bar{\pi}^{ger} \qquad \bar{r}_t^* = i_t^* - \bar{\pi}^{ger} + e_t - e^* \qquad \sigma_{r_t}^{2*} = \sigma_{\pi}^{2ger}$$

(since the nominal interest rate is known exactly at date t, the variance of the real interest rates for the investor at date t depends only on the variance of inflation).

To simplify, we make two more hypotheses on the stochastic law of π_t^{us}, π_t^{ger} and e_{t+5}. We assume that there is no correlation between those three variables (so $\sigma_{\pi_t^{us} e_{t-5}} = \sigma_{\pi_t^{ger} e_{t-5}} = 0$). That is clearly not true in the short run where inflation between countries and exchange rates evolutions are strongly correlated, but is more acceptable in the long run since one of the main determinants of the long-term inflation rate must be the monetary authorities' tolerance for inflation. In fact, other hypotheses would have complicated the formal analysis without greatly changing the conclusions.

Thus:

$$\sigma^2_{r_t \bar{r}_t^*} = 0$$

$$\sigma^2_{\bar{r}_t r^*_t} = 0$$

$$\sigma^2 = \text{var}\,(r_t - \bar{r}_t^*) = \sigma_{\pi}^{2us} + \sigma_{\pi}^{2ger} + \sigma_e^2$$

and

$$X_t^{us,\,ger} = \frac{(i_t^* - \bar{\pi}^{ger}) - (i_t - \bar{\pi}^{us}) + (e_t - e^*)}{2\theta\sigma^2} + \frac{\sigma_{\pi}^{2us}}{\sigma^2}$$

$$X_t^{ger,\,us} = \frac{(i_t - \bar{\pi}^{us}) - (i_t^* - \bar{\pi}^{ger}) - (e_t - e^*)}{2\theta^*\sigma^2} + \frac{\sigma_{\pi}^{2ger}}{\sigma^2}$$

Now that we have specified the way investors in the USA and Germany diversified their portfolios taking account of $i_t - \bar{\pi}^{us}$ (real long-term interest rate in the US), $i_t^* - \bar{\pi}^{ger}$ (real long-term interest rate in Germany), $e_t - e*$ (over evaluation of the dollar at date t), σ_{π}^{2us} (uncertainty about the future US inflation), σ_{π}^{2ger} (uncertainty about the future German inflation rate) and σ_e^2 (uncertainty over the future exchange rate), we can look at the equilibrium in the exchange market.

We call U_t the net American deficit (measured in real dollars) which has to be financed by long-term capital. U_t is the accumulation of past current account deficits as well as any other shocks (such a short-term speculative movement) which might affect the US and German balance of payments. We assume that U_t may be described as a random variable: $U_t = N\,(0,\,\sigma_u^2)$.[6] At the equilibrium on the exchange market, U_t is equal to the German demand for US bonds *less* the US demand for German bonds. Let us call W the real

American wealth in bonds (US and German) and W^* the real German wealth (both with respect to US prices).[7]

$$U_t = X^{ger,\,us}\, W^* - X^{us,\,ger}\, W$$

Let us call $dr_t = (i_t - \overline{\pi}^{us}) - (i_t^* - \overline{\pi}^{ger})$; dr_t is the difference between the real long-term interest rate in the USA and in Germany.

The above equation thus becomes:

$$\frac{dr_t - (e_t - e^*)}{2\sigma^2}\left[\frac{W^*}{\theta^*} + \frac{W}{\theta}\right] + \frac{\sigma_\pi^{2ger}}{\sigma^2}\,W^* - \frac{\sigma_\pi^{2us}}{\sigma^2}W = U_t$$

$$e_t = e^* + dr_t - A\sigma^2 U_t + B \tag{1}$$

with

$$A = 2/\left[\frac{W^*}{\theta^*} + \frac{W}{\theta}\right]$$

$$B = (\sigma_\pi^{2ger}W^* - \sigma_\pi^{2us}W)\,A$$

We can take the variance of both sides of the above equation,[8] which leads to:

$$\sigma_e^2 = V + \mu\,(\sigma_\pi^{2us} + \sigma_\pi^{2ger} + \sigma_e^2)^2\,\sigma_u^2{}^9 \tag{2}$$

with $\mu = A^2$, $V = \mathrm{var}\,(dr_t)$

This equation is easy to interpret. The variance σ_e^2 depends on the variance of the relative real interest rates in the two countries (V), which sets a floor for σ_e^2; and on the shocks which affect the US balance of payments. The effect of these shocks depends on the substitutability between the bonds of the USA and Germany (i.e., it depends on σ_π^{2us}, σ_π^{2ger} and the variance of e itself).

This equation is quadratic in σ_e^2 and admits two solutions. These solutions are examined in detail in the Appendix (p. 172). Figure 8.1 shows σ_e^2 as a function of σ_u^2, following the analysis of the Appendix. Figure 8.2 is computed exactly, with the empirical values of V, $\sigma^2{}_{\pi us}$ and $\sigma^2{}_{\pi ger}$ measured in the sample for the floating exchange-rate period. The following points should now be made.

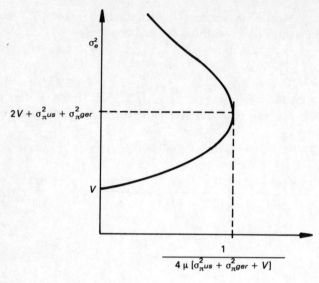

Figure 8.1 σ_e^2 as a function of σ_u^2

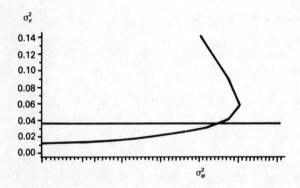

Figure 8.2 δ_e^2 as a function of δ_u^2 based on empirial values for V, $\sigma_{\pi us}^2$, $\sigma_{\pi ger}^2$

- The existence of solutions supposes that the volatility of U_t is not too large. If this is not the case, the stabilising power of long-term investors is sufficient.
- The smaller solution is such that σ_e^2 increases with σ_u^2 while the

bigger solution does the opposite. When σ_u^2 is small (i.e., the shocks to the US balance of payments are small) σ_e^2 is very large for the second solution. This solution is a rational equilibrium where long-term investors think that the exchange rate is very volatile, so long-term capital flows are small and the exchange rate is indeed volatile even for small shocks to the balance of payments.[10]

This possibility of two solutions gives an argument in favour of the intervention of Central Banks on the exchange market. By showing their determination to stabilise exchange rates, Central Banks may be able to avoid the high-volatility solution. In other words, the intervention of Central Banks, even sterilised, may play a stabilising role by increasing the stabilising power of long-term private investors (i.e., by making sure the exchange rate stays within the range for the low-volatility solution). Intervention would thus be done parsimoniously if indications are that a high-volatility solution exists (i.e., if for whatever reasons long-term capital flows are low, despite a strong over- or underevaluation of the exchange rate, because of a high uncertainty about future exchange-rate movements). Intervention would have been called for in 1985 to lower the dollar and at the beginning of 1988 to sustain it, on this ground.

As to the question of whether stabilising inflation helps to stabilise the real exchange rate, we show in the Appendix that the results from our models are ambiguous.

On the one hand, the sign of the correlation depends on the kind of equilibrium (high-volatility or low-volatility) that we have. We restrict ourselves to the low-volatility case, on the supposition that nowadays with the presence of Central Banks on the exchange market this equilibrium is the most plausible.[11]

On the other hand, this sign depends on the link between V, the variance of the relative real interest rate in the USA and Germany, and $\sigma_{\pi^{us}}^2$, the variance of the US inflation. If stabilising inflation increases the volatility of real long-term interest rates, we are not sure of the effect on the exchange-rate volatility of such a policy. It tends to increase the substitutability between bonds of the two countries, but increases the volatility of exchange rates due to real interest rate shocks. However, Section 8.3 tends to show that, both on theoretical and empirical grounds, there is probably no trade-off between stabilising inflation and stabilising real interest rates, and so no trade-off between stabilising inflation and stabilising the real exchange rate.

8.3   AN ANALYSIS OF THE TRADE-OFF BETWEEN STABILISING INFLATION AND STABILISING THE REAL INTEREST RATE

On *a priori*, one would expect a trade-off between stabilising inflation and stabilising the real interest rate. To stabilise inflation, Central Banks are supposed to accept large movements in both nominal and real interest rates. In other words, one suspects that those Central Banks who are less concerned about stabilising inflation are also those who want to stabilise real activity and real interest rates.

But there are good theoretical reasons to expect no trade-off. First of all, in our model we are concerned about the long-term inflation and not about the short-term price increase. The stabilisation of long-term inflation does not lead to large movements in short-term real activity. If the long-term Phillips curve exhibits a vertical slope, the cost of a progressive reduction of the inflation rate to the Central Bank target may be rather small. In fact, it may be possible for Central Banks to display their long-term target for inflation and to commit themselves to respect it without much cost to the stability of real activity. However, we must acknowledge that a long-term commitment may lack credibility and that a better short-term control of inflation may be the condition for long-term credibility. On the one hand, it may be a case for legal constraints on long-term inflation, as is discussed regularly in the USA, which helps to establish long-term credibility and to impose on Central Banks the obligation to reveal their long-term target. On the other hand, long term credibility may be progressively secured in the case of independent Central Banks as investors look year after year to the record of the monetary authorities fulfilling their commitment.

The second point is that stabilising long-term inflation may limit the extent of the increase in real long-term interest rates when a restrictive monetary policy is required. The point is that stabilising long-term inflation may increase the substitutability between productive capital and financial investment in bonds, since the real yield of bonds is better known and so better compared to the yield (by nature a real one) of productive capital. If this is true, a given modification in investment needs a smaller variation in real long-term interest rates if the Central Bank has stabilised the long-term inflation rate.

This can be illustrated in a small model. We assume that the authorities have a target for short-term real activity Y_t and that that, taking into account shocks to other components of demand, means a target I_t for real investment. This target is assumed to be described by a random variable on the capital stock $K_t = N(K, \sigma_k^2)$. We assume also, which is a strong assumption, that investment is determined by arbitrage between bonds and productive capital. Investors think that the real yield of productive capital over the long term is a random variable $r_c = N(\bar{r}_c, \sigma_{rc}^2)$. As in Section 8.2, π, long-term inflation, is also a random variable: $\pi = N(\bar{\pi}, \sigma_\pi^2)$. We have assumed $\sigma_{\pi r_c} = 0$. Let us call W the total wealth of investors i_t the nominal long-term interest rate. This is not directly controlled by the monetary authorities but we assume that through modifications of short-term interest rates they can use it to control real investment $r_t = r_t - \bar{\pi}$ is the real long-term anticipated interest rate.

$$ K_t = \left[\frac{\bar{r}_c - i_t + \bar{\pi}}{2\,\theta\,\sigma^2} + \frac{\sigma_\pi^2}{\sigma^2} \right] W $$

where

θ = relative risk-aversion of investors

σ^2 = variance of the relative yield between bonds and capital
$(\sigma^2 = \sigma_{r_c}^2 + \sigma_\pi^2)$

$$ r_t = r_c + 2\,\theta\,\sigma_\pi^2 - \frac{K_t}{W}\,2\,\theta\,\sigma^2 $$

$$ \sigma_{r_t}^2 = \left[\frac{2\,\theta\,\sigma^2}{W} \right]^2 \sigma_k^2 $$

$$ \sigma_{r_t}^2 = \left[\frac{2\,\theta}{W} \right]^2 \left[\sigma_{r_c}^2 + \sigma_\pi^2 \right]^2 \sigma_k^2 \tag{3} $$

From equation (3), we can discuss the link between volatility of long-term inflation and the volatility of real anticipated long-term interest rate. Equation (3) shows that the volatility of long-term interest rates (real) decreases when long-term inflation is stabilised since in the long run there should be little trade-off between stabilising inflation and stabilising the return on capital (i.e., $\sigma_{r_c}^2$ and σ_π^2 are not closely correlated).

Table 8.1 shows the covariance matrix between US and German

Table 8.1   Covariance matrix

US inflation	German inflation	US real interest rate	German real interest rate	Real exchange rate
0.0010873	5.4E-04	−0.001075	−.5.1E-04	0.0037649
5.4E-04	4.5E-04	−5.3E-04	−4.2E-04	0.2E-04
−0.001075	−5.3E-04	0.0010659	5.0E-04	−0.003955
−5.1E-04	−4.2E-04	5.0E-04	4.0E-04	−9.5E-04
0.0037649	9.2E-04	−0.003955	−9.5E-04	0.0366424

inflation, and the US and German real interest rates, amongst other variables. It is a well-known empirical fact that there is a negative correlation between the levels of the real interest rate and expected inflation (see the survey by Mishkin, 1988). But a negative covariance of the levels does not say anything about covariance of the variances. However, in Germany, the variance of inflation and the real interest rate is lower, whereas the USA has a higher variance for inflation and the real interest rate. Even if the real interest rate is here the result of a conventional calculation using past inflation, this can be interpreted as a strong sign of no trade-off between stability of inflation and stability of real interest rates.

8.4   CONCLUSION

This paper shows that if long-term expectations and long-term investment are stabilising and short-term speculation destabilising in the exchange market, diminishing the uncertainly that faces the investor due to inflation in different countries probably stabilises the exchange rate. An anticipated return to PPP allows investors who correctly anticipate this to play their stabilising role. It was found, in empirical justification of our model, that decreasing the variance of inflation accelerates the returns to the level justified by the real interest differential. Uncertainty about future inflation has two origins. In the first place, there may be some uncertainty about the reaction function of Central Banks, particularly in countries where Central Banks have a very discretionary policy. Secondly, even if the reaction function is well-known, uncertainty will come from the existence of shocks to the economy: if the Central Bank is not concerned very strictly only with inflation, these shocks create movements in price increases. But, here again, we must stress the difference between long-term and short-term inflation. What matters in this paper is only long-term inflation. From this paper, we make the argument for (1) the obligation for Central Banks to reveal their long-term inflation targets, or at least to provide the means for investors to learn their targets, and (2) to restrict their objective function, as far as the long term is concerned, to the stabilisation of inflation. Since it is generally believed that the trade-off between inflation and real activity is less pronounced at the long term than at the short term, such an orientation may have little cost in terms of destabilising real activity.

That is what this paper is about. What it is not is a plea for a so-called conservative Central Bank and freely floating exchange rates. First a conservative Central Bank is better characterised by its short-term reaction function than by the long-term one which is important in this paper. In a word, we gave no special argument to choose between a Central Bank which acts to create a very fast reduction of the inflation rate after an inflationary shock and a Central Bank which prefers gradual one. It is also the volatility of inflation, not the level, which we are concerned about. However, short-term control of inflation may be seen as a condition for long-term control if the Central Bank is not seen as very credible – for example, if it is not independent from fiscal policy and its dictates. Secondly, our feeling is indeed that the working of the exchange-rate system may be improved by the intervention of Central Banks in case of excess volatility and by better anti-inflation long-term credibility. The relative stability of the exchange rate system since 1987 has probably a lot to do with the progress made by monetary authorities along these lines. In this regard, there is a growing feeling that the present system of informal management of exchange rates is perhaps the best one (see Frenkel and Goldstein, 1989, for a general analysis of exchange-rate systems which concludes implicitly in this way). However, this better international monetary system yet suffers from some flaws traditionally associated with freely-floating exchange rates (the risk of inefficient non-cooperative equilibrium seems to be the greatest). In fact, this paper does not give too many arguments for the general debate between fixed and floating exchange rates.

Appendix: Analysis of the Solutions of Equation (2)

$$\sigma_e^2 = V + \mu \, (\sigma_{\pi us}^2 + \sigma_{\pi ger}^2 + \sigma_e^2)^2 \, \sigma_u^2 \tag{2}$$

The two solutions are:

$$\sigma_e^2 = \frac{1 - 2\,\mu\,\sigma_u^2\,[\sigma_{\pi us}^2 + \sigma_{\pi ger}^2] \pm \sqrt{1 - 4\mu\sigma_u^2\,[\sigma^2\pi^{us} + \sigma^2\pi^{ger} = V]}}{2\,\mu\,\sigma_u^2} \tag{3}$$

There are two real solutions iff:

$$0 < \sigma_u^2 < \frac{1}{4\,\mu\,[\sigma_{\pi us}^2 + \sigma_{\pi ger}^2 + V]}$$

when

$$\sigma_e^2 = 1/4\,\mu\,[\sigma_{\pi us}^2 + \sigma_{\pi ger}^2 + V]$$

there is one solution:

$$\sigma_e^2 = 2\,V + \sigma_{\pi us}^2 + \sigma_{\pi ger}^2$$

when

$$\sigma_u^2 = 0$$

there is one solution:

$$\sigma_e^2 = V$$

If we take the derivative of equation (2) with respect to s_u^2, we find:

$$\frac{d\sigma_e^2}{d\sigma_u^2} = \mu\,(\sigma_{\pi us}^2 + \sigma_{\pi ger}^2 + \sigma_e^2)^2 + 2\,\mu\,\sigma_u^2 \;\frac{d\sigma_e^2}{d\sigma_u^2}(\sigma_{\pi us}^2 + \sigma_{\pi ger}^2 + \sigma_e^2)$$

$$\frac{d\sigma_e^2}{d\sigma_u^2} = \frac{\mu\,(\sigma_{\pi us}^2 + \sigma_{\pi ger}^2 + \sigma_e^2)^2}{1 - 2\,\mu\,\sigma_u^2(\sigma_{\pi us}^2 + \sigma_{\pi ger}^2 + \sigma_e^2)}$$

The sign of $\dfrac{d\sigma_e^2}{d\sigma_u^2}$ is the sign of

172

$1 - 2 \mu \sigma_u^2 (\sigma_{\pi us}^2 = \sigma_{\pi ger}^2 = \sigma_e^2)$

If we look at the value of σ_u^2 such that

$1 - 2 \mu \sigma_u^2 (\sigma_{\pi us}^2 + \sigma_{\pi ger}^2 + \sigma_e^2) = 0$

taking into account equation (2), we find:

$$\sigma_u^2 = \frac{1}{4 \mu \left[\sigma_{\pi us}^2 + \sigma_{\pi ger}^2 + V \right]}$$

(i.e. the largest value acceptable for σ_u^2). The tangent is vertical at this point. We can conclude that the sign of the derivative is constant for each of the solutions (since $\dfrac{d\sigma_e^2}{d\sigma_u^2}$ is a continuous function which has no zero value for σ_u^2 included between 0 and

$$\frac{1}{4 \mu \left[\sigma_{\pi us}^2 + \sigma_{\pi ger}^2 + V \right]} \ )$$

The smaller solution

$$\sigma_e^2 = \frac{1 - 2 \mu \sigma_u^2 \left[\sigma_{\pi us}^2 + \sigma_{\pi ger}^2 \right] - \sqrt{1 - 4 \mu \sigma_u^2 \left[\sigma_{\pi us}^2 + \sigma_{\pi ger}^2 + V \right]}}{2 \mu \sigma_u^2}$$

is monotonous growing from V, for $\sigma_u^2 = 0$, to $2 V + \sigma_{\pi us}^2 + \sigma_{\pi ger}^2$ for

$$\sigma_u^2 = \frac{1}{4 \mu \left[\sigma_{\pi us}^2 + \sigma_{\pi ger}^2 + V \right]}$$

The larger solution is monotonous decreasing from $+ \infty$, for $\sigma_u^2 = 0$, to $2 V + \sigma_{\pi us}^2 + \sigma_{\pi ger}^2$, for

$$\sigma_u^2 = \frac{1}{4 \mu \left[\sigma_{\pi us}^2 + \sigma_{\pi ger}^2 + V \right]}$$

Another question is to find how σ_e^2 vary with $\sigma_{\pi us}^2$ or $\sigma_{\pi ger}^2$. Let us take the derivative of equation (2) with respect to $\sigma_{\pi us}^2$:

$$\frac{d\sigma_e^2}{d\sigma_{\pi us}^2} = \frac{dV}{d\sigma_{\pi us}^2} + 2\mu \left(1 + \frac{d\sigma_e^2}{d\sigma_{\pi us}^2} \right) (\sigma_{\pi us}^2 + \sigma_{\pi ger}^2 + \sigma_e^2) \sigma_u^2$$

$$\frac{d\sigma_e^2}{d\sigma_{\pi us}^2} = \frac{\dfrac{dV}{d\sigma_{\pi us}^2} + 2\mu (\sigma_{\pi us}^2 + \sigma_{\pi ger}^2 + \sigma_e^2)\sigma_u^2}{1 - 2\mu (\sigma_{\pi us}^2 + \sigma_{\pi ger}^2 + \sigma_e^2) \sigma_u^2}$$

The sign of this expression is ambiguous because of the sign both of the numerator and of the denominator. For the numerator, $2\mu\,(\sigma_{\pi us}^2 + \sigma_{\pi ger}^2 + \sigma_e^2)\,\sigma_u^2$ is positive but the sign of $\dfrac{dV}{d\sigma_{\pi us}^2}$ is unknown.

The sign of the denominator is positive if we are in the low-volatility solution and negative in the other case: the sign of $1 - 2\mu(\sigma_{\pi us}^2 + \sigma_{\pi ger}^2 + \sigma_e^2)\,\sigma_u^2$ is the same as the sign of $[1/2\mu\sigma_u^2 - [\sigma_{\pi us}^2 + \sigma_{\pi ger}^2]] - \sigma_e^2)$ i.e.,

$$\frac{\pm\sqrt{1 - 4\mu\,\sigma_u^2\,[\sigma_{\pi us}^2 + \sigma_{\pi ger}^2 + V]}}{2\mu\,\sigma_u^2}$$

as one can see from equation (3).

So we must consider the four cases in Table A8.1

Table A8.1   High- and low-volatility solutions

Sign of $\dfrac{d\sigma_e^2}{d\,\sigma_{\pi us}^2}$	*High-volatility solution* Low-volatility solution	+ − $\dfrac{dV}{d\,\sigma_{\pi us}^2}$ Very negative	− + $\dfrac{dV}{d\,\sigma_{\pi us}^2}$ Positive or not too negative

Notes

1. Sachs (1985) exploited the flatness of the yield curve for maturities beyond 5 years to measure return to PPP. Sachs's maintained hypothesis is true for maturities between 5 and 20 years. The 30-years rate behaves differently than the other long-term rates.
2. The existence of eventual mean reversion is also compatible with speculative bubbles, which in their turn could be completely rational. See, notably, Meese (1985). On the other hand, short-term random walk behaviour could be compatible with long-term mean reversion if the random walk behaviour is near random walk.
3. Empirical studies of anti-inflation reputations are a relatively new phenomenon. See, for instance, Weber (1989) where he compares Germany's undisputed anti-inflation reputation with both EMS and non-EMS countries. He finds Germany's reputation somewhat moderated in recent years, whereas that of a country like the US compares with that of a country like France, especially in recent years.
4. This model relies on Dornbusch (1983).
5.
$$\theta = \frac{-U_2}{U_1} W \text{ and } \theta^* = \frac{-U_2}{-U_1} W^*$$

   where U_1, U_2 are the derivatives of the utility function of the investor with respect to the level of wealth and variance, and W, W^* are the real American and German wealth.
6. We consider as exogeneous all capital flows which are not investment in long-term bonds. We assume that long-term investment in bonds is the only stabilising power in the exchange market. All other flows do not depend on the real exchange rate and result in an *ex ante* disequilibrium on the exchange market which has to be financed by long-term capital flows. This is a very strong simplification: the real exchange rate influences, albeit slowly, the current-account deficit and direct investments are long-term investments which depend on the real exchange rate.
7. In the rest of this paper, we will assume that W and W^* are constant. There is, of course, an inconsistency in assuming that real German wealth with respect to US prices is constant or evolves like the 'true' German real wealth (i.e., with respect to German prices) since it is influenced by modifications of the real exchange rate. Using this assumption, we limit our analysis to only one of the ways in which the exchange rate is balanced. We take into account that modifications of the exchange rate change the relative yield of investment in different countries, and thus affect capital flows, but we forget that there is a 'wealth effect' which helps to clear the market: a fall in the dollar must lead to an increase of the foreign real wealth expressed in dollars, and thus to a new demand for US currency.
8. This equation deserves a brief comment. It means that the overevaluation of the dollar ($e_I - e^*$) varies as the real long-term differential between the USA and Germany. See Coe and Golub (1986) for an empirical test of a similar model. Note that the constant B depends on

the uncertainty about German and US inflation. If this uncertainty changes – that is, if investors think that the Central Bank has changed its reaction function – the constant is modified and there is a shock to the real exchange rate. However, it should also be noted that another channel which has not been mentioned is the effect of a change in Central Bank inflationary policy on the differential of real interest rates (dr_t in the equation).

9. This result needs two comments:

   - Strictly speaking, the term σ_e^2 on the left-hand side of this equation is not the same as the term σ_e^2 on the right-hand side. The former refers to the variance of the real exchange rate at date t and the latter at date $t + 5$. This is not a real problem since we assumed that the variance for the real exchange rate was constant.
   - The variance of the relative real interest rate

   $$dr_t = (i_t - \bar{\pi}^{us}) - (i_t^* - \bar{\pi}^{ger}), \ (V = \text{var } dr_t)$$

   is the 'true' variance of the stochastic process, not the variance of dr_t taking into account the information known at date t. If it is assumed, as we assumed, that anticipations for inflation are constant over time, V is also the variance of the relative nominal interest rate, whereas the portfolio balance model starts out with the nominal rate constant and all the action coming from inflation uncertainty.

10. A close examination of the model shows that this point – and, more generally, the existence of two solutions – depends crucially on the fact that it is the variance of wealth which is important to the individual, and not something else, like the standard deviation of wealth.

11. All the results are inverted in the case of a high-volatility equilibrium since the more bonds are substitutable in this case, the more volatile must be the real exchange rate if it is to be rational in face of the potential stabilising power of long-term investors.

References

Coe, T. and Golub, S. (1986) 'Exchange rates and real long-term interest rate differentials: evidence for eighteen OECD countries', OECD, Working Paper, no. 28, Paris, OECD.

Dornbusch, Rudiger (1976) 'Expectations and exchange rate dynamics', *Journal of Political Economy*, 84 (December) pp. 1161–74

Dornbusch, Rudiger (1983) 'Exchange rate risk and the macro-economics of exchange-rate determination', in *Research in International Business and Finance*, vol 3, JAI Press, pp. 3–27.

Frankel, F. and Froot, K. (1987a) 'Short-term and long-term expectations of the yen/dollar exchange rate: evidence from survey data', NBER, Working Paper, no. 2216 (April).

Frankel, F. and Froot, K. (1987b) 'Understanding the US Dollar in the Eighties: the expectations of chartists and fundamentalists', *Economic Record*, no. 63, pp. 24–38

Frankel, F. and Meese, R. (1987) 'Are exchange-rates excessively variable?', NBER, Working Paper, no. 2249 (May).

Frankel, F. and Goldstein, M. (1989) 'Monetary Policies, Capital Market Integration, and the Exchange Rate Regime', Paper prepared for the Bank of France – University Conference (December).

Meese, R. (1985) 'Testing for bubbles in exchange markets: a case of sparkling rates?' *Journal of Political Economy*, vol. 94, no. 2, pp. 345–73.

Mishkin, Frederic S. (1978) 'Efficient markets theory: implications for monetary policy', *Brookings Papers on Economic Activity*, n.s. pp. 707–68.

Mishkin, Frederic S. (1988) 'Understanding Real Interest Rates', Cambridge, Mass., NBER, Working Paper, no. 2691.

Sachs, Jeffrey D. (1985) 'The dollar and the policy mix: 1985', *Brookings Papers on Economic Activity*, 1, pp. 117–85.

Weber, Axel A. (1989) 'The role of policymakers' reputation in the EMS deflation: an empirical evaluation (October) (manuscript).

Discussion

Ernst Baltensperger

Davanne and Vijayraghavan start with the observation that recent work on exchange markets suggests that, while short-term expectations may be destabilising (exhibit 'bandwagon' effects), long-term expectations appear to be stabilising (mean-reverting). They wish to examine the implication of this for Central Bank policy directed at stabilising the real exchange rate. The authors are especially concerned with the question of a trade-off between two possible goals of Central Bank policy: stabilising inflation and stabilising the real exchange rate. They attempt to show, in a portfolio balance model of real exchange-rate determination, that such a trade-off probably does not exist. Rather, lowering the volatility of inflation is likely to lower also the variability of the real exchange rate. It must be emphasised that in all this the authors take a long-term perspective (i.e., they are concerned with average inflation and exchange rates over a time span of about 5 years, not with short-run variability). The existence of two solutions for the determination of real exchange-rate volatility (a high-volatility solution and a low-volatility solution), finally, leads the authors to advocate a Central Bank intervention policy on exchange markets as an instrument to make sure (or at least increase the likelihood) that the low-volatility solution is obtained.

I find the paper interesting and competent. Furthermore, I have much sympathy for most of the conclusions and views to which it leads. Nevertheless, let me point out a few areas where I believe the approach of the paper to be limited, and even potentially misleading in its conclusions.

The model employed treats the US net real deficit *vis-à-vis* the rest of the world as a stochastic variable (with mean 0 and variance σ_u^2). Equilibrium in the exchange market requires that this net deficit equal the difference between the foreign demand for US bonds and the US demand for foreign bonds, which is explained in terms of the expected real long-term interest differential, the overestimation of the dollar, and uncertainty about US inflation, foreign inflation, and the exchange rate. The model is quite restrictive in some of its assumptions. The stochastic processes for US and foreign inflation

178

(means and variances) are given exogenously and remain constant over time. The same holds for the net US difícit, and for the real exchange rate, except that in the latter case the variance is solved for endogenously in the model. (This is not made very clear to the reader at first: on p. 162, σ_e^2 appears to be exogenous as well; only on p. 165 does it become clear that it is treated endogenously.)

One question I have here is: what happens if these stochastic processes are allowed to change? This would introduce an additional dimension of expectations formation, a dynamic dimension not dealt with in the paper. The paper assumes that, for example, the inflation process in the US is given and constant (although in a stochastic specification). If it can change, which should certainly be possible in reality, the formation of inflationary expectations becomes more complex than is assumed in the paper. For empirical and policy applications, this problem could, I believe, be quite important.

In particular, this kind of problem seems relevant to me with regard to the issue of exchange-market intervention taken up by the authors. They advocate an intervention policy as an instrument able to ensure a 'low-volatility' solution for the real exchange rate. This appears to be relatively unproblematic, as long as the equilibrium value of the real exchange rate (e^*) is constant and known. If it is not, however, there is a danger of trying to stabilise e at a disequilibrium level, which involves a risk of destabilising the real economy, a risk not captured in the model. Personally, in spite of the argument in the paper, I would remain rather sceptical about such an intervention policy.

In equation (2) on p. 165, as the authors correctly note themselves, the σ_e on both sides of the equation are not identical in principle. On the left-hand side, we have var(e_t), on the right-hand side the variance of the long-run exchange rate, var(e_{t+5}). The authors discard this problem by referring to their assumption that the stochastic process of e (and thus the variance of e) is constant in their model. In principle, I can accept that (although, as already mentioned, this type of assumption restricts the model's range of application). However, I ask myself whether this does really do justice to the view stressed in the introduction, according to which there are different forces at work in the short and in the long run (destabilising ones in the former case, stabilising ones in the latter, probably reflecting different sectors with different information sets). I realise that it would be difficult to incorporate this in an explicit manner into a model such as the present one. But it appears to me that the introduction raises expectations which are in this case not fulfilled.

A final point: the advice for Central Banks' long-term policy given in the concluding Section 8.4 is well taken. Only, it should be added that long-term developments are always necessarily the result of a multitude of short-term decisions: if you want to realise appropriate long-term goals, you have to think of them in the context of short-term decisions, too.

Part III
European Monetary Union

9 Economic and Monetary Union (EMU) in Europe: A UK Perspective

Charles A.E. Goodhart

9.1 INTRODUCTION

The subject of this paper is the current state of progress towards economic and monetary union (EMU), as seen from a UK viewpoint. (The conference for which this contribution was actually written took place in February 1990.) Progress was swift in 1985, which witnessed the publication of the Delors Committee report in April and its discussion at the Madrid Conference of Heads of State in June.

With agreement having been reached in Madrid, at least in principle, to proceed to Stage 1, as had been proposed by Delors in July 1990, the focus of argument shifted to the advantages (or otherwise) of moving on to the subsequent stages – first irrevocably-fixed currencies, and then to a single European currency, and associated with that, a single European system of Central Banks. This would, indeed, represent a major change in monetary regime, perhaps the most important since the *de facto* abandonment of the gold standard on the outbreak of war in 1914. It is this major change in monetary regime that I shall focus on in most of the rest of this paper.

First I should, perhaps, expand slightly on my earlier comment that the move to Stage 1 had been agreed only in principle at Madrid. The requirements for the achievement of Stage 1 are that all member states should enter the Exchange-rate Mechanism (ERM) with the narrower 2¼ per cent bands and without the protection of exchange controls. The British government's position now is that we will enter the ERM, but only after two conditions have been satisfied: first that our inflation has come down into rough equality with that of other members of the EC, and second that the ERM has been shown to work satisfactorily even after all the major participating countries have abandoned exchange controls.

Achievement of the first condition seems even further away in the distant future, following adverse developments on the UK inflation front. But the second condition is more important. It is clear that Sir Alan Walters (e.g., 1986, Chapter 7) sees the relatively satisfactory performance of the ERM to date as depending significantly – indeed, perhaps crucially – on the protection afforded to many of the major countries by such exchange controls. It is likely, therefore, that compromise within the British government was achieved on this second condition precisely because Mrs Thatcher expected this condition *not* to be met, while both Sir Geoffrey Howe and Nigel Lawson expected it actually to be achievable, and to be achieved in the near future.

There may soon be some important tests of this second condition. A lower rate of increase in unit labour costs in (West) Germany than in the other member countries has been tending to bring about a divorce in *real* exchange rates within the EC (so long as their nominal rates remain pegged and fixed against each other), leading to considerable divergences in bilateral current account positions among ERM members. There have been suggestions that West Germany would actually favour such a realignment, and that could indeed provide a recipe for future market instability. Whereas the French economy has, perhaps, now converged sufficiently to that of (West) Germany to weather such pressures, it is arguable how long Italy could so do without the protection of exchange controls, particularly now that it has also adopted the standard narrow ERM bands (January 1990). All these considerations have, however, been upset by the moves towards German reunification, the ramifications of which upon the future development of both ERM and EMU will no doubt be considerable, but remain as yet difficult to discern in the current state of flux in East Germany, and East Europe more widely.

So, for a variety of reasons, I do not share the conventional view that the achievement of Stage 1 will necessarily be simple to achieve, and requires only the necessary political will. But let me now turn to the main theme of my paper, which is the pros and cons of the further subsequent moves towards EMU.

9.2 THE BENEFITS OF MONETARY UNION

The Delors committee (1989) did not attempt to itemise, far less to quantify, what the respective benefits and costs of a move to a monetary union might be; not only would any attempt at a quantified cost–benefit analysis have been extremely difficult to undertake, and highly contentious and debatable, but the commitee were able to claim, self-protectively, that their remit had already accepted the desirability of the move towards monetary union, leaving them with only the job of setting out which route to that agreed end would be best. While that may have been convenient for the committee, most of the rest of us will want to have some account of what the respective benefits and costs may be, even though the quantification of these is, indeed, extremely difficult.

There are, perhaps, four main benefits. The first, and most obvious of these, which could certainly in principle be quantified, is the reduction in the transaction costs of having to change from one currency to another, via exchange rates, in the process of making transfers of goods and services, tourism, etc. in moving from one country to another within the EMS; this also comprises, of course, the resource costs involved for the commercial (and indeed for the Central) banks, which could be released for other functions once a single currency had been adopted. The savings that might be achieved in this way, and the consequential enhanced (public good) value of the single European currency as a medium of exchange, are of some considerable importance, but are not by any standards massive.

Probably a much more important feature would be the reduction in uncertainty about future exchange-rate (step) changes that would occur. This reduction in uncertainty would provide investors, whether direct or portfolio, with a somewhat greater ability to allocate the geographical siting of resources in order to achieve maximum efficiency. The reduction of this uncertainty, and the lessening of the costs of trying to obtain information about likely foreign exchange-rate developments, and of monetary policies in other European countries, would facilitate the greater unification of the European economic system. This benefit can, however, also be overstated. The key factor in deciding on the geographical allocation of resources is the likely development of relative *real* costs; stability – indeed, fixity – of *nominal* exchange rates does not eliminate (and may not even reduce) uncertainty about the future longer-term path of *real* exchange rates.

The third main benefit of the adoption of a single-currency system would, indeed, be the greater unification of the market that would result. It is extremely difficult to quantify this, but the best way of visualising what is involved is to think what might have happened, counterfactually, if each of the US states had had a separate currency and a separate Central Bank – with, for example, a Texan dollar, and a New York dollar, and a Virginia dollar, etc. It is quite likely that the unification and unity of the economic and political system within the US would have been impaired by the disparity in currencies and monetary policies.

The fourth main advantage of having a single currency is that it is a necessary part of any move towards greater (economic and political) unification, as was demonstrated in the earlier histories of Germany and Italy themselves (as well as in certain other European states such as Switzerland).

9.3   THE COSTS OF A SINGLE CURRENCY SYSTEM

The ability to print money provides a revenue seigniorage to the monetary authorities. This source of revenue is higher in those cases where the monetary base – consisting of currency outstanding and the reserves required to be held by the commercial banking system – is large, and where the rate of increase in the monetary base is high, particularly in cases of high inflation. In practice, now that most countries in (Northern) Europe have managed to achieve quite low inflation rates, and also have low required reserve ratios, the proportion of tax revenues represented by seigniorage is low in most of these countries. Seigniorage has, at times in the past, provided a significant proportion of total revenues to certain Southern European countries, but now that inflation has been brought down in Italy, Spain, etc. this source of revenue has quite markedly decreased.

Moreover, in most of these Southern European countries, a significant proportion of such seigniorage is due to the high required reserve ratios which their banking systems are currently forced to maintain. Such high required ratios represent, in practice, a tax burden on the banking system. Once exchange controls are competely lifted (in 1990, or 1992) it will be increasingly difficult in any case for countries to tax their own national banking systems more heavily than in other areas of the EMS, because it will be possible for borrowers and lenders to intermediate very simply, even in their own national currencies, outside their own borders. The potential for disintermediation is thus in any case going to restrict the ability of national governments to impose a seigniorage tax on their banking systems after 1992, whether or not EMU is to be achieved. So the argument that has been put forward – that a move towards EMU will simply be too expensive, in fiscal terms, for the Southern European countries to accept – would seem to be incorrect; nevertheless it is true that the Southern European countries will face considerable difficulties after 1992 in having to dismantle the high required reserve ratios and other constraints on their repressed national banking systems, a difficulty which will arise as a result of the move to a single financial market, and *not* essentially from the subsequent move to EMU. The seigniorage cost argument is thus not, in practice, of any major importance within the context of a discussion of EMU.

A much more serious problem is raised by the potential difficulties of economic adjustment to shocks in the face of market imperfections – in particular, imperfections in labour markets. If all markets, including labour markets, were perfectly flexible, so that full employment would be restored virtually immediately after any shock hitting a particular locality, then it is hard to see what economic advantages there could be from having separate (and adjustable) currencies. A common currency over the widest possible range of areas would provide the public good of reducing transactions costs and maximising the role and usefulness of money as a medium of exchange. The economic – as contrasted with the political – value of having separate exchange rates and independent monetary policies is that it provides another route for adjusting relative wages and relative prices if the markets fail to do so, or at least fail to do so quickly enough. If labour markets should prove inflexible, and/or labour itself relatively immobile, then it may be possible to adjust relative real wages and competitiveness so as to restore full employment by an appropriate adjustment in exchange rates. If wages and prices are sticky, then monetary policy and exchange-rate adjustments can have desirable *real* effects. If markets work perfectly, then monetary policy and exchange-rate movements can have only nominal effects. Proponents of a rapid move, first into the ERM, and subsequently to EMU, tend to argue that (1) labour markets are sufficiently flexible, or (2) that they will quite quickly become so, once accommodating adjustments in monetary/exchange-rate policies have been removed as an option, or (3) that you cannot now change real wages by devaluation because of real-wage rigidity.

The third possible source of perceived costs from the abandonment of national monetary control and the acceptance of a common currency arises from the loss of national sovereignty that would result. The true costs of such loss of sovereignty, however, depend greatly on the extent to which monetary policy can be used for adjustment purposes, and have real effects in the context of imperfect labour markets, as outlined above. If markets worked perfectly, then all that sovereignty would achieving would be the choice of the inflation rate, though that would bring with it some command over resources through seigniorage, again as outlined above. The Germans may, indeed, fear that an European Central Bank System, with voting proportional (presumably) to the comparative size of the participating economies, might result in a more expansionary or inflationary choice of policies than would currently be chosen by the Bundesbank. For the remaining countries within Europe, it is hard to see why an ECBS should lead to greater inflation than they themselves have suffered in the past. It is consequently, hard to see that there is much merit in the argument that each country needs to have national control over its own inflation rate. Indeed, I believe that the merit of the argument of the need to maintain some command over national monetary policy depends almost entirely on the associated view that there are considerable imperfections in wage and price adjustment within national markets, the adverse effects of which can at times be ameliorated by judicious use of national monetary policies.

9.4   ADJUSTMENT FOR LABOUR-MARKET RIGIDITIES

The Delors committee recognised that the failure of markets to adjust efficiently and rapidly in certain regions could lead to excessive deflationary or inflationary pressure. The most direct measure which they suggested for meeting possible problems whereby (peripheral) regions became uncompetitive was to double the existing structural programmes. However, these programmes are not really aimed at dealing with adjustment problems, but are rather intended to improve the physical infrastructure in the currently poorer regions of the EC. The report, in para. 29, thus states that, 'The principal objective of regional policies should not be to subsidise incomes and simply offset inequalities in standards of living, but to help to equalise production conditions through investment programmes in such areas as physical infrastructure, communications, transportation and education so that large-scale movements of labour do not become the major adjustment factor. A common problem with this kind of approach is that the bureaucratic choice of physical investment programme, frequently in public-sector infrastructure projects, becomes decided more on political than on economic grounds. This is known in the USA by the graphic term 'pork barrel'. Experience in other federal countries, such as Australia, indicates quite clearly that such investments are frequently traded for political support; and, indeed, the political horse-trading in the course of the Madrid summit of June 1989 suggests that the structural funds will be used largely as a high-cost carrot to persuade the smaller members of the EC (i.e., Ireland, Portugal and Greece) to go along with the decisions of the larger countries and to renounce their potential ability to play an obstructive political role.

If such structural funds are too small and in any case badly designed to play a role in alleviating the problems that may arise from market imperfections, and national monetary policies can no longer do so once a single common currency and European monetary policy has been adopted, can one turn to fiscal policies, either within the EC or at the national country level, to undertake such an adjustment function?

9.5   FISCAL POLICY AND THE DELORS COMMITTEE

Within a fully federal system, such as holds in the USA, fiscal policy does play a considerable role in alleviating the regional problems that would otherwise be caused by market imperfections. Even so, it is important in this context to recall that labour mobility is considerably greater within the USA, and wage flexibility probably also somewhat greater, than in Western Europe. Even so, there are limitations in the USA on such labour mobility, and there do remain constraints on the speed and flexibility with which wages can adjust to restore full employment after some local shock. There are thus clearly times when certain regions (such as the oil-producing regions, or the rust-belt, or the North Eastern states of the USA) have found themselves facing difficulties and deflationary pressures. Under these circumstances, within a fully federal system, the existence of a federal income tax and a common federal level of certain social security and unemployment benefit payments provides for an automatic invisible transfer from the more prosperous regions and states to those suffering deflationary pressures, offsetting about a third of any negative shock (see Sachs and Sala-I-Martin, 1989). Moreover, this transfer does not lead to the accretion, or any increase, in the debt position of the more depressed regions, nor to the building up of an associated credit position in the more prosperous states; in that sense, it is an unrequited transfer. This transfer offsets the current-account deficit in the region with the deflationary shock, and serves to support their economy and to soften the pressure of the adverse shock. So a fully federal fiscal system would act as an automatic built-in system for balancing the disparate economic pressures on the various parts of the community at large.

This will not, for the time being, be politically possible within the EC; it has not, so far, proven politically possible to channel any fiscal resources through the centre in Brussels in the form of commonly-applied income taxes that would be applied on a common basis to all countries, and it would seem that there are political constraints in the wealthier countries to a proposal to divert any significant proportion of income taxes to the federal centre. At the same time, the extent and degree of divergence in economic development between the present members of the EC make it quite difficult – possibly impossible at this stage – to introduce common centralised social and unemployment benefit payments over the whole EC. For example, a level of unemployment benefit which was regarded as socially minimal within the context of the former West Germany might seem so handsome in the context of Portugal and Greece that a significant proportion of the labour force in these latter two countries would voluntarily leave employment. In any case the Delors committee recognised that 'the centrally managed Community budget is likely to remain a very small part of total public sector spending and that much of this budget will not be available for cyclical adjustments'.

This means that any attempt to use fiscal policies in order to bring about economic adjustments in the face of labour-market imperfections in the various local regions would have to be undertaken through *national* fiscal policies. This would have the added disadvantage, as compared to federal fiscal policies, that the use of national fiscal policy to increase expenditures in deflationary regions would add to their future debt burden. So the constraints on the use of national fiscal policy for adjustment purposes within a common-currency area might be somewhat greater than on the quasi-automatic use of federal fiscal policies for that purpose within a fully federal system. The poorer regions of the USA, such as some of the Southern states, have probably received massive continuing transfers of funds from the more prosperous states over many decades, without that increasing their own debt. If they had had to rely entirely on their own state budgets in order to maintain an improved living standards, the degree of fiscal assistance would probably have been considerably less.

In any case, concern about rising debt/income ratios is thus liable to lead to (market) discipline on the willingness of national governments to use fiscal policy for internal adjustment purposes. Rather than showing any concern with the possible resulting limitation on the use of fiscal policy for internal adjustment purposes, the Delors committee goes to the other extreme of trying to limit and constrain the ability of national governments to use fiscal policies for their own purposes. Instead, the Delors committee repeats, again and again, its insistence that national fiscal policies must be constrained by 'binding rules' and limits on the size of the deficit that each national country may run. Indeed, they assert that it will not be possible to operate a single monetary union satisfactorily unless there are associated controls of this kind over the national countries' ability to vary their own fiscal policies. The call for 'binding rules' on national fiscal policies is made time and time again within the report. Why?

A number of reasons for this insistence on centralised control over national fiscal policies are put forward. First, there is a clear underlying feeling in the report that certain countries may seek to borrow excessively, especially now that they would have greater access to a wider European pool of savings, and would thereby raise real interest rates relative to their more conservative neighbours, which would put strains and tensions on European coordination. A second reason which is put forward is that market discipline on governments seeking to borrow more would not work efficiently. It is specifically argued (in para. 30) that 'The constraints imposed by market forces might either be too slow and weak or too sudden and disruptive'. The obvious analogy is with the problems that were experienced in the mid-1980s by New York City; the concern appears to be that a slow realisation by markets that some governments were borrowing excessively would not lead to a significant increase in their costs initially, but would lead at some stage to a complete cessation of their ability to borrow, which would have very disruptive effects on the EC as a whole. It may be felt that there is some slight moral hazard, in that the individual national countries might believe that there was some chance of their own taxpayers getting bailed out by the remainder of the EC in cases when the markets might become closed to them.

The Central Bank members of the Delors committee were all familiar with the well-versed claim that the external imbalances in recent years have been largely due to an inappropriate fiscal/monetary mix within the USA. If the EC were to seek to coordinate monetary policies with the USA and Japan in pursuit of greater worldwide external stability, it would clearly be necessary for the EC itself to have some command over its aggregate fiscal/monetary policy mix. But with the aggregate size of fiscal policy within the EC being almost entirely determined simply by the sum of national fiscal deficits, it would clearly be necessary for the EC to have some command over such national fiscal deficits in order to be able to have any control at all over the aggregate EC fiscal/monetary policy mix.

9.6   ARGUMENTS AGAINST THE DELORS COMMITTEE'S FISCAL SUGGESTIONS

Whereas the Delors committee appears to regard it as self-evident that a currency union must involve some control over national fiscal policies as well, it may be remembered that the gold standard did provide such a common currency union, and in the latter there was no international coordination, or constraint, whatsoever on domestic fiscal policies. Why, then, is it impossible to envisage a currency union under current circumstances, in the form of a gold standard-type system, with a monetary union but no fiscal constraints? One reasonable counter-argument is that, during the gold standard period, governments played a very much smaller role in the economies of their respective countries, and generally abided by a balanced budget objective, which could be regarded, in effect, as representing the required fiscal constraint on national policies. Indeed, it is probably naive to hark back to the gold standard; the structure and nature of our economies has changed markedly since that time, notably with the much larger role of public sectors. But, in some part, the rationale for the larger role of public sectors may have been that, for various reasons, markets (particularly labour markets) have tended to work less flexibly in the twentieth than they did in the nineteenth century. There was certainly much greater labour migration (in particular across the Atlantic and at times of particular stress in Europe) during the nineteenth century than has occurred since 1945. Again, it is arguable that the growth of trades unions and other factors have made labour markets work less flexibly in recent decades than in the nineteenth century. This would suggest that some part of the growth in the public sector has been called forth by the need to play a greater adjustment role within the economy than was necessary earlier. If that is true, then there is *more* need now, rather than less, for there to be some other macro-economic method and instrument for undertaking adjustment, in those cases when monetary policy and exchange rates cannot be so used. Accordingly, if the adoption of a common monetary union should also rule out national fiscal adjustment mechanisms, in the absence of any federal fiscal adjustment mechanism, then the problems caused by imperfect labour markets leading to pockets of regional distress could become acute.

There will then be a need for the alleviation of regional distress, though without removing all pressures for adjustment. The Delors committee does not seem to have appreciated the potential importance of this need for an adjustment mechanism. Indeed there is a phrase, which I find rather chilling (in para. 30), that, 'in setting [fiscal] limits the situation of each member country might have to be taken into consideration'! It is, perhaps, worth noting *en passant* that the Delors committee would also rule out any attempt by governments to adjust for labour-market imperfections by direct intervention in the prices and incomes-setting modalities of their own countries. Earlier in the same para. 30 the committee states that 'Governments, for their part, would refrain from direct intervention in the wage and price formation process'. (It is not, however, clear how a government, which in its role in the public sector provides direct employment for a significant proportion of the labour force, could entirely withdraw from any role in the wage and price formation process.)

Undoubtedly there are some valid concerns here about the possibility of national governments using fiscal policy in a manner which could more widely disrupt EC developments. The experience of local authorities in various countries indicates that it is possible for them to be taken over by politicians who may pay little or no regard to the ultimate financial consequences of unfunded expenditure programmes. Indeed, markets may initially allow them excessive credit, in the belief that they come under the umbrella of the higher-level governmental body (e.g., at the federal level). Moreover, even when there is no specific guarantee, the local politicians (and possibly their voters) may believe that ultimately their current expenditures will be financed by tax payers elsewhere. While that is certainly a potential danger, it is arguable that there are better ways of dealing with it than through transferring the main decision on the size of fiscal deficits to the EC centre. The extent, and nature, of the interference from the centre in the process of national fiscal policy decision-making is likely to become a very sensitive issue.

There may also be better ways of dealing with the policy-mix issue than through requiring deficit countries to limit the extent of such deficits. For example, it might be possible to require each of the member countries broadly to decide simultaneously on their preferred optimal budget deficit or surplus for the forthcoming year, and then to review whether the sum of these deficits/surpluses matches the required aggregate preferred policy-mix position. Rather than having all the adjustment taken by the deficit countries, the achievement of the preferred aggregate policy mix might be accomplished by requiring all countries to shade their own national preferred positions by a common percentage amount.

Admittedly, there are difficulties (e.g., in the encouragement of strategic games-playing in the above suggestion), but this particular area seems to be the locus for the greatest future problems in reconciling the continuation of some remaining national control over the well-being of their own citizens with the adoption at the same time of a common monetary system.

Let me reiterate once again: if one seriously believes that wage flexibility or labour mobility within the EC is sufficient to allow all markets, but especially labour markets, to adjust pretty efficiently, then we should move to currency unification with all due deliberate speed. If one, however, believes that labour markets work very imperfectly – imperfections that the proposed Social Charter may even worsen – then one must be concerned whether the remaining national and regional economic instruments would be sufficient, under the Delors committee proposals, to prevent serious economic strains and imbalances developing between regions and nation states.

9.7   THE UK TREASURY'S 1989 PROPOSALS FOR 'AN EVOLUTIONARY APPROACH TO ECONOMIC AND MONETARY UNION'

Let me turn next to the UK Treasury's proposals for 'An Evolutionary Approach to Economic and Monetary Union' (November 1989). This was described by Nigel Lawson as involving competition between currencies, but this is a misnomer. So long as any recipient of a payment in a foreign currency has to exchange it at uncertain and variable exchange rates in return for his own currency, he will charge a higher comparative price for a sale effected in foreign than in domestic currencies. If, however, the relative values of differing currencies were pegged for payment purposes (say, by giving them a legal tender value) while their actual market value could still show fluctuations, then Gresham's Law would come into operation (see also Chapter 10): rather than the best currency, the worst currency would come to dominate. But, in practice, we can be sure that there will be no competition among hand-to-hand currencies.

There is, of course, already full competition between deposits on free markets, notably the Euro-currency market; and there is again of course no tendency for the Euro-markets to move towards single-currency domination precisely because the differential between equilibrium nominal interest rates exactly offsets the expected faster rate of depreciation of one (more inflationary) currency than another. Indeed, one possible source of bias – the ability to charge nominal rather than real interest rates against tax – could once again tend to make borrowers prefer to borrow the most, rather than the least, inflationary currency, but I would doubt whether, given the risks of foreign-currency borrowing, this would be a serious cause of bias.

The Treasury's plan rests on the political and economic unpopularity, within the ERM, of accepting a devaluation *vis-à-vis* the central currency, the Deutsche Mark. While I accept that there is some such incentive to hold currencies pegged and fixed against the Deutsche Mark, the Treasury's plan faced three main problems. First, it lead logically to acceptance of the Deutsche Mark as Europe's eventual single currency and to the Bundesbank as the single European Central Bank. While I myself would applaud that, many of the authors of the Delors committee would not. Second, it rests on a very favourable interpretation of the ERM – which is, to say the least, odd coming from the UK. Third, and worst, it provides no guarantee whatsoever of actually achieving the ultimate objective of monetary union by any given deadline.

9.8 DELORS AND THE EMERGENCE OF EASTERN EUROPE

Although the move towards the achievement of EMU within Western Europe is a matter of great importance, and would represent a

radical change of (economic) regime and structure, the politico-
economic importance of that has been dwarfed in by the emerging
changes in Eastern Europe, in particular with the developing shift
away from command economies towards a more market-oriented
system. Since this latter development burst onto the scene with
remarkable speed, it is doubtful how much the authors of the Delors
committee report were able to take it into serious consideration in
their own deliberations. Nevertheless, there is some considerable
potential interaction between the structural measures suggested in
the Delors report and the emerging development of Eastern European states. As already indicated, the proposals outlined in the
Delors committee report would involve the transfer of a significant –
perhaps the major – proportion of macro-economic policy instruments to the EC centre in Brussels. With the majority of macro-
economic policy decisions and initiatives being taken in Brussels, it
would seem only logical and sensible that international macro-
economic policy coordination be undertaken by the EC, rather than
by its separate member governments, as indeed the Delors committee specifically proposed in para. 38. If, however, the EC is going
to run international economic (foreign) policy on behalf of its member countries, can such international policy-making within the economic sphere be divorced from diplomacy and foreign policy more
widely in other spheres: or, alternatively, will there be a tendency for
the EC to play a wider role, on behalf of national governments, in
setting foreign policy more broadly? Indeed, given the EC's wider
role in international policy-making, and its concern with the coordination of fiscal policies, will it be possible to achieve all of this
without there being increasing EC concern over expenditures on
defence – and, indeed, defence policies – more widely, as well?

But if these various powers are to be transferred increasingly to the
EC centre, beginning with macro-economic powers going on to the
ability to determine international economic policy, and subsequently
foreign and defence policy, more broadly, how will that fit with the
apparently growing desire of non-aligned, or socialist, countries to
have a relationship with the EC? Will the greater centralisation and
integration of Western Europe make it more difficult to achieve
detente with such Eastern European countries as wish to have an
economic relationship with the EC – for example, Hungary and
Poland? In view of the greater movement in the politico–economic
systems in Eastern Europe, is it currently wise for the Western
Europe countries to move towards greater centralisation of powers

and decision-making? Will these greater transfers of power to Brussels aid and assist, or will they have the contrary effect, on the possibility of bringing about some greater reunification of Europe than has been possible since 1945? This is both an important and a sensitive subject. At this moment of flux and uncertainty in future wider economic developments, it would seem wise to be cautious, gradual and hesitant about making far-ranging and sweeping changes to the economic (and ultimately to the political) structure of Western Europe without thinking about the potentially wider consequences that these may have for Europe and the rest of the world.

9.9   EMU AND GERMAN REUNIFICATION

It was reported in the *Financial Times* (8 February 1990, p. 2) that, on hearing of the expedited move to monetary unification between the former West and East Germany, a European Commission official remarked that he hoped to hear fewer lectures in future from Mr Pöhl on the need for convergence as a pre-requisite for EMU. Indeed, there may be some common tendency to believe that, if it is possible for such markedly different economies as the two Germanies to move to monetary unification, then it should be a far simpler matter to progress to EMU among the more similar economies of Western Europe.

But this superficial argument is totally incorrect, and monetary unification between the two Germanies will be in many (possibly most) respects simpler, easier and more desirable, than is the case for EMU. The crucial point to grasp is that the process of price- and wage-setting does not generally take place in perfect markets, dependent only on local demand/supply and rational expectations of future inflation, etc. but is conditional on a complex nexus of backward-looking comparative relationships. So long as that nexus remains a powerful influence over wage- and price-setting, it is virtually impossible to drive wages and prices down quickly and flexibly to a level that is consistent with a country with a lower trend growth of unit labour costs, without in the meantime running the risks of a major recession. If the trend rate of growth of unit labour costs in West Germany in tradeable goods industries is 0, or negative, and UK trend productivity in such industries is, say $3\frac{1}{2}$ per cent, we have to get our trend growth of nominal wages in such industries down to $3\frac{1}{2}$ per cent p.a. (or below) also, in order to be able to sustain irrevocably-fixed exchange rates. No doubt we must try to achieve such an outcome in due course, since that is also a minimum condition for zero inflation, but what kind of recession would it take to do that in the immediate future with our present labour market, trades unions, etc.?

The key point is that that backward-looking nexus of comparative wage and price relationships has broken down in the former East Germany. As has been widely reported the East German economic structure is on the point of collapse; there will need to be a complete shift to a new regime of price and wage relationships, a completely different structure of ownership, a new financial system, and revived markets. This must be the moment, *par excellence*, when a whole-scale accompanying monetary regime change is both essential and comparatively easy to accomplish.

This is not to suggest that there will not be problems. Reunification has caused a sharp increase in demand pressure and government expenditures, so the Bundesbank has to cope with inflationary impulses (with, or without, monetary unification). There is the well-aired question of what exchange rate to choose for the currency transfer, and also several other transitional problems. But there are also many features of the German scene that will make monetary unification comparatively easy and painless. The collapse of any nexus of backward-looking comparative relationships should allow for some considerable flexibility in wage levels in East Germany for some years to come. The mobility of labour and capital between the two parts of the country will remain high. Germany will form not only a single monetary union, but also become a unified federal fiscal system, so that any area buffered by an adverse economic shock will obtain a partial fiscal offset. These conditions are precisely those that make monetary union viable and beneficial. They will exist in a reunified Germany; they do not yet exist in Western Europe, at least not to anything like the same extent.

The fact that monetary unification in Germany is both necessary and desirable, and will be successfully achieved, does not, alas, throw much light on the different (and actually more difficult) issue of the road to EMU; it is a mistake to believe that it does. A similar mistake was made, for example, in the analysis of how to stop inflations. Sargent (1986, especially Ch. 3) noted that a number of interwar hyperinflations had been ended, more or less at a stroke, without causing any additional unemployment, by a credible monetary regime change. The inference was then often drawn that it should be even easier to end comparatively mild inflations by a credible monetary regime change. That is not correct; the difference in the two cases is that under hyperinflation the nexus of backward-looking comparative relationships will already have disintegrated.

For somewhat different reasons it has also disintegrated in the former East Germany. That makes monetary unification with West Germany both more desirable and (some might find paradoxically) easier to implement. The success of such unification should not be seen as implying a similarly easy passage for EMU.

References

Delors committee (1989) *Report on economic and monetary union in the European Community*. Office for Official Publications of the European Communities, Luxembourg.

Sachs, J.D. and Sala-I-Martin, X. (1989) 'Federal Fiscal Policy and Currency Unions: Some Lessons for Europe from the United States', paper presented at the NBER Conference on 'European Economic Integration: Towards 1992', Cambridge, Mass. (August).

Sargent, T.J. (1986) *Rational Expectations and Inflation*, New York, Harper & Row.

UK Treasury (1989) 'An Evolutionary Approach to Economic and Monetary Union', London, HM Treasury (November).

Walters, Sir A. (1986) *Britain's Economic Renaissance: Margaret Thatcher's Reform 1979–1986*, Oxford University Press.

Discussion

Erich W. Streissler

I find myself in full agreement with many of the basic points of Professor Goodhart's fine paper. Indeed, the savings in transaction costs that may be achieved by monetary union 'are not by any standards massive'; the cost of seigniorage foregone in the case of monetary union are not 'of any major importance'; and regional policies in order to alleviate distributional distortions due to monetary union are much more likely to become a hugh 'pork barrel' racket than anything else. What might be considered Professor Goodhart's main point is very memorable: 'If the adoption of a common monetary union should also rule out national fiscal adjustment mechanisms', then Europe is likely to get into real trouble.

In fact, all historical experience shows that fiscal autonomy (in the sense of deciding what to use public funds for) is fully compatible with monetary union. The historical case most relevant to our present problems is, I think, the old German Reich from the sixteenth century to 1866: each German prince had full fiscal autonomy and also minted his own money; but the coins were of a common standard weight (with some variation in terms of multiples) and of common fineness determined by the '*Reichsmünzfuß*' and later by so-called mint conventions. In consequence, coins of *other* principalities, which were expressly called 'foreign' coins, were accepted at par in each principality, as I can show for the archbishopric of Salzburg. In modern parlance we should, I think, call the system of the old German Reich one of *long-term fixed exchange rates* rather than one of full monetary union. And we can learn from this case that long-term fixed exchange rates, in convenient multiples of each currency to the other are, as the mathematician would say, within an ϵ-surrounding of full monetary union; and it is therefore not worth all the trouble and cost of erecting any expensive institutions of full monetary union.

I turn now to the points where I beg to differ from Professor Goodhart. My first criticism of his paper is that in places it is misled by the fiction of political power in the face of market forces, where hardly any political power is left. Formerly, it is true, exchange

200

controls mattered. But once trade is freely and fully integrated
exchange controls on capital movements are just hollow trappings of
their former self; or, to put it in economic terms, they impose only
small additional transaction costs. Traders can shift around any
amount of capital via the balance of trade; and no-one can control
them effectively. Thus I do not agree with the author that removing
exchange controls in the summer of 1990, could prove a rather severe
test of the stability of the ERM system.

My second criticism of Professor Goodhart's paper is that in his
long list of the advantages of a single currency – most of which
appear, in fact, on his own reckoning to be rather piddling – Professor Goodhart does not mention a lower level of real interest rates.

Now it is frequently argued that monetary union increases the
variability of interest rates rather than decreasing it; and that it thus
on average raises rather than lowers the rate of interest. This is due to
the fact that after monetary integration the interest rate is the only
macro-economic price that can adjust in order to equilibrate shocks.
But this interest-raising effect occurs only as long as markets *do not
yet fully believe* that exchange rates are going to be fixed for all the
forseeable future and as long as lenders to a country have therefore
to be compensated by a risk premium in the interest rate for the risks
of devaluation. Once expectations are *fully* adjusted to nearly permanently fixed exchange rates the schedules shift: *capital markets become highly interest-elastic*. Tiny interest differentials are then
enough to attract large amounts of capital, as we in Austria see. As
the British used to say in the nineteenth century, at 7 per cent interest
one can get any amount of gold, even from the moon!

Which brings me to my third and last criticism. This concerns what
Professor Goodhart takes as given. I am anything but a monetarist,
above all because I think that monetarism is fundamentally wrong in
taking money to be exogenously determined while it is once again
today mostly endogenous as to its nominal quantity. But even so we
should face up to Robert Lucas's fundamental point: *economic agents
do adjust to policy*. And in particular: markets adjust to the monetary
regime. Professor Goodhart says: 'If wages and prices are sticky,
then monetary policy and exchange-rate adjustments can have desirable *real* effects . . . The true costs of . . . a loss of sovereignty . . .
depend greatly on the extent to which monetary policy can be used
for adjustment purposes, and have real effects in the context of
imperfect labour markets'. True enough, though such statements
smack a little of the bygone 1960s. But I would put it exactly the

other way round: long-term fixed exchange rates (or full monetary union) are the way to make *both goods and labour markets more perfect!* In fact monetary integration is the paramount way of making markets behave more competitively. Everybody then learns to think in terms of *permanent prices.* All price changes become *relative* price changes, *real* price changes in a much more competitive, because much larger, market. Thus the problem Professor Goodhart addresses changes, though fully so perhaps only after a decade; and there may, indeed, be nasty transitional problems. I thus do not think that the modern situation differs from the nineteenth-century gold standard because today we have large trade unions. If trade unions mind about unemployment, labour markets can react just as flexibly in the face of the same monetary regime as they did in the nineteenth century, and possibly even more flexibly, then formerly.

I do agree with Professor Goodhart that one of the great differences today relative to the nineteenth century is that we have a much bigger public sector. But again monetary integration brings about important changes even here. The most important lesson of the financial crisis of New York is, to my mind, that New York was, indeed, forced by private lenders to reform its budget in the end. Overlending for some time there may be; but both the Austrian and the German communities, which had gone on spending sprees in the 1970s, do have now on average a balanced budget! I mention the communities as the relevant example because local authorities do not have the ability to finance themselves by creating money. With monetary integration governments are going to be in much the same position as local authorities are in today. In fact, financially, they will not differ much from big private enterprises: They will be able to provide very differentiated products, and I think that is good; but financially they will be constrained to remain solvent in the eyes of private creditors. The great difference monetary integration makes to fiscal policy is that the opinion of *international capital markets* about the long-term financial position of a government becomes possibly even more important than the momentary preferences of the voters.

10 Good Money Driving Out Bad: A Model of the Hayek Process in Action

Erich W. Streissler

1

An old adage has it that 'bad money drives out good'. Under the name of Gresham's Law, this is well known to students of monetary theory and amply attested by historical experience. The precise conditions for it to rule have, however, to be borne in mind: 'Where by legal enactment a government assigns the same nominal value to two or more forms of circulatory medium whose intrinsic values differ, payments will always, as far as possible, be made in that medium of which the cost of production is least, and the more valuable medium will tend to disappear from circulation' (Harris, 1987, p. 563).

Gresham's Law is thus actually only one more case of the possible perverse effects of state regulation, and a typical case to boot of the impotence of a government in imposing its will upon reluctant economic agents. Gresham's Law is the consequence of a policy which is, in the resounding ancient phrase of Thomas Mun, 'not only fruitless but also hurtful'[1] – fruitless in its main aim and hurtful in its side-effects. We would be wise to remember this and other historical 'impossibility theorems' of state action in monetary matters at a time when Europe may once more be on the verge of establishing a currency union by political fiat and by constructivist action. For money is much rather a creature of custom and of social consensus. As Menger (1976/1871, p. 261) put it more than a hundred years ago: 'The origin of money . . . is . . . entirely natural and thus displays legislative influence only in the rarest instances. Money is not an invention of the state. It is not the product of a legislative act'. The first origins of money and no less the establishment of a new common

203

currency are a consequence of self-interested optimising behaviour: 'As *each* economizing individual becomes increasingly more aware of his economic interest, he is led by this *interest, without any agreement, without legislative compulsion, and even without regard to the public interest*, to give his commodities in exchange for other, more saleable, commodities, even if he does not need them for any immediate consumption purpose' (Menger, 1976/1871, p. 260). Thus the commodity with the greatest degree of 'marketability' becomes money by and by; or perhaps we should rather say in these times of imminent currency union: it becomes the paramount money, and thus our common currency. This fundamental notion of Menger's has been echoed by the entire Austrian School; it is not by accident that it was once more taken up by Hayek (1976). Hayek avers that if different distinct and distinguishable currencies are allowed to compete freely, economic agents will opt for the best, in the sense of the most stable, currency. What Hayek describes is not at all a utopian situation. In fact, we see it happening everywhere today, particularly in Europe, though it is rather different national currencies than different private 'currencies' which compete. I shall call this the Hayek process, a process already suggested by Menger.

On the face of it, currency competition appears to be in flat contradiction to Gresham's Law; for it can be summed up in the adage that 'good money drives out bad'. But on closer view it is, in fact, only another manifestation of this 'law'; or, perhaps more appropriately, it is merely the obverse of Gresham's Law: while Gresham's Law states that, given the advantage of the uses of money, eventually that kind of money will be used exclusively by the public which secures these advantages at the lowest price, the Hayek process avers that, given a uniform price between different species of money, eventually that species of money will alone be used that secures the highest advantage of use.

This paper attempts to formalise in a simple way the economic advantages of using a common medium of exchange, hinted at in the arguments of Menger and Hayek. In other words, it tries to model the likely establishment of a common currency by mere social action and thus the achievement of a currency union as 'a result of human action though not of human design'. Section 2 will try to model the advantage of using a medium of exchange that is more and more widely accepted. A positive external effect of using a specific currency will be shown. Section 3 will model the partial equilibrium situation of the representative individual who needs a 'temporary abode of purchasing power' before buying the average commodity bundle, desired for consumption or production purposes, after a fixed or a stochastic time interval. That currency will give the greatest advantage as a 'temporary abode' which shows both the most predictable and the least variable rate of inflation. In Section 4, I shall show that the variance of inflation is likely to be a positive monotonic function of the average rate of inflation, and that furthermore inflation with high variance is likely to be underestimated. The conclusion of these two sections will be that the most 'stable' currency will attract the largest number of customers and will therefore achieve the cost advantage of being also the most acceptable. Section 5 will then present the general equilibrium features and show that in a long-run equilibrium the most stable and thus generally preferred currency must also have the lowest *real* rate of interest. The creation of a stable currency is thus a case of super-non-neutrality of money. In fact, the achievement of the lowest possible real interest rate is the great economic advantage of a currency union, if this arises naturally due to the common choice of the most stable currency. Section 6 will finally draw policy conclusions.

2

In the spirit of Menger, let us suppose that in a given society there are many potential media of exchange and that several of them are actually used by some individuals. In such a society there is thus not one unique kind of 'money'; there are many distinct currencies (and not only different states of the same currency and dollars in the form of cash, dollars in the form of deposit accounts, time deposits, saving accounts, etc.).

Such a situation is not at all far-fetched. Try any shop in Austria and you will find that you can pay at least in two and probably in half a dozen different currencies; and, furthermore according to Austrian civil law, which fortunately was framed in 1811 during the inflationary Napoleonic period, if you like you can legally contract repayment of a loan in gold or silver coin of the realm;[2] in fact, Austria has today two types of gold coins and many types of silver coins that are such admissible legal tender. These gold and silver coins, as legal tender, cannot fall below the value of the 'paper' Austrian Schilling shown on their face; but they will normally exchange at the much higher market price linked to their gold or silver content. Thus for all economic intents and purposes these gold and silver coins, though also called

Schillings, are perfectly legal parallel currencies in Austria.

If you prefer less exotic examples than the case of Austria, go to any Eastern European country and you will find basically the same situation, possibly with the slight difference that the sole currency nobody will accept is the actual local currency! Or, if you are historically inclined, think back to the seventeenth and eighteenth centuries, where in many countries. England not excepted,[3] foreign currencies circulated freely beside the official local one.

The choice between different admissible currencies is thus already a fact of present and past everyday life. Let us now consider an individual who wishes to buy a given commodity using the currency with the index i. There are N (other) individuals ('shops') in this society who can supply him with this commodity, n_i of which accept currency i, while $N-n_i$ do not accept this currency at all or at any price. The reason for this may be that it appears simply too costly for these $N-n_i$ individuals to inform themselves[4] about the quality of currency i: how should the general Yugoslav trader, for instance, know about Polish Zlotys, when even the Poles do not seem to be too sure about them? (It would make little difference to our discussion if we assumed that currency i is, indeed, accepted by everyone, but by many only at a discount. For such a discount would be nothing but the expected cost of the search, here to be described, for someone willing to take currency i at its face value, the search being now undertaken by the seller of the real commodity instead of the buyer.)

Let us assume that our individual randomly samples all the shops dealing in his desired commodity to find out whether they will take currency i in payment. With probability $p_i = n_i/N$ he will be successful already in the first shop. If not, he incurs an additional transaction cost in excess of the minimum necessary cost (going to the first shop and buying there), the cost of searching for some seller of his desired commodity who will accept currency i. To keep things simple let us assume that there is a search cost c_i, which remains constant for each search step – i.e., the visit of one more shop (c_i may, for instance, be the cost for the time of visiting one shop); and one can think of the shops as being equally spaced on the perimeter of a circle, our customer visiting one shop after the other in order to find out whether it accepts currency i. Let us for the sake of easy calculation make the further (inessential) assumption that our customer samples shops 'with replacement' (i.e., the probabilities of finding a shop willing to accept currency i do not change in the course of sampling). For a large N, which should be realistic, there is practically no appreciable quantitative difference to sampling without replacement. Remembering that our customer has to be unsuccessful in the first shop with probability $(1-p_i)$, and that the probability of success is constant at p_i, the expected total excess search cost (beyond entering the first shop) in order to find a shop willing to accept currency i, $E(C_i)$, will be:

$$E(C_i) = (1 - p_i) \{c_i p_i + 2c_i p_i(1 - p_i) + 3c_i p_i(1 - p_i)^2 \qquad (1)$$
$$+ 4c_i p_i(1 - p_i)^3 + \ldots \}$$

$$= \frac{1 - p_i}{p_i} \, c_i = \frac{N - n_i}{n_i} \, c_i$$

The total expected cost for traders in society added up for all individuals using currency i, $E(TC_i)$, will be:

$$E(TC_i) = n_i \, E(C_i) = (N-n_i)c_i \qquad (2)$$

To derive approximate results for comparative static analysis we use calculus, which we may do with only a small error for a large N. Then the effect of one more individual, individual $(n_i + 1)$, becoming willing to trade in currency i on the expected search cost of each individual is given by

$$\frac{dE(C_i)}{dp_i} = \frac{1}{p_i^2} \, c_i \qquad (3)$$

Thus each individual who decides to trade in currency i generates a cost reduction of search for all other individuals willing to trade in this currency and thus creates a positive external effect for them. In fact, in the binominal case he even reduces the total search cost for traders in this currency for all individuals, including himself: as can be seen from equation (2), TC, falls from $(N-n_i)c_i$ to $(N-n_i-1)c_i$ through the increase by one trader. In other words, there are economies of scale of many individuals using a given currency.

In our model, search cost is proportional to search time. Instead of expressing search in cost terms we can therefore also express it in extra time foregone. Let us define $a_i t \equiv c_i$ as the time necessary to visit one more shop in order to inquire whether this shop is willing to sell against currency i. For one individual the total additional transaction time necessary to find a shop supplied with the desired commodity and willing to accept currency i shall be called ΔT_i and its expected value is, using equation (1):

$$E(\Delta T_i) = \frac{1 - p_i}{p_i} \, a_i t = \frac{N - n_i}{n_i} \, a_i t \qquad (4)$$

In what follows I shall mainly be interested in this time dimension of search. This angle also suggests, once the essentials of the previous discussion are grasped, a somewhat simpler probabilistic formulation of search for a shop willing to accept currency i. So far, we have worked quite naturally with a binomial distribution of shops either willing or unwilling to accept i. As is well known, with $N \to \infty$ and simultaneously $n_i \to 0$ the binomial approaches a Poisson distribution. But, as is also well known, 'a Poisson process is one in which the intervals between successive events have independent identical exponential distributions'.[5] We can thus imagine the following *alternative* search model: our trader desirous of buying a given commodity against payment in currency i walks randomly through a town and meets in his path shops supplying this commodity according to a Poisson distribution with parameter m_i, given by equation (5a) below, where x is the number of stores found. The time t which elapses between finding one store and the next is, independent of the number of stores x already visited, given by the exponential distribution in equation (5b):

$$\text{prob}(x = k) = e^{-m_i} m_i^k / k! \qquad (5a)$$

$$\text{prob}(dt) = m_i e^{-m_i t} dt \qquad (5b)$$

If we now call ΔT_i the total time which elapses till the first shop willing to accept currency i in exchange for the commodity is found, then the expected value of this search time is nothing but the mean of the exponential distribution in equation (5b). Thus:

$$E(\Delta T_i) = \frac{1}{m_i} \qquad (6)$$

If the Poisson probability m_i changes (i.e., if more and more shops become willing to accept currency i), this average search time declines, as in equation (3), with the square of the probability. In the limit, with all shops accepting currency i, there is no search.

3

In Section 2 we asked what happens to a trader who wishes to use currency i as a medium of exchange and how long it takes – or how costly it is for him – to find a similarly-minded trading partner. This is only a small variation on a well-known problem: the finding of the right trading partner in general. We are, however, interested in a different question to which the above is only preliminary. Why does our trader wish to use currency i in the first place? To this question we now turn.

Let us picture the transaction structure of a representative individual as follows: after a technically and exogenously determined period, call it T, our individual purchases the average final commodity, a unit bundle of the social product. The period T can be further explained. As is well known from the quantity equation of money, our representative individual purchases his average bundle V times per unit time period, where V is the velocity of circulation. The average period for holding money is therefore k, where $k \equiv 1/V$; and thus the desired time interval $\hat{T}$ is $\hat{T} \equiv k$ in unit time. For if M is the quantity of money, P the price level and Y real income, the quantity equation can be expressed alternatively as in equation (7):

$$M = \frac{1}{V} \cdot P \cdot Y = k \cdot P \cdot Y \tag{7}$$

We shall think of the period T (or k) till purchase is effected as fixed in the tradition of the 'old' quantity theory of money.[6] It is immaterial whether we think of it as a constant (e.g., the period from one harvest to the next or wages which have to be paid once a month) or, once more, as the average of a stochastic process, the need for a commodity purchase being 'revealed' to our individual at some unknown moment but according to some known probability law: the car breaks down suddenly and needs repair work; or an entrepreneur receives an unexpected order, the completion of which requires the purchase of certain material inputs. The decisive point to our argument is only that purchase time is independent of the parameters of the financial decision to whose optimisation we now turn.

Until this moment of the next commodity purchase our individual will wish to hold money as a 'temporary abode of his purchasing power'. We assume he chooses currency i as such a temporary abode. Furthermore, we assume that our individual can deposit this currency i in a fixed-interest time account (and with no fixed charges for deposit and withdrawal) till the moment of the desired purchase. This fixed interest rate is determined in advance at the moment of deposit, time 0. Using the Friedman–Fisher notion of the nominal interest rate, call it r_i, being in equilibrium, the real rate of interest, to be called θ, plus the expected rate of inflation, to be called $\hat{\pi}_i$ – (or $r_i = \theta + \hat{\pi}_i$) a sum S_o, deposited at time 0 in this i-currency time account will then accumulate with instantaneous compound interest up to the end of period T to the following sum S_{iT}:

$$S_{iT} = S_o \exp r_{iT} = S_o \exp (\hat{\pi}_i + \theta)T \qquad (8)$$

Notice that the expected rate of inflation $\hat{\pi}_i$ is currency-i-specific, while the real rate of interest θ is the common real return on all assets.

The decision problem of our individual is now basically that of any forward contract.[7] He wishes to purchase commodities with a delay at the expected moment in time $T = k$. His capital S_o accumulates by earning interest in his time account. But the desired amount K_o of the commodity valued at time 0 (which, without loss in generality we shall set equal to the sum of money S_o, thus $K_o = S_o$) also 'rises' in price in an inflationary world. It will rise over the period T at a rate of inflation specific to the currency i up to a value K_{iT}. Now, the problem of our representative individual is to make S_{iT}/K_{iT} as large as possible (i.e., to find a currency i which yields the highest possible real interest return expressed in the purchasing power relative to the general commodity to be purchased later).

Basically, currency i, deposited in a time account, is a fixed-interest asset while the commodity to be purchased is a variable-price asset similar to a stock company share. Since the persuasive argument of Black and Scholes (1973) it has been generally assumed that such variable-price assets change in value over time according to a stochastic process following a log normal distribution. In other words, it is assumed that the percentage price change of the asset follows a Brownian motion in continuous time, where the mean change for an infinitesimally short period is given by π_{oi} and the variance of change in this infinitesimally short period of time by σ_i^2. This is a good model for an inflationary price change (relative to currency i) and will therefore be assumed here. Using the well-known mean for a log normal destribution, the expected value of the price of our commodity at time T, $(E(K_{iT})$, is given by:[8]

$$E(K_{iT}) = K_o \exp(\pi_{oi} + \tfrac{1}{2}\sigma_i^2) \, T \tag{9}$$

Both the mean and the variance of the Brownian motion rise proportionately with time T.[9] Note that the mean inflation rate (e.g., the change in the logarithm of the asset price) in such a log normal model depends upon the variance of the Brownian motion σ_i^2 as well as upon the mean relative change in each infinitesimal time interval, π_{oi}. This is due to the fact that the geometric and the arithmetic means differ, the former being in general lower than the latter for strictly positive variates.

In consequence a currency that is not inflationary on geometric average ($\pi_{oi} = 0$), but has a variance in price change, is inflationary: the logarithm of an asset denominated in it rises over time with $\tfrac{1}{2}\sigma_i^2 t$! The mean for a unit period of the inflationary process relative to currency i, π_i, is:

$$\pi_i = \pi_{oi} + \tfrac{1}{2}\sigma_i^2 \tag{10}$$

Gathering expressions, we find that the relative expected purchasing power of currency i in purchasing commodities after time T, $S_{iT}/E(K_{iT})$, is:

$$\begin{aligned} S_{iT}/E(K_{iT}) &= \exp[(\theta + \hat{\pi}_i) - (\pi_{oi} + \tfrac{1}{2}\sigma_i^2)]T \\ &= \exp[\theta - (\pi_{oi} - \pi_i) - \tfrac{1}{2}\sigma_i^2]T \end{aligned} \tag{11}$$

The second term in the second bracketed expression, $(\pi_{oi} - \pi_{\cdot i})$, is the excess of the actual instantaneous average rate of inflation over the estimate of the rate of inflation which enters into the determination of the nominal rate of interest. A currency whose rate of inflation is underestimated by the nominal interest rate is not 'safe'. Note that if nominal interest does not fully adjust to the rate of inflation this is all the more true. The third term, $\tfrac{1}{2}\sigma_i^2$, is (half) the variance of the inflationary process. Thus, given the real rate of interest θ a currency will be the better temporary abode of purchasing power *the better its rate of inflation can be estimated and the lower the variance of its rate of inflation*.

Only if purchase can immediately be effected (i.e., if currency i is immediately accepted), however, will T equal the technically necessary delay k, unknown precisely in advance. With a currency that is not commonly accepted we find, combining equations (8) and (6):

$$T = \hat{T} + \Delta T_i = k + 1/m_i \tag{12}$$

$$S_{iT}/E(K_{iT}) = \exp[\theta - (\pi_{oi} - \hat{\pi}_i) - \tfrac{1}{2}\sigma_i^2]\,[k + 1/m_i] \tag{13}$$

We can assume that the real rate of interest, θ, corresponds to the representative rate of time preference and should thus be earned per period of time. This can be achieved only if $(\pi_{oi} - \hat{\pi}_i)$ and σ_i^2 are zero. In trying to minimise the inflationary loss from equation (13) individuals will thus seek out the currency with the most easily predictable rate of inflation; and this basically depends upon a long-term continuity in the monetary policy pursued. They will also seek out the currency with the least inflationary variance; and this will depend upon the absence of erratic changes in policy. But even so there is a trade-off: it will also have to be a currency in general acceptance: $1/m_i$ will have to be low or even zero, if $(\pi_{oi} - \hat{\pi}_i)$ and σ_i^2 are given and bounded away from zero. Otherwise, one may lose by waiting longer even with a less inflationary currency (unless, of course, we are in the extreme case and both $(\pi_{oi} - \hat{\pi}_i)$ and σ_i^2 are zero – when one does not lose through waiting as one earns the real rate of interest throughout).

In this model of currency competition we are thus faced with the common problem of entry of a competitor in a market with economies of scale.[10] Either the new competitor has to be much better in order to compete: the inflationary performance of a small new currency has to be much better in order to overcome the disadvantage that few people use it. Or, on the other hand, with equal inflationary performances the currency which is used to a greater extent by mere chance, that is to say most likely the currency of a larger country, will prevail. Thus we see that it is not very easy for good new currencies to come up against bad old ones: and not (only) for the reason that the 'market' for currencies is not informationally efficient, a feature which has been assumed away in our model.[11] The difficulty faced by a new currency is already due to the fact that the market for currencies is not competitive because search for a trading partner accepting a new currency creates external effects and economies of scale.

Still, historical experience does show that either by chance or by a much lower inflationary potential relative to other currencies certain currencies do establish themselves as predominant. A currency union comes about by mere market forces. Actual political 'currency unions' are mainly the official recognition and consolidation of an already established state of the world. At present we can again witness the establishment of a currency union by market force: more and more the Deutsche Mark develops into the common currency of Europe. The important point to be realised is that every individual who recognises the low-inflationary potential of a certain currency and starts to deal in it exerts a powerful pull on all other individuals to do the same and deal in this currency, because then it becomes cheaper to use it.

4

Can we say that a high average rate of inflation and not only a high variance of inflation reduces a currency's attractiveness? So far in our analysis it does not do so: it is only the forecasting error of inflation which is relevant – and that only in a one-sided way, only the underestimation of inflation in the determination of the nominal interest rate is causing a loss. But there are two possible ways in which the average rate of inflation might enter expression (13). First the variance σ_i^2 might be a positive monotonic function of the average rate of inflation ($\sigma_i^2 (\pi_i)$ having everywhere a derivative $d\sigma_i^2/d\pi_i > 0$). For this there is good empirical evidence.[12] And it is easy to show that an explicit formulation of the stochastic process of the (inflationary) change in the commodity price leads quite naturally to such a dependence. Secondly the forecasting error of inflation might be a positive monotonic function of the variance of the rate of inflation, which itself might be a positive monotonic function of the average rate of inflation. The well-known signal-extraction problem of a noisy inflationary process gives a good argument for this latter possibility as well. I shall take up these two aspects in turn.

Let us assume the following unrestricted random walk for the logarithm of the price of the commodity to be bought: in any one unit time period and independently from the position reached and previous change the price logarithm either takes a unit jump upwards with probability p, or takes a unit jump downwards with probability q or stays constant with probability $(1-p-q)$. In other words, the logarithm of price moves according to the multinominal probability law stated, whose first moment around zero for one step is $(p-q)$ and whose second moment around zero is $(p+q)$. (Going to the limit for continuous time and infinitesimally small unit jumps this process yields, for $p+q = 1$, the Wiener process.[13] Let us call the mean unit jump μ and the variance of the unit jump σ^2. These are:

$$\mu = p-q \tag{14a}$$

$$\sigma^2 = (p+q) - (p+q)^2$$
$$= \mu + 2q - \mu^2 = \mu(1-\mu) + 2q \tag{14b}$$

If we assume the probability of a downward jump of the logarithm of price, q, to be zero, as is not unreasonable for inflationary processes with some price rigidity (i.e., if we assume the price either staying put or rising) or, slightly more generally, if we assume q independent of μ – i.e., a higher probability of a downward movement in price being exactly balanced by a higher probability of an upward movement – then σ^2 becomes for $\mu < \frac{1}{2}$ an exact positive monotonic function of μ: The variance of inflation is then the higher, the higher its mean rate. However the variance is not simply proportional to the mean: its elasticity with respect to μ falls short of unity.

The argument can be extended to many jumps, say n in number. For if we call x_n the position of the logarithm of price after n jumps, then $E(x_n) = n\mu$, $\text{var}(x_n) = n\sigma^2$.

The variance of inflation is thus likely to be a positive monotonic function of its average; and particularly so for more inflationary currencies, where a fall in price is unlikely. We now turn to the estimation problem of the inflationary process of a currency. The problem is that changes in the rate of return of the time account in currency i cannot be assigned unambiguously to changes in the average rate of inflation of this currency; they might also be due to variations in the real rate of return over time.

To find out whether the nominal interest on his time account in currency i, given a constant real rate 0, fully reflects the rate of inflation of currency i, our agent might then want to regress the logarithm of the value of his time account, $\log S_{it}$, on the logarithm of the price in terms of this currency of the commodity to be bought, $\log K_{it}$, thus:

$$\log S_{it} = \alpha + \beta \log K_{it} \tag{15}$$

If the rate of inflation of currency i has no variance but only the mean rate π_{oi} per period, $\log K_{it} = \pi_{oi}t$. In such a case (and with the classical regression assumptions) the regression would yield the following unbiased estimates, if $\log S_{it}$ reflected this constant rate of inflation correctly:

$$E(\hat{\alpha}) = 0, \ E(\hat{\beta}) = (\pi_{oi} + \theta)/\pi_{oi} \tag{16}$$

However if, as we assumed, K_{it} is a log normally distributed variate, then $\log K_{it} = N(\pi_{oi}t, \sigma_i^2 t)$. Putting it differently, the rate of inflation per period π_{it} would then be given by

$$\pi_{it} = \pi_{oi} + w_t \tag{17a}$$

or possibly

$$\pi_{it} = \bar{\pi}_{oi} + v_t + w_t \tag{17b}$$

The second expression, (17b), allows for the possibility that the average rate of inflation also varies over time ($\pi_{oi} = \bar{\pi}_{oi} + v_t$) due to changes in monetary policy. This would make it even more difficult to estimate inflation. (The inflation rates per period are then drawings from different normal distributions with different means but constant variance.) On the other hand w_t reflects the variability of inflation and is an i.i.d. variable, $w_t = N(0, \sigma_i^2)$.

In both cases $\log K_{it}$ would then not measure correctly the relevant rate of inflation to be used for the adjustment of the nominal rate of interest, which would be π_{oi} or $\bar{\pi}_{oi} + v_t$. We have a problem of regression estimation with errors in variables[14] or the signal-extraction problem of inflation (the mixture of real and nominal price movements) first analysed by Robert Lucas (1973). If we take the simpler model (17a) for the inflationary process of currency i, we find that the regression coefficients β and α will not be estimated without bias even asymptotically. Rather, the estimate $\hat{\beta}$ will *underestimate* the true parameter β and be related to β in the probability limit for many repeated samples of length T as

$$p\lim \hat{\beta} = \frac{1}{1 + \dfrac{\sigma_i^2}{\sigma_t^2}} \beta \tag{18}$$

σ_t^2 is the variance of time, the basic independent variable in the above regression. For a given T the bias will be the larger, the larger the variance of inflation, σ_i^2, that is to say the larger the variance of the stochastic variable w_t. As $\sigma_t^2 = 1/12 \ [(T-1) \ T \ (T+1)]$ for a sample of time length T we can also express the above asymptotic bias approximately as

$$\beta \approx \cfrac{1}{1 + \cfrac{12\sigma_i^2}{T(T-1)\,(T+1)}} \, \beta \qquad (19)$$

(The approximation is due to the fact that equation (18) is correct only for an infinitely large sample.) Thus the bias would indeed vanish as $T \to \infty$, if the inflationary process remained stationary. This is very cold comfort, however, as it is most unlikely that for a currency picked at random the inflationary process would indeed remain constant over any very long period. Fears of the non-stationarity of the stochastic processes involved are the usual rationale for not extending the sampling period of regressions too much. Our agent will thus want to choose samples of finite length T for estimation, and possibly even of relatively short time periods T.

There are, of course, also other methods for estimating β, which would indeed estimate it consistently.[15] But they are likely to have large sampling errors, and doubly large ones in the case of a large underlying theoretical variance of the inflationary process. And there are also other estimation procedures, which do have a bias even in the limit and usually underestimate the regression coefficient β, for instance differencing the logarithms in the regression equation (regression of $\Delta \log S_{it}$ on $\Delta \log K_{it}$).

It is thus the case that the rate of inflation of a currency with greater inflationary variance can be assessed only with difficulty; and, furthermore, it is likely that its inflationary potential will be underestimated. This would imply that in expression (13) the estimation error $(\pi_{oi} - \hat{\pi}_i)$ is likely to be positive (inflation being underestimated) and the larger, the larger σ_i^2. We have also given both theoretical reasons and quoted empirical evidence that σ_i^2 itself is likely to be the larger, the larger the average rate of inflation. This would justify the following simplification of expression (13). Calling π_i the true mean rate of inflation we can write:

$$(\pi_{oi} - \hat{\pi}_i) + \tfrac{1}{2}\sigma_i^2 = f\left(\sigma_i^2(\pi_i)\right) \frac{df}{d\sigma_i^2} > 0, \frac{d\sigma_i^2}{d\pi_i} > 0 \qquad (20)$$

$$S_{iT}/E(K_{iT}) = \exp\left[\theta\, f(\sigma_i^2(\hat{\pi}_i))\right] [k + 1/m_i] \qquad (21)$$

Equation (21) Summarises our discussion in Sections 5 and 6: the greater the variance of inflation and the greater the average rate of inflation of given currency i, the more is it likely that the use of this currency as a temporary abode of purchasing power will yield a rate of return that falls below the common real rate of return θ.

5

The above result was derived only from expected values and thus without any resort to utility considerations of our representative economic agents. In other words, it was derived even for risk-neutral agents: basically our agent has to face expected losses if he uses a more inflationary currency. The whole argument could be strengthened in an obvious way, if our agent were risk-averse as well. Then the fact of the less accurate estimation of an inflation with a larger variance (and not only the likelihood of its underestimation on average) becomes crucial. In the latter case of a risk-averse agent it would be even more true that a currency with greater and more variable inflation is an inferior temporary abode, and equation (21) would *a fortiori* hold. Furthermore the results of Section 2 were derived purely on transaction-cost grounds. Once more equation (21) would *a fortiori* hold if there were high information costs in informing oneself about either a less well-known or a more inflationary currency.

Note, furthermore, that unless there is a currency that is totally uninflationary (or, alternatively, unless there exists a currency whose rate of inflation is non-stochastic), then the real rate of return on transaction balances held even in the 'best' currency always falls short of the real rate of return θ (see equation (21)). Such a dominance in the rate of return of the monetary medium by other assets is typical of many monetary models.[16] To close our model we have therefore to assume (a) that the real rate of return θ is achievable only by individuals who produce as entrepreneurs and only as far as they produce; (b) that non-entrepreneurs cannot fully achieve this rate of return as stock holders because of the agency problems of stock holders vs. managers (Jensen and Meckling, 1976); (c) that they cannot achieve it themselves as creditors of enterprises because of a lack of sufficient information about firms but can achieve it only via an informed intermediary, the bank.[17]

Let us consider the 'best' currency available, and one which has also come into common use, calling this currency 1. It is the currency for which $f(\sigma_i^2(\pi_i))$ is minimal and for which $m_1 \rightarrow \infty$. The use of this currency yields the highest possible return among all currencies. In this sense, this best currency assures the highest rate of return of money as a temporary abode of purchasing power, given the basic real rate θ.

Let us now turn to very long-run equilibrium considerations. This paper does not attempt to derive the long-run equilibria or to prove their existence. But it seems plausible that multiple equilibria exist. Let us then assume that an equilibrium exists in which for some reason or other two or more currencies of different inflationary tendencies are used simultaneously. The best example would probably be the case of two different national economies with two different national currencies where the individuals can deal freely in one country or the other and where with equal returns (indifferent currency cost) they use both currencies. Furthermore, I assume that in this long-run equilibrium both currencies are fully acceptable, so that there are no transaction costs; these would only further complicable the following argument without adding anything new. For reasons of arbitrage the expected rates of return on these two currencies have then to be equal. Taking the best currency i and some other currency i it must therefore be true that

$$\theta_1 - f(\sigma_1^2(\pi_1)) = \theta_i - f(\sigma_1^2(\pi_i)) \text{ given } \sigma_i^2(\pi_i) > \sigma_1^2(\pi_1) \tag{22}$$

As the inflationary variances differ by assumption, the variance (and the mean) of inflation of currency i being larger than that of the best alternative, currency 1, the arbitrage equality (22) can be achieved only if the real rates of return θ (indexed now for the different 'economies' or the different currency usages) are different. In long-run equilibrium we have to have

$$\theta_1 < \theta_i \quad \text{given } f(\sigma_1^2(\pi_1)) < f(\sigma_i^2(\pi_i)) \tag{23}$$

The most fundamental consequence of finding a less inflationary currency (and one with a less variable rate of inflation) is thus to *lower the real rate of interest of an economy*; at least as long as other currencies are still around in long-run equilibrium and their relative returns have been made equal by arbitrage. In the spirit of monetary growth models, this lower real rate of interest of the less inflationary economy is the effect of this economy becoming more capital-intensive, most likely due to an real capital inflow into the country with the lower rate of inflation; but in contrast to the usual monetary growth models this higher capital intensity is the result of an exogenously fixed price as well as an exogenously fixed money-creation process, the fixed price implied by the arbitrage condition towards another currency. If, as usual, we call the absence of an effect of money on the real rate of interest super-neutrality[18] then we may say that the establishment of a best non-inflationary currency and also the creation of a new and better currency, which replaces others, is a case of the lack of monetary super-neutrality: a new kind of money that is better has long-run real effects on an economy. The ultimate aim of a currency union, which is achieved by the optimising behaviour of private individuals, is thus to realise the lowest possible time cost of capital.

Historical evidence supports this conclusion. The heyday of the gold standard around 1900 coincides with a historical low in the real rate of interest in all the countries concerned. The relatively non-inflationary and relatively predictable Deutsche Mark once more seems to support a lower real rate of interest than the volatile US dollar.

6

The then developed world achieved the last effective currency union (i.e., the Gold Standard) by chance and not by design. England, the dominant power of the eighteenth century, started that century with a parallel currency in gold and silver. 'On the advice of Sir Isaac Newton, in December 1717, a proclamation was issued reducing the value of the guinea from 21*s*.6*d*. to 21*s*. and prohibiting the payment or receipt of gold coins at any higher rate . . . This measure, however, proved inadequate: The drain of silver could have been checked only by a reduction that would have brought the ratio close to that in the Far East' (Ashton, 1966/1955, p. 71). In this wrong adjustment of price, Sir Isaac, the Master of the Royal Mint, proved a worse economist than physicist. But as the price of silver to gold remained fixed from then on up to the very end of the eighteenth century a 21*s*. to the guinea, something else was achieved: gold replaced silver and became the sole currency of the dominant economic power. In recognising this, Newton proved much more perspicacious, remarking already in 1717: 'Gold is now become our standard money, and silver is a commodity which rises and falls here in its price as it does in Spain'; and this was legally recognised – nearly half a century later! – when in 1774 gold was made sole legal tender for larger payments in Britain (Ashton, 1966/1955, pp. 176, 177).

The gold standard was thus established in Europe by chance and by the working of market forces – if not to say by the miscalculation of a great scientist. The Gold Standard was established as a common currency by Gresham's Law proper, but reinforced in the nineteenth century also by the Hayek process, as silver proved much more inflationary and much more unpredictably inflationary. The currency union of the gold standard came about not because gold was a completely uninflationary currency but because its rate of increase, and thus its rate of inflation, were relatively predictable.

At present we are once more witnessing the establishment of a currency union in Europe by the forces of the market and by currency competition: the process of the Deutsche Mark becoming the common currency in Europe. Not that this currency is completely non-inflationary, either; but, once again, its rate of inflation is low and this rate is relatively predictable.[19] As the case of the Deutsche Mark has also once more demonstrated, the attempt to establish a new currency first of all involves the expense of creating a reputation for trustworthiness and predictability.[20]

In face of this rare and happy occasion of a better currency actually establishing itself, it appears quite incomprehensible that at the same time attempts should be made to create another common European currency by artifical means, a currency whose success is not at all assured and which in any case is certainly going to be costly in economic terms – costly in once more establishing a reputation, and costly in terms of higher real interest rates demanded by agents in order to safeguard themselves against as yet unpredictable inflation, at least during a transition period.

Notes

1. Mun, (1949/1664), written about 1623, Chap. XII, p. 42 and Chap. XXI, p. 87, and similarly also Chap. X, p. 36 and IX, p. 33.
2. Para. 987, *ABGB* (*Allgemeines bürgerliches Gesetzbuch*) says: 'Wenn ein Darleiher sich die Zahlung in der besonderen, von ihm gegebenen Münzsorte bedungen hat; so muß die Zahlung in eben dieser Münzsorte geleistet werden'. See also para 988 und para 989, *ABGB* which secure the contract in the case of legal changes in the coinage. Para 986, *ABGB* makes it clear that all this applies to coined money ('klingende Münze'), not the mere 'equivalent' in paper.

   The doctor of Legal Sciences in Austria, Friedrich A. von Hayek should have remembered from the legal studies of his youth that at least as far as public currencies are used the currency competition described by him could already legally exist in his native country, Austria: though as far as coin is concerned, the different potentially competing currencies are, in fact, not used: different national currencies, on the other hand, are freely used in various contracts.

3. Pepys (1985) passim, where Pepys is paid in Dutch money, receives a ducket (of unspecified origin), speaks of Portuguese crusados as current in England, etc.
4. For a much more elaborate transaction search model see Diamond (1982).
5. Johnson and Kotz (1969, p. 103). See also Cox and Miller, (1965, p. 6).
6. See as an example of the 'old' quantity theory, which takes velocity as an institutional constant, for instance Holtrop (1933).
7. See on the pricing of a forward contract, for example, Rubinstein (1987).
8. Johnson and Kotz (1970, p. 115).
9. See Cox and Miller (1965, p. 205ff).
10. See, for example, Tirole (1988, Ch. VIII).
11. Taub (1985), argues that firms supplying private money cannot credibly commit themselves to a non-inflationary issue of this brand of money and that therefore no Nash equilibrium exists. In addition to dynamic inconsistency of currency competition Fischer (1986) argues that any type of money is a product that is not well defined.
12. The correlation between the variability of inflation and its average rate was first seriously discussed by Lucas (1973).
13. Cox and Miller (1965, p. 26), and for the limiting Wiener process p. 205ff.
14. See any textbook of econometrics, for example, Johnston (1973, Ch. 9.4, p. 281ff, especially p. 282).
15. See, for example, Johnston (1973, p. 284ff) with particular reference to Abraham Wald's method of fitting a straight line.
16. On the difficulty of modelling an exchange economy where money is not dominated in its rate of return see Sargent (1987, p. 289ff and passim), and resolving this difficulty King and Plosser (1986).
17. See for a formal analysis of this problems the unpublished paper by Krasa and Kubitschek (1988).
18. A monetary growth model embodying 'superneutrality' of money (a term introduced by him) was presented by Sidrauski (1987).
19. An examination of eight currencies, the German Mark (DM), the Swiss Franc (sfr), the Austrian Schilling (AS), the pound sterling (£), The French Franc (ffr), the Italian Lira (lir), the United States dollar ($) and the Japanese Yen (¥) for the longer period 1960–88 (28 years) and the more recent shorter period 1974–88 (14 years) shows the following picture for yearly inflation rates of the consumer price index:

Over the whole period the German Mark shows the lowest average rate of inflation and also the lowest variance of inflation. Apart from sfr and AS all the other currencies were far more inflationary. For the period 1974–88 the Swiss Franc is slightly better on average than the Deutsche Mark, but slightly worse in its variance.

	DM	sfr	AS	£	FFr	lir	$	¥
Mean inflation rate, 1960–88 (%)	3.66	3.87	4.57	7.97	6.85	9.24	5.07	5.77
Standard deviation of inflation, 1960–88 (%)	2.04	2.31	2.08	5.61	3.70	6.39	3.37	4.51
Mean inflation rate, 1974–88 (%)	3.34	3.12	4.57	10.18	8.55	13.21	6.45	4.24
Standard deviation of inflation, 1974–88 (%)	2.05	2.23	2.00	6.41	3.75	5.49	3.46	3.56

Source: Jahresgutachten 1989/90, Sachverständigenrat zur Begutachtung der gesamtwirtschaftlichen Entwicklung, *Weichenstellungen für die Neunziger Jahre*, Metzler-Poeschel, Stuttgart 1989, Table 14, p. 234).

   Only the Deutsche Mark (slightly), the sfr and the Yen have reduced their rate of inflation in the period 1974–88, while the Austrian Schilling was the only currency with a constant rate of inflation over the two periods. The German Mark has kept its variance constant, only the Swiss Franc and the Yen reducing it. The Austrian Schilling has increased its variance slightly in the latter period. All other currencies (£, FFr, lir and $) have increased both their average rate of inflation and their variance in the period 1974–88 with respect to 1960–74.
   In both samples the variance (or its root, the standard deviation) of the rate of inflation is highly correlated with the mean rate of inflation. For the 1960–88 sample the rank correlation coefficient is $R = 0.976$, for the period 1974–88 $R = 0.926$, both significantly different from zero at the 99.9 per cent level.
20. See, for example, Barro (1986).

References

Ashton, T.S. (1966/1955) *An Economic History of England: The 18th Century*, London, Methuen (reprint).

Barro, Robert (1986) 'Reputation in a Model of Monetary Policy with Incomplete Information', *Journal of Monetary Economics*, 17.

Black, Fischer and Scholes, Myron (1973) 'The Pricing of Options and Corporate Liabilities', *Journal of Political Economy*, 81.

Cox, R.D. and Miller, H.D. (1965) *The Theory of Stochastic Processes*, London, Methuen.

Diamond, Peter A. (1982) 'Aggregate Demand Management in Search Equilibrium', *Journal of Political Economy*, 90.

Fischer, Stanley (1986) 'Friedman versus Hayek on Private Money', *Journal of Monetary Economics*, 17

Harris, C. Alexander (1987) 'Gresham's Law', in Earwell, J. *et al.* (eds), *The New Palgrave – A Dictionary of Economics*, vol. 2, London, Macmillan.

Hayek, Friedrich A.v. (1976) *Denationalization of Money*, London, Institute of Economic Affairs.

Holtrop, M.W. (1933) 'Die Umlaufgeschwindigkeit des Geldes', in HAYEK, Friedrich A.v. (ed.), *Beiträge zur Geldtheorie*, Vienna, Springer.

Jensen, Michael C. and Meckling, William H. (1976) 'Theory of the Firm: Managerial Behaviour, Agency Costs and Ownership Structure', *Journal of Financial Economics*, 3.

Johnson, Norman L. and Kotz, Samuel (1969) *Distributions in Statistics: Discrete Distributions*, New York, Houghton Mifflin.

Johnson, Norman L. and Kotz, Samuel (1970) *Distributions in Statistics: Continuous Univeriate Distributions – 1*, New York, Houghton Mifflin.

Johnston, J. (1973) *Econometric Methods*, 2nd edn, New York, McGraw Hill.

King, Robert G. and Plosser, Charles J. (1986) 'Money as the Mechanism of Exchange', *Journal of Monetary Economics*, 17.

Krasa, Stefan and Kubitschek, Josef (1988) 'Direct Financing, Intermediation and Credit Rationing', *Research Paper, no. 983*, Graduate School of Business, Standord University.

Lucas, Robert E. (1973) 'Some International Evidence on Output–Inflation Tradeoffs', *American Economic Review*, LXIII.

Menger, Carl (1976/1871) *Principles of Economics* (trans by Dingwall, James and Hoselitz, Bert F. of *Grundsätze der Volkswirthschaftslehre*, Vienna), New York and London, New York University Press.

Mun, Thomas (1949/1664) *England's Treasure by Forraign Trade – or The Ballance of Forraign Trade is the Rule of Our Treasure*, Oxford, Basil Blackwell (reprint).

Pepys (1985) Robert Latham (ed.), *The Diary of Samuel Pepys*, shortened version, London, Bell & Hyman.

Rubinstein, Thomas J. (1987) 'Derivative Asset Analysis', *Economic Perspectives*, 1 (Fall).

Sargent, Thomas J. (1987) *Macroeconomic Theory*, 2nd edn, Boston, Academic Press.

Sidrauski, Miguel (1967) 'Rational Choice and Patterns of Growth in a Monetary Economy', *American Economic Review*, Papers and Proceedings, LVII.

Taub, Bart (1985) 'Private Fiat Money with Many Suppliers', *Journal of Monetary Economics*, 16.

Tirole, Jean (1988) *The Theory of Industrial Organization* Cambridge, Mass., MIT Press.

Discussion
Claude Dupuy

The novel feature of Professor Streissler's paper is the framework he proposes for discussing the issue of European monetary policy. Following a neoclassical approach, he suggests that monetary and financial integration – which aims to ensure a nominal stability by controlling inflation and exchange-rate fluctuations – would best be achieved by promoting efficient competition among national currencies. Such competition, he contends, would lead to an orderly convergence of monetary policies.

Admittedly, Professor Streissler's argument is not entirely new. It is rooted in a long tradition of neoclassical economic thought, most notably embodied by Hayek. A very similar expression of these ideas is also found in the British Treasury working papers on European monetary union. But the author's intention is deliberately provocative. While everyone agrees with the final aims of the neoclassical approach, the method Professor Streissler advocates – *currency competition* – runs counter both to the prevailing theoretical analyses and to the practical measures already implemented or envisaged in the Delors report. Indeed, all these studies and measures rest on the notion of *coordination* among national monetary policies.

Let us review the monetary cooperation versus competition debate. To begin with, it is worth briefly recalling Hayek's views on the matter, which have served as a guideline for the neoclassical school.

D10.1 INTER-CURRENCY COMPETITION ACCORDING TO HAYEK

As Professor Streissler emphasises, one cannot tackle the issue of monetary competition without referring to the theoretical framework put forward by Hayek in his book *Denationalization of Money*. Hayek begins by raising the question of nominal stability in a free-banking context. Monetary assets are issued by credit institutions acting without any Central Bank supervisory control. Taking the neoclassical philosophy to its extreme, he denies the authorities any right to manage money. For Hayek, however virtuous the Central Bank, a monetary policy is neither desirable nor possible. It is not desirable, for history proves that no Central Bank can resist government pressure (an example that corroborates this view is the domestic political pressure exercised on the Bundesbank in 1990 to adopt a one-for-one Deutsche Mark/Ostmark parity against its will). Neither is a monetary policy possible, for financial innovation makes it unrealistic to attempt an accurate definition of money – and, more importantly, of an adequate money supply. Hayek therefore rejects the very idea of centralised money management. For him, individual trade-offs between private, competing currencies are the only way to ensure monetary stability.

What is the relevance of Hayek's framework? If we take money supply in the narrow sense (M1), the only example available is America's brief experiment in 'free banking' before the Civil War. However, the introduction of new money-market instruments has given fresh relevance to the neoclassical theory. Some of these assets are not included in the aggregates monitored by the Central Banks and thus escape their supervisory control. We can, therefore, legitimately regard them as private currency and analyse them by applying the competition principle. In other words, we can say that these assets are subject to individual trade-offs according to their capacity to maintain purchasing power.

However, the analogy with private currency is limited by the fact that the price of these assets, which varies on the secondary markets depending on offered yields, is closely linked to the interbank market rate. The latter, in turn, is strongly guided by Central Bank rates. This considerably restricts the credit institutions' autonomy for managing such assets. As a result, Hayek's private-currency model is hard to apply here, and we agree entirely with Professor Streissler's more realistic choice of competition among national currencies as an analytical framework.

D10.2 COMPETITION AMONG NATIONAL CURRENCIES

What particular meaning does 'competition' acquire in the national-currency context? As before, it naturally implies the total absence of regulatory limits to the free flow of capital. But, unlike Hayek's contruct, competition must coexist with legal limits to the currencies' use as legal tender outside their countries. Indeed, a currency cannot serve as legal tender beyond its borders unless it is convertible under exchange rates that are fixed but adjustable according to inflation differentials. Moreover, when currencies are managed by public authorities, the prices of national currencies are determined by economic policies and not by managerial acts, as would be the case with private currencies.

Despite these differences, the practical mechanisms of competition remain identical. The transposition of the neoclassical model to this managed-currency framework is simple and continues to rest on individual agent behaviour. Agents' risk-aversion causes them to abandon the least stable currencies and to focus their choice on currencies enjoying the most efficient monetary policies, which guarantee their continued purchasing power. The most stable currency becomes the dominant unit. This monopolistic trend makes it possible to reach an economic optimum. Unless they want to be eliminated from the money market, the other Central Banks are forced to supply agents with a currency at least as stable as the dominant one. They must therefore eradicate any inflationary tendencies. As a result, inter-currency competition necessarily leads to a convergence of monetary policies.

In practice, this reasoning is fallacious. Reality is complicated by the Central Banks' managerial autonomy in this system. Because of competition, their policies are non-transparent. This generates disturbances that, instead of promoting policy convergence, create instabilities driving interest rates up. We would point out three causes of instability.

First, despite capital mobility, such a system induces a highly imperfect currency substitutability, for peripheral currencies are perceived as riskier than the dominant unit. This prevents the harmonisation of real interest rates, since fixed parities require these currencies to be sustained by higher interest rates. As experience has taught us, distortions between real rates inside a single monetary zone are a factor of instability, triggering speculative movements of capital that are difficult to control.

Second, the lack of monetary cooperation leaves the dominant country free to manage its currency in accordance with domestic targets. In particular, its authorities will try to export inflation to peripheral countries by boosting the exchange rate.

Third, the combination of non-cooperation, fixed parities and perfect capital mobility means that, in the event of asymmetrical inflationary shocks or inter-country savings transfers, all the adjustment measures will affect the variability of domestic interest rates. Econometric studies show us that markets react highly negatively to monetary-policy instability, which increases financial risks. In such cases, the markets will demand additional premiums, which translate into a general rise in real interest rates.

To conclude, it does not seem that competition among domestic currencies can help to reach the twin goals of monetary policy convergence and a decline in interest rates. On the contrary, it fosters policy instability and pushes interest rates higher.

11 A European Central Bank: The Issue of Independence

Rolf Caesar

11.1 INTRODUCTION

One statement of the Delors report refers to the idea that once the economic and monetary union is established the body responsible for monetary policy 'should be independent of instructions from national governments and Community authorities' (Delors *et al.*, 1989, para. 32). Although the committee decided on this recommendation unanimously it turned out to be one of the most disputed points of the report. On the one hand, it is emphasised by those arguing that Central Banks' independence provides the first essential of a sound monetary policy. On the other hand some political leaders – especially in France and Great Britain – vehemently criticise this proposal. The question of independence of a possible future European Central Bank System (ECBS) will thus certainly remain an important matter of debate in the process of European monetary integration.

Three aspects seem to be particularly worth discussing. First, it has to be asked what is to be understood by 'independence' (Section 11.2). In this context it will become apparent that there are considerable discrepancies in the interpretation of 'independence' in literature as well as in political discussions. Secondly, judging 'independence' requires considering carefully the principal arguments in favour of and against independence of Central Banks *vis-à-vis* the government (Section 11.3). Finally, when talking about the political reality in the EC the central question is whether – and if yes how far – there is a true chance for the establishment of an independent ECBS (Section 11.4). The results of the paper will then be briefly summarised (Section 11.5).

11.2   WHAT IS 'INDEPENDENCE'?

'Autonomy', 'independence', or something else?

Traditionally, the position of a Central Bank in the political arena has been discussed under headings such as 'autonomy' and 'independence'. As a rule, both terms are treated as synonymous. However, the respective meaning of 'autonomy' and 'independence' (and their counterparts 'subordination' and 'dependence') changes with the subject. In fact, it is possible to distinguish at least four levels of interpretation (cf. Caesar, 1981, pp. 56–8). First, independence (or autonomy, respectively) is used as an approach to characterise the institutional relations between the Central Bank and political decision-makers. In this context, further differentiation is sometimes made between the legal aspect of independence (on which nearly all relevant studies concentrate) and the actual relations (which are definitely even more important in reality but which are mostly excluded from consideration in the literature). Secondly, independence is discussed with respect to possible rules for the conduct of monetary policy. The Chicago School, for example, and Walter Eucken in Germany treated this aspect comprehensively. Thirdly, in a broader sense the words 'independence' and 'autonomy' are meant to describe the possibilities for the Central Bank to neglect external restrictions for its internal monetary policy resulting from the existence of fixed exchange rates (i.e., to pursue an 'autonomous' internal monetary policy). In this sense, the terms 'independence' and 'autonomy' have already been used by Keynes (cf. the detailed study of Lück, 1939) especially in the context of the debate on the Bretton Woods system and its aftermath. Finally, in an even wider context an independent, or autonomous, Central Bank is understood as an institution able to enforce its intentions on monetary policy in an effective way; in this context, the term 'power' of a Central Bank is quite popular (cf. Duwendag, 1973).

Taking into account the ambiguity of the traditional terminology the author has, in some earlier studies (1981, 1983) preferred to circumscribe the totality of all these aspects – legal, political, and economic – of Central Banks' 'independence' by using the term 'room for manoeuvre' (this is the literal translation of the German word 'Handlungsspielraum', a term which Hansmeyer, 1968, introduced in order to describe the discretion of Central Bankers). Here the actual room for manoeuvre of a Central Bank is defined as an amalgam of political latitude and economic options. Although the legal provisions form an important basis for this, the actual room for manoeuvre is determined ultimately by the extent to which political and economic reality enables the Central Bank to reach its aims. The actual room for manoeuvre thus comprises two elements: the political element consists in the scope for the Central Bank to take independent decisions or actions without provoking conflicts that it would be politically incapable of withstanding, while the economic element describes the scope for the Central Bank to translate its economic intentions into effective action (Caesar, 1983, pp. 3–4).

This paper will concentrate on the first element (i.e., the institutional and political aspect of Central Banks' 'independence'). While questions related to the economic element of central banks room for manoeuvre will be widely neglected. In this narrower sense the term 'independence' will also be used in the following paragraphs.

Dimensions of independence

A Central Bank's independence (or room for manoeuvre) may be a matter of investigation under various aspects. A first aspect – which might be summarised by the question 'independence in what sense?' – is based on the traditional sub-division of the monetary decision-making process into the determination of the objectives of monetary policy and the measures to be chosen in order to implement these objectives. From this point of view a realistic degree of independence of a Central Bank requires either a considerable degree of freedom to decide on the objectives of monetary policy or clear provisions on the priorities of these objectives in its statute protecting the bank from outside pressure. Compared to that, it would make little sense to use the term 'independence' with respect to the implementation phase alone,[1] (i.e., if the objectives of monetary policy could be changed more or less arbitrarily by influences from the government or other outside actors).

The second aspect to which much attention is devoted in traditional studies concerns the actual factors determining a Central Bank's freedom of action. This question could be condensed as '(in-)dependence by what means?'. An answer to the question certainly needs an analysis of the legal regulations which mainly refer to the 'functional' aspect (i.e., provisions pertaining to the objectives of Central Bank policy; rights of direction, rights of approval, rights of control, etc.; Central Bank lending to the government) and to the 'personal' aspect (i.e., appointment and possible recall of the Central Bank's leading officials). These regulations will tend to restrict a Central Bank's actual independence, though at least some of them may also contribute to an enlargement of the room for manoeuvre (e.g., by offering the Central Bank additional ways to influence the behaviour of other actors relevant to the results of monetary policy). But even more important than the legal regulations are certainly the actual conditions for a Central Bank's political room for manoeuvre which are, however, much more difficult to judge. Some indicators useful for such an attempt may be, for example, the factual application of the legal restrictions, the number and outcome of conflicts between the Central Bank and other actors, a comparison of the objectives of monetary policy with that of other economic policies (cf. Caesar, 1981, pp. 125–49). These indicators show quite clearly that the actual political room for manoeuvre of a Central Bank is not determined so much by the Central Bank's law and its statute as by the political 'climate', historical traditions, and experiences of the country concerned.

In a third dimension those actors who are able to influence a central bank's decisions and operations could be considered. Under this aspect – which could be labelled as 'independence from what?' – it is mainly the Central Bank's relation with the government on which the relevant studies and suggestions have focused. However, the Central Bank's contact with the parliament, with the banking sector, and with actors from abroad may also be of relevance and interest.

While the three dimensions of the independence problem discussed so far are mainly topics of empirical analysis, a fourth dimension – which could be summarised by 'independence, why?' – seems to be rather a question of ideology. The question put here is whether an independent Central Bank is desirable and justifiable at all. Of course, this question should be affirmed on principle before discussing any concrete provisions to realise an independent status for the Central Bank. Thus for our specific subject (i.e., a possibly independent European Central Bank) the arguments in favour of, and against, independence should be summarised first. The following remarks will concentrate on the Central Bank's relation to the government, as this is the main point of debate in theory as well as in politics.[2]

11.3   WHY INDEPENDENCE FOR THE CENTRAL BANK?

Arguments in favour of independence

Reflections on the pros and cons of Central Bank independence are nearly as old as the existence of Central Banks themselves. Moreover, this discussion has been determined by considerably changing viewpoints and opinions during the last two centuries. This already gives occasion to suppose that it will be very difficult to give a clear and objective answer to the question of the optimal room for manoeuvre for a Central Bank. In fact, on the whole the debate on this subject can be characterised as a normative and ideological one with the arguments pro and con lying at differing levels of consideration.

On behalf of the postulate of independence three main arguments must be taken into consideration which could be named the 'economic', the 'political' and the 'technical' arguments (for further references cf. Caesar, 1980, pp. 351–61). The 'economic' argument is the oldest and, as a rule, also estimated as the most important. It amounts to the statement that a subordination of the Central Bank to political bodies entails the danger of a 'fiscal inflation'. The underlying idea is that politicians tend to look at the Central Bank as a source of budget financing neglecting the risks and detrimental effects of inflation (cf. Hawtrey, 1932, pp. 266–7; Harris, 1961, p. 88, Buchanan and Wagner, 1977, pp. 93–105). This argument – which is basically of a political–psychological nature – is further supported by reference to numerous historical examples.

Closely connected with the 'economic' argument is the 'political' one. According to it an independent Central Bank is recommended because it can operate regardless of the political day-to-day business which government and parliament cannot avoid (cf. Burns, 1976, p. 493). An independent central bank is thus seen as a guarantor of a continuous stabilisation policy because of its longer-term policy horizon. This view has been supported in the literature by the idea that a government's discretionary economic policy might be subjected to an 'inflationary bias' resulting from 'time inconsistency' and leading to a 'credibility problem' (cf. Kydland and Prescott, 1977; McCallum, 1984; Cukierman, 1986; Rogoff, 1987). This problem could be solved by transferring monetary decision-making competences to an independent Central Bank which should, however, be bound in addition to the objective of price stability.

In the last analysis, the 'economic' as well as the 'political' argu-

ment are rooted in a fundamental mistrust of the politicians' willingness to give sufficient weight to the objective of price stability, or in a
greater confidence in central bankers' preparedness to pursue that
objective, respectively. The latter aspect has been supplemented by
the view of the theory of bureaucracy that independent Central
Banks will give priority to price stability also for their own interests
(for a survey, cf. Toma and Toma, 1986). If the prevention of
inflation is regarded as a Central Bank's primary task such an institution will maximise its own reputation (as well as that of its leading
officials), and thereby safeguard its (independent) position in the
political arena, by striving for price stability. This view is empirically
supported by a number of analyses which conclude that inflation rates
tend to be considerably lower in countries with independent Central
Banks than in countries with dependent ones (cf. Parkin, 1978; Fair,
1979; Caesar, 1981; Banaian, Laney and Willett, 1983).

In addition to the arguments discussed so far the 'technical' argument recommends an independent Central Bank because of its faster
decision-making process and maybe because of superior economic
qualification of central bankers compared to politicians (cf. Der
Wissenschaftliche Beirat beim Bundesministerium für Wirtschaft,
1977, p. 44).

It is true that a number of serious objections have been put forward
in literature which question the validity of the arguments quoted
above, at least to a certain extent. But at the same time it seems
hardly possible when looking at reality to deny a true core of all three
of them.

Arguments against independence

In contrast to these attempts to justify an independent Central Bank
there are other, and equally important, arguments postulating
exactly the opposite (i.e., a Central Bank dependent on the government). Leaving aside some rather irrelevant points such as the risk of
a Central Bank independent of the government but more dependent
on the banking system (cf. Narr-Lindner, 1984), two key opinions have
to be quoted here which could be called the 'democratic' argument and
the 'economic policy' argument (Caesar, 1980, pp. 361–7).

The first one, which is taken particularly seriously in jurisprudence
and political science, is founded on an (alleged) missing political
justification for an independent Central Bank in a democratic society. From this point of view such an institution is regarded as a

'foreign body' in a political system, demanding all public institutions with substantial executive power to be controlled by the government (which has in turn been determined by the parliament) or by the parliament itself. Hence a Central Bank able to conduct its monetary policy without being responsible (or 'accountable',[3]) to any political representatives legitimated by democratic rules would not be acceptable (cf., *inter alia*, Committee on the Working of the Monetary System, 1959, pp. 273–4).

The 'economic policy' argument is primarily advocated by economists sympathising with Keynesian philosophy. They postulate a subordination of the Central Bank to the decision-makers of fiscal policy because of serious 'friction losses' resulting from a monetary policy not necessarily coordinated with fiscal policy actions (cf. Committee on the Working of the Monetary System, 1959, p. 273; Bach, 1971, p. 205). The most recent proposals in the USA to give the Secretary of the Treasury a seat and vote on the Board of Governors of the Federal Reserve System clearly reflect such a view, aiming at an economic policy which is a uniform whole.

Certainly, an attempt to assess the validity of these two arguments has to take into account a number of quite reasonable objections (cf. Caesar, 1980). But it would again be difficult to deny the relevance of both arguments completely. In any case the question of sufficient political justification remains a crucial one for an independent Central Bank. And no serious economist should entirely deny the possible positive effects of an effective coordination between the monetary and fiscal authorities.

Preliminary conclusions

Accepting, therefore, at least in principle, the main points made in favour of independence as well as the arguments made against it, one is in the awkward position that the pros and cons can hardly be compared to each other as they lie at different levels of consideration. There are, on the one side, those who demand price stability to be the most relevant task of a Central Bank. They fear that, in the absence of an independent Central Bank, the achievement of this objective may be endangered by the 'structural weaknesses of a pluralistic decision-making process' (von Arnim, 1977, p. 356). On the other side, their opponents argue that these dangers are much exaggerated and, above all, that a democratic state should not resign the right to change priorities in monetary policy (possibly even at the expense of price stability). In the final reckoning, it therefore remains a question of individual assessment which one of these differing judgements is regarded as more relevant in practice for a 'sound' economic policy.

Offering his personal point of view, the author of this paper is of the opinion that, as a rule, the advantages of an independent Central Bank do outweigh the possible risks connected with such an institution. Hence the following considerations, based on the conviction that for a future ECBS a status of independence is desirable, too, with respect to national governments of the ECs member states as well as in relation to the respective political decision-making bodies at the Community level. Contrary to that, it might be acceptable to introduce a certain duty for a European Central Bank to report from time to time before the European Parliament. However, this should not go as far as to put the Bank under serious parliamentary pressure.

11.4 ACTUAL INDEPENDENCE FOR AN ECBS?

The recommendations of the Delors report

As mentioned above the statements of the Delors report pertaining to the independence aspect of a future ECBS were particularly welcomed by the proponents of the independence idea, for two reasons.

First, the recommendations of the report were made unanimously by the members of the Delors group (i.e., including the Central Bank governors of countries with traditionally highly dependent Central Banks (such as France, Great Britain, and Italy). Secondly, the passages in the report on the issue of independence seem to be remarkably clear and unambiguous in nearly all respects crucial for a legally independent status of a ECBS for the final stage of EMU: according to the report (para. 32) the ECBS 'would be committed to the objective of price stability'; moreover, it 'should be independent of instructions from national governments and Community authorities', and its leading representatives should 'have appropriate security of tenure'; finally, the system should 'not . . . lend to public-sector authorities'. All these proposals are similar to the often-praised formulations of the German Bundesbank Law, and in some points they go even beyond the German Law. Therefore, from a legal standpoint, the ECBS designed by the Delors group would in fact be 'more German than the German Bundesbank' (Harbrecht, 1989, p. 169). It thus seems that the advocates of independence should be quite happy with the report of the Delors group (and probably none of them would have expected those outcomes when establishing the Delors group in 1988).

However, two important reservations have to be made here. First, there are some other formulations in the report referring, directly or indirectly, to the independence problem which are considerably more ambiguous. And, secondly, it is a crucial question how far the provisions suggested in the report can really secure an actual independence for the ECBS.

As to the first aspect, the report is very distinct on the point of independence for the final stage, but much less clear for the stages one and two of the EMU. There is a recommendation for stage one only that 'consideration should be given to extending the scope of central banks' autonomy' (para. 52). This rather careful wording – which was taken up exactly in the October 1989 proposal for a revised statute of the Committee of Central Bank Governors – is certainly not as strict as the passage on the ECBS's independence in stage three; moreover, it should be mentioned in this context that in the October 1989 proposal the respective passage was changed in a very instructive way to 'adequate autonomy' for the final stage of EMU.

Another suggestion of the Delors report which would restrict the ECBS's legal independence is the provision that the system 'should support the general economic policy set at the Community level by the competent bodies' (para. 32). Though this provision (which is again similar to one in the Bundesbank Law) is meant to be 'subject' to the already-quoted priority for price stability, it nevertheless opens a door to political influence on the ECBS.

Moreover, the proposal that the ECBS should be organised in a federal way (para. 32) is not without problems. In this context it might be less important whether the federal character of the system were mainly oriented along the lines of the Federal Reserve System, or the Bundesbank, or the former Bank deutscher Länder (cf. Gros and Thygesen, 1988, pp. 59–60; Kloten, 1988a, pp. 13–14). But it would be a serious menace to the actual independence of the ECBS if its main decision-making body were composed of representatives (i.e., probably the presidents in office) of the existing Central Banks of the individual countries. For in that case any legal independence of the ECBS on the European level could become meaningless because of a surviving influence of the national governments on their respec-

tive Central Bank officials on the national level (cf. Der Wissenschaftliche Beirat beim Bundesministerium für Wirtschaft, 1989,
p. 4). It would therefore be desirable to establish the central body of
the ECBS only from (competent) persons not retaining any additional functions in their national Central Banks. As a matter of
course, the extent of the actual independence of this body would also
be determined by the much cited 'element of personality' (which
seems, however, often to be slightly exaggerated).

Finally, the demand for a 'Community's exchange rate policy
vis-à-vis third countries' (para. 32) may entail heavy restrictions for
the ECBS's effective scope of action. As the passages on the distribution of responsibilities are not very clear in this respect (the ECBS
is thought to 'manage' the external policy but there is nothing said
about which body ought to set the guidelines for this policy), the
'external flank' of an ECBS's monetary policy could be laid open,
which in turn would make the ECBS's formal independence a matter
of little practical relevance.

The other problem with the Delors report's recommendations on
independence is even more important. Though the suggested legal
provisions should (with the exceptions just quoted) certainly be
welcome to the proponents of Central Banks' independence, they
could of course not prevent the (formally) independent status in
reality still being endangered. This is true with respect to all the
points regarded as essential in the report: the explicit responsibility
for price stability depends in fact on the actual interpretation of that
objective permitting a wide range of variations (from 'zero inflation'
to any form of 'relative stability'). The 'independence of instructions'
may be questioned in reality by 'political appointments' and heavy
'informal pressure' from political actors. Lastly, the prohibition of
(direct) lending to public-sector authorities can easily be circum-
vented by extensive open-market operations in public securities.[4]

Any legal stipulations on a Central Bank's independence can
therefore at best be a factor of support for an effectively great room
for manoeuvre. In any case, what has to be added to this in order to
secure an actual independence is a widely-accepted consensus across
the society on two points: (1) on the fundamental importance of price
stability among the objectives of economic policy, and (2) on the
sustainability of an institution pursuing that objective even at the risk
of conflicts with the government. Hence the prospects for the actual
room for manoeuvre of a ECBS depend on the extent to which this
kind of double consensus is already existent, or may grow, in the

member countries of the EC. A closer look at the conditions in these
countries should therefore be useful.

**Central Bank laws and the effective room for manoeuvre of Central
Banks in Europe**

Legal regulations and effective circumstances in the other EC
countries besides Germany little reason to believe that the prerequisites for an independent ECBS could be given, or created, in the
foreseeable future.

To begin with the legal room for manoeuvre, no Central Bank
except the Bundesbank – which is often characterised as the 'most
autonomous in the world' (Opie, 1962, p. 91; Sayers, 1967, p. 78) –
disposes of the degree of independence suggested by the Delors
group. Only the Bundesbank is expressively 'independent of instructions of the Federal Government' (Bundesbank Law, para. 12 II) so
that a direct influence of the government on monetary policy decisions is excluded. It is true that even the Bundesbank is obliged 'to
support the general economic policy' of the government (Bundesbank Law, para. 12 I). But this is subject to the 'maintenance of its
task', stipulated as 'safeguarding the currency' (Bundesbank Law,
para. 3) which the Bundesbank itself has, as a rule, interpreted in the
sense of giving priority to price stability as its 'principal duty' (Emminger, 1968, p. 3). The legal position of the Bundesbank vis-à-vis
the government is further determined by a number of other provisions, referring, for example, to the right of participation of members of the government in meetings of the Central Bank Council as
the Bundesbank's main decision-making body (even with the possibility of a suspensive veto), to some general duties of the Bundesbank to give advice and information to the government, and to the
(strictly limited) possibilities of direct Central Bank lending to
public-sector authorities. But, on the whole, all these provisions
pertaining to the 'functional' aspect do not constitute any decisive
restrictions for the Bundesbank's scope of decision on monetary
policy. The chances for massive political influences rather occur on
the 'personal' level as only political bodies are responsible for the
appointment of the member of the Central Bank Council. But, again,
this fact is at least moderated by a number of other specifications
(term of office, irrevocability, 'pluralism' of appointing bodies).

Compared to the Bundesbank most other Central Banks in Europe
are in a much weaker legal position (for details cf. Caesar, 1981;

Hasse, 1989, pp. 209–27; and several contributions in Toniolo, 1988). Their scope of decision on the determination and realisation of monetary objectives is confined more or less, for example, by rights of directives, of approval, and of control, given to the respective governments. It is thereby of minor importance whether these rights refer directly to the relations between the Central Bank and the government (as in Great Britain) or whether they are based on indirect ways of influence via other political bodies which are in turn dominated by the government (as in France and Italy). In addition, on the personal level leading Central Bank officials are replaceable in a number of countries (e.g., Belgium, France, Italy, Spain). Finally, the stipulations concerning the Central Bank's lending to the public sector in many countries open an important foothold for political influence on monetary policy.

In view of this clearly restricted room for manoeuvre a realisation of the Delors group's proposals would presume a fundamental change of opinion on the issue of independence in the countries mentioned above. It is true that in some countries proposals have been made to extend the legal scope of freedom of the respective Central Banks. This was the case in France in the mid-1980s when the Chirac government made such a proposal during the election campaign. But after the election (won by the Socialists) this proposal was quickly junked again. And especially in the context of the discussions on a European Central Bank the idea of independence has been rejected very clearly by leading French politicians, such as Mrs Cresson and Mr Bérégovoy (cf. Caesar, 1989, p. 275).

Similarly, the British prime minister vehemently attacked the Delors group's ideas on independence as well as the initiative taken by Mr Lawson, the former Chancellor of the Exchequer, to extend the Bank of England's legal status. That this critical view of independence is quite popular with politicians in the UK can be further demonstrated by the results of a hearing on the Delors report held by a 1987 committee on the House of Commons during which the Governor of the Bank of England was blamed very aggressively for having signed the report. The situation may be partly different in some other EC countries, such as the Benelux countries, or Italy (especially since the appointment of the former Governor of the Bank of Italy, Guido Carli, as the Italian Minister of the Treasury). But on the whole it seems that the chances for widening the legal independence of the Central Banks in the EC are rather small.

Even more important than any reforms of the legal regulations however, would be changes in some fundamental circumstances which are at present opposed to an enduring enlargement of the Central Bank room for manoeuvre in the countries concerned. Following our considerations above, this mainly refers (1) to the weight given to the objective of price stability, and (2) to the estimation of Central Banks' independence 'as such'.

Starting again from the German situation, it is certainly true that the legal provisions in the Bundesbank Law quoted above are an important factor of support for the bank in cases of conflict. But the legal stipulations would have little meaning – and, probably no chance to continue – if they were not in reality based on a widespread consensus in the German society that an 'independent' Bundesbank were the best protection against a repetition of the experiences of two great inflations during this century. It is of secondary importance in this context whether this point of view is correct or not as such (cf. above, p. 000). But the particular confidence in the Bundesbank connected with this view has become a sort of a 'national taboo' which estimates the Bundesbank as an 'institutional counterweight' against any inflationary aspirations in German economic policy (for further references cf. Caesar, 1981, pp. 201–5). And at the same time it forms the decisive bulwark against any propositions coming up occasionally also in Germany which suggest restricting the legal scope of action of the Central Bank (cf. Ehrenberg, 1988; Zinn, 1988).

Looking at the other EC countries the situation is no doubt very different, with respect to both factors relevant in this context. First, as to the ranking of price stability compared to the other aims of stabilisation policy it is certainly true that monetary policies in the majority of the EC countries have become more stability-oriented since 1983 and that remarkable success has been achieved in fighting inflation. Nevertheless, the ideas on the appropriate degree of price stability still differ widely in the various countries (and are definitely not comparable to the German view). It is very indicative that the Germans are recurrently reproached for suffering from an 'inflation trauma' and for pursuing an excessively restrictive monetary policy (a reproach particularly relevant in view of the rather expansive course of German monetary policy since 1987). From this perspective one would have to conclude that the quick realisation of a common European body for deciding on monetary affairs in the Community would imply considerable risks for price stability.

And, as already mentioned, with respect to the idea of independence as a matter of principle there is probably not much sympathy for the German institutional solution in the majority of the EC

countries (cf. also Sachverständigenrat zur Begutachtung der gesamtwirtschaftlichen Entwicklung, 1989, p. 183). Especially in France and
Great Britain it is not only the government which regards its Central
Bank as an obsequious tool of policy. It is also the Central Banks'
understanding in these countries that they are hardly more than an
executive organ of the government which stands in opposition to a
radical change of responsibilities (cf. the popular characterisation of
the Bank of England as the 'East-End Branch of the Treasury'). And
it may be instructive that, as a rule, in both countries a possible
career within the Treasury is clearly preferred by ambitious young
academics to a corresponding rise within the Central Bank. This
should (in spite of the undoubted respect offered to the Central Bank
by the public) still be taken as an indicator reflecting the real distribution of power between the government and the Central Bank, and
its assessment by the society.

Taking into account such deep-rooted traditions, those who believe that a considerable and rather rapid change in the understanding of independence might be possible in the course of European
monetary integration do not show much realism. For the foreseeable
future European monetary policies will probably still remain confronted with 'deep-seated dissents in the basic positions as to the
institutional side' (Kloten, 1988b, p. 416).

11.5 SUMMARY

- Central Banks' 'independence' (or 'autonomy') has been a topic
  of discussion in literature and politics since the existence of privi-
  leged Central Banks themselves. However, the actual meaning of
  these terms is not clear at all, and quite different (legal, political,
  and economic) aspects have been treated under the heading of
  'independence' which might better be circumscribed by the term
  'room for manoeuvre'.

- Reflections on the independence problem have mainly concentrated on four questions: the level of the monetary decision-
  making process concerned ('independence in what sense?'); the
  actual factors determining a Central Bank's freedom of action
  ('(in-)dependence by what means?'); the actors who may influence
  a Central Bank's behaviour ('independence from what?'); the pros
  and cons of independence as a matter of principle ('independence,
  why?').

- As to the last dimension, a number of serious arguments in favour of independence (the 'economic' argument, the 'political' argument, and the 'technical' argument) as well as against Central Banks' independence of the government (the 'democratic' argument, and the 'economic policy' argument) have to be taken into account. However, the pros and cons can hardly be compared to each other as they are at different levels of consideration.

- It therefore remains a question of individual assessment whether an independent Central Bank is advocated, or not. Offering his personal point of view, the author is of the opinion that, as a rule, the advantages of an independent Central Bank do outweigh the possible risks connected with such an institution. Hence the considerations of this paper based on the conviction that for a future ECBS a status of independence is desirable, too.

- On the whole, the suggestions of the Delors report seem to be remarkably clear in nearly all respects crucial for a legally independent status of a ECBS in the final stage of an EMU. But there are some formulations in their report which might still open a door to political influence on the ECBS.

- Even more important is the fact that the suggested legal provisions can of course not prevent a formally independent status of the ECBS being endangered in practice. The actual independence of the system will depend on the degree of a social consensus on (1) the ranking of price stability as compared to other aims of economic policy, and (2) on the sustainability of an institution pursuing this objective even at the risk of conflicts with the government.

- A look at the present circumstances in the EC countries except Germany gives little occasion to believe that this kind of double consensus already exists, or may grow quite rapidly. In spite of some indisputable success in a number of EC countries in fighting inflation the ideas on the appropriate degree of price stability doubtless still vary considerably.

- With respect to the idea of independence as a matter of principle there is, apparently, not much sympathy for the German institutional solution in the majority of the EC countries. In France and the UK leading politicians have expressively rejected the Delors group's proposals on this point.

- The prerequisites for an actually independent, and stability-oriented, ECBS therefore seem hardly to be present in the foreseeable future. From this perspective the quick realisation of a common European body for deciding on monetary affairs in the Community would imply considerable risks for price stability.

Notes

1. This might be the 'independence' meant by a formulation sometimes used in Anglo-Saxon literature saying that a Central Bank should be 'independent' within government, rather than 'independent' of government (cf. Board of Governors, 1963, p. 250; de Kock, 1974, p. 318).
2. As to a Central Bank's relations with the parliament it is a matter of course that a Central Bank can never be entirely independent of parliamentary influence because every law stating 'independence' is always alterable by decision of the parliament. Therefore any discussion on 'Central Bank independence from the parliament' would make sense only with respect to the question of some permanent contacts between both institutions. A Central Bank's independence in this sense might be restricted more or less, for example, by a decisive role for the parliament in settling cases of conflict between the Central Bank and the government (as in the Netherlands), or by a parliament's right to recall the Central Bank's leading officials (as in Sweden), or by a Central Bank's obligation to give reports to the parliament on a regular basis (as in the USA).
3. This term has also been used in some other studies (Thygesen, 1989; *The Economist*, 1990). But the actual meaning of 'accountability' is rather unclear, too, and it seems as if it might include quite weak as well as very strong restrictions on a Central Bank's room for manoeuvre. This term will therefore not be used in the paper.
4. It is certainly worth mentioning in this context that in the recent catalogue of questions developed by the Guigou group (a group of high-ranking officials from the ministries of Finance and of Foreign Affairs) on the EMU there is one question explicitly asking whether it should be interdicted to the ECBS to finance public-sector deficits. One should at least be surprised that this question has been brought up again after the clear rejection of such ideas by the Delors group.

References

Bach, G.L. (1971) 'Making Monetary and Fiscal Policy', 'Washington', Brookings Institution.

Banaian, K., Laney, L.O. and Willett, T.D. (1983) 'Central Bank Independence: An International Comparison', Economic Review, Federal Reserve Bank of Dallas (March), reprinted in: Toma and Toma, (1986).

Board of Governors of the Federal Reserve System and the United States Treasury Department (1963) *The Federal Reserve and the Treasury: Answers to questions from the Commission on Money and Credit*, Englewood Cliffs, N.J., Prentice-Hall.

Buchanan, J.M. and Wagner, R.E. (1977) *Democracy in Deficit. The Political Legacy of Lord Keynes*, New York, San Francisco and London, Academia Press.

Burns, A. (1976) 'The Independence of the Federal Reserve System', *Federal Reserve Bulletin* (June).

Caesar, R. (1980)   'Die Unabhängigkeit der Notenbank im demokratischen Staat. Argumente und Gegenargumente', *Zeitschrift für Politik*, N.S., vol. 27.

Caesar, R. (1981)   'Der Handlungsspielraum von Notenbanken. Theoretische Analyse und internationaler Vergleich', Baden-Baden, Nomos Verlagsgesellschaft.

Caesar, R. (1983)   'Central Banks in the Political Arena', *Wirtschaftsdienst*, vol. 63.

Caesar, R. (1989)   'Der Delors-Bericht: ein wegweisendes Dokument? Fortschritte sind unverkennbar', *Wirtschaftsdienst*, vol. 69.

Committee on the Working of the Monetary System (1959)   'Report. Presented to Parliament by the Chancellor of the Exchequer by Command of Her Majesty', Cmnd. 827, London, HMSO.

Cukierman, A. (1986)   'Central Bank Behavior and Credibility: Some Recent Theoretical Developments', *Review*, Federal Reserve Bank of St. Louis (May).

De Cecco, M. and Giovannini, A. (eds) (1989)   *A European Central Bank? Perspectives on monetary inflation after ten years of the EMS*, Cambridge, Cambridge University Press.

De Kock, M.H. (1974)   *Central Banking*, 4th edn, London, Staflas Press.

Delors, J. *et al.* (1989)   'Committee for the Study of Economic and Monetary Union: Report on economic and monetary union in the European Community', Luxembourg.

Der Wissenschaftliche Beirat beim Bundesministerium für Wirtschaft (1977) 'Gutachten vom 9. und 10.3.1973: Grundfragen der Stabilitätspolitik', in Gutachten, 8. Bd., ed. by Bundesministerium für Wirtschaft, Göttingen.

Der Wissenschaftliche Beirat beim Bundesministerium für Wirtschaft (1989) 'Stellungnahme zum Bericht des Delors-Ausschusses vom 5.6.1989', *BMWI-Schriftenreihe*, no. 63, Bonn.

Duwendag, D. (ed.) *Macht und Ohnmacht der Bundesbank*, Frankfurt/ Main, Athenäum Verlag.

The Economist (1990)   'What kind of EMU?', *The Economist* (10 February 1990).

Ehrenberg, H. (1988)   'Autonom bis zum europäischen Ende?', *Wirtschaftsdienst*, vol. 69.

Emminger, O. (1968)   'Zwanzig Jahre deutsche Geldpolitik – Rückblick und Ausblick', Deutsche Bundesbank, Auszüge aus Presseartikeln, no. 22/20.3.1968.

Fair, D. (1979)   'The Independence of Central Banks', *The Banker*, no. 644 (October).

Gros, D. and Thygesen, N. (1988)   'The EMS. Achievement, Current Issues, and Directions for the Future', CEPS Paper, no. 35, Brussels.

Hansmeyer, K.-H. (1968)   'Wandlungen im Handlungsspielraum der Notenbank?', in Andreae, C.A. *et al.* (eds), *Geldtheorie und Geldpolitik*, Berlin, Dunchers Humblot.

Harbrecht, W. (1989)   'Wege zur Errichtung einer Europäischen Zentralbank: Zum Delors-Bericht', *Integration*, vol. 12.

Harriss, C.L. (1961)   'Le Trésor et la Banque Centrale', in Institut International de Finances Publiques (ed.), *La gestion de la trésorerie publique*, Madrid/ Brussels, Derecho Financiers/Emile Bruglant.

Hasse, R.H. (1989) *Die Europäische Zentralbank: Perspektiven für eine Weiterentwicklung des Europäischen Währungssystems*, Göttinger, Venlenhoeck & Ruprecht.

Hawtrey, R.G. (1932) *The Art of Central Banking*, London, New York and Toronto, Layman Caen.

Kydland, E.C. and Prescott, E.C. (1977) 'Rules Rather than Discretion: The Inconsistency of Optimal Plans', *Journal of Political Economy*, vol. 85.

Kloten, N. (1988a) 'Moving towards a European Central Bank System', Deutsche Bundesbank, Auszüge aus Presseartikeln, no. 46/23.6.1988.

Kloten, N. (1988b) *Zur Anatomie geldpolitischer Entscheidungen des Zentralbankrates*, in Dürr, E. and Sieber, H. (eds), *Weltwirtschaft im Wandel*, Bern and Stuttgart, Paul Hauft.

Lück, W. (1939) 'Monetäre Unabhängigkeit. Untersuchung der Vorschläge von J.M. Keynes für unabhängige nationale Währungssysteme', Leipzig.

McCallum, B.-T. (1984) 'Credibility and Monetary Policy', NBER Working Paper, no. 1490, Washington, D.C.

Narr-Lindner, G. (1984) *Grenzen monetärer Steuerung. Die Restriktionspolitik der Bundesbank 1964–1974*, Frankfurt and New York, Camfur Verlag.

Opie, R.G. (1962) 'Western Germany', in Sayers, R.S. (ed.) *Banking in Western Europe*, Oxford, Clementa Press.

Parkin, M. (1978) 'In Search of a Monetary Constitution for the European Communities', in Fratianni, M. and Peeters, T. (eds) *One Money for Europe*, New York, McMillan.

Rogoff, K. (1987): 'Reputational Constraints on Monetary Policy', Carnegie-Rochester Conference Series on Public Policy, vol. 26.

Sachverständigenrat zur Begutachtung der gesamtwirtschaftlichen Entwicklung (1989) 'Jahresgutachten 1989/90', Stuttgart/Mainz.

Sayers, R.S. (1967) *Modern Banking*, 7th edn Oxford, Clementa Press.

Thygesen, N. (1989) 'Decentralization and Accountability within the Central Bank: Any Lessons from the US Experience for the Potential Organization of a European Central Banking Institution?', in de Grauwe, P. and Peeters, T. (eds), *The ECU and European Monetary Integration*, London, Macmillan.

Toma, E.F. and Toma, M. (eds), (1988) *Central Bankers, Bureaucratic Incentives, and Monetary Policy* Dordrecht, Boston and Lancaster, Kluwer.

Toniolo, G. (ed.) (1988) *Central Banks' Independence in Historical Perspective*, Berlin and New York, Walter de Guye.

Von Arnim, H.H. (1977) *Gemeinwohl und Gruppeninteressen*, Frankfurt/ Main, Metzner.

Zinn, K.G. (1988) 'Wie autonom ist die Bundesbank?', *Sozialismus*, vol. 14, no. 102.

Discussion

Hermann-Josef Dudler

Rolf Caesar's paper represents a good example of traditional German mainstream thinking on the issue of Central Bank independence. Representatives of this school of thought take it more or less for granted that the predominant ultimate objective of monetary policy ought to be the maintenance of price stability. This proposition results from the analytical presumption that the pursuit of stable prices constitutes the optimal use of monetary management as a tool of economic stabilisation policy and is, moreover, based on the conviction that conservative Central Banks exhibit a general predilection for anti-inflationary policies. The methodology applied in these German contributions may be linked to the traditional German 'historical school' and its modern applications, in which political and sociological lines of reasoning play an important role. In such a framework it can be shown relatively easily that Central Bank independence seems to be the least costly institutional solution for controlling a socially harmful bias in modern societies: the propensity of parliaments, elected governments and social pressure groups to resort to inflation as a temporary device for solving open or hidden social conflicts.

Adherents of this line of thinking tend to dislike the 'activist' use of monetary policy for short-run stabilisation purposes broadly in accordance with neoclassical tenets. At the same time, the democratic accountability of independent Central Banks does not appear to pose a fundamental problem to them, because the political interaction of the Bundesbank with German society seems to prove, as a model case, that Central Bank autonomy and the smooth working of a democratic system can, as a matter of principle, be regarded as fully compatible. These considerations tend to override typical arguments that frequently militate against complete political independence of Central Banks in the context of industrial societies outside Germany. In fact, authors like Caesar clearly recognise that the 'German model' might not be easily applied elsewhere and, therefore, doubt whether the project of a European Central Banking System (ECBS) is desirable or at all feasible from the German point of view. Incor-

246

porating these characteristic features, Caesar's contribution is highly instructive, since it confronts European readers with a typical sceptical German way of thinking on European monetary integration. In some respects, the paper is, however, rather incomplete from the viewpoint of international academic communication. It does not discuss the relevant international literature on Central Bank 'credibility', public choice, the game-theoretic analyses of Central Bank behaviour, or the potential credibility benefits of EMU as analysed in rigorous academic contributions during the last few years. The paper also pays too little attention to the 'Achilles's heels' of the independent Bundesbank: self-imposed exchange-rate constraints and the influence of both sides of industry on price/wage determination in Germany. Finally, the author underestimates the degree to which Germany can positively influence the thinking of her neighbours in the field of central banking, if German politicians, technocrats and academics actively contribute to paving the way towards European monetary integration. The success of the EMS, the Delors report and the conservative 1989 Mandate, which put the policy coordination of EC Central Banks during stage one of the planned EMU on a sound basis, are good cases in point. In an attempt to allay apprehensions of German central bankers that European monetary integration could undermine monetary stability in Germany, a European Central Bank official remarked that 'In every European central banker's chest beats the heart of the Bundesbank'. Such encouraging attitudes belong to European political reality today and should be appreciated by German policy-makers and academics, since they constitute a promising basis for future European monetary integration.

12 Economic Policy and European Integration

Anthonie Knoester, André M.M. Kolodziejak and Guus Muijzers

12.1 INTRODUCTION

'Project Europe 1992' refers to the intention to have the European internal market completed on 1 January 1993 at the latest, which means that from that date on persons, goods, services and capital will be able to move freely within the EC. The measures to be taken in this context can be defined as examples of negative integration (i.e., abolition of intra-European constraints). In this paper, the main point we wish to make is that this negative integration should be followed by a process of positive integration (i.e., harmonisation of national policies). In our view, uncoordinated macro-economic and monetary policies are a serious threat to the forthcoming European internal market.

In addition, harmonisation of national policies is a necessary condition for further steps on the road towards a complete European EMU, as described in the resolution adopted by the European Council and representatives of the members states on 22 March 1971. In Hanover, in June 1988, the European Council asked for a report setting the agenda for a road towards economic and monetary union. This report, which became well-known as the Delors Report, stressed the importance of parallelism of economic and monetary integration. It also pointed to the subsidiarity principle, which says that every task that can be performed at the national level should stay with the member states. The Delors report was discussed by heads of state and government at the European Council in Madrid in June 1989, and from that time on the difficult political transformation into reality began.

In some European countries – for example, in the UK under the Thatcher administration until 1990 – political willingness to reduce national autonomy with regard to macro-economic and monetary policies was very small. Related to this, there was a tendency to use

248

the subsidiarity principle as an instrument to change the original
Delors concept aiming at parallelism at large. As a result, the
question is whether in the Europe of the future we can expect only a
Currency Union instead of a complete EMU. If so, European integration itself will be in danger.

To put it simply, Europe and its economy do not need an internal
market which remains imperfect, hardly credible and rather unstable
because of the absence of positive integration in the form of forthcoming economic and monetary union. It should be noted that even a
Currency Union can operate successfully only when a stable consensus on economic development and policy has been achieved within
the Community. In our view, lasting monetary stability can be
achieved only with more parallelism (i.e., with more harmonisation
of national policies).

The plan of our paper is as follows. In Section 12.2 we will discuss
briefly the incomplete European macro-economic integration. Section 12.3 deals with the loss of national macro-economic and monetary autonomy which in reality has already taken place. The case of
the Netherlands will be presented as an example. In addition, we will
argue that national sovereignty is widely confused with the still
widespread illusion of national autonomy in both small and large
European countries. National autonomy is heavily constrained by
strong economic and financial interdependences. These interdependences will even be stronger after the completion of the internal
market in 1992. Section 12.4 deals with the question whether cooperation in general, and especially cooperation within the framework of
the EMS and EC, can restore the effectiveness of economic policies.
Sharing the European Council's view that completion of the internal
market should be an irreversible process, we will put forward proposals for ways of institutionalising strengthened European macro-
economic and monetary cooperation. In Section 12.5 one of our
proposals is a gradual introduction of a European Federal Bank
System after the model of the United States Federal Reserve System.
In addition, the possible shape of the statute governing such a system
will be discussed, as well as the implications of a European Federal
Bank System for national fiscal policies. We will end with a summary
and conclusions in Section 12.6.

12.2   INCOMPLETE EUROPEAN MACRO-ECONOMIC INTEGRATION

Macro-economic coordination and monetary cohesion have largely been neglected in the European effort towards unification since the Rome Treaty of 1958, with the exception of a period at the end of the 1960s and the beginning of the 1970s. The Treaty provisions in this respect, laid down in Articles 103–109, have hardly been given substance. It must be admitted that the turbulent 1970s, beset by economic problems, were hardly the most fertile period for developing common or supranational monetary and macro-economic policies. On the other hand, it is evident that the main difficulty is that the member countries are particularly sensitive about retaining sovereignty in this field.

In 1983, when both the economic recession and European unification had reached their nadir, a European Parliament document – the Albert–Ball report – marked a revolution in thinking about European integration, which was of the utmost importance for monetary and macro-economic cooperation (Albert and Ball, 1983). The authors pointed to the cost of 'non-Europe' to the member countries in the macro-economic area. The 'cost of non-Europe' awareness has imparted new dynamics to European integration in that it has raised questions about national and *communautaire* macro-economic and monetary policies (Ball, 1988, pp. 18 ff). The new dynamics is connected with the completion of the internal market along the lines set out in the Commission's White Paper of 1985. A common market allowing free movement of goods, services and production factors must be established by 1 January 1993, at the latest. In its progress report of November 1988, the European Commission set great store by completion of the internal market, which it considered to be the key not only to the Community's prosperity but also to its future (Cecchini, 1988). At the Hanover European Council meeting (June 1988), the heads of state and government declared that the establishment of the internal market, the chief objective of the Single European Act, 'has now reached the point of no return, which is accepted as a fact by everyone playing an active role in economic and social life'. The Commission, basing itself on the Cecchini report (1988) said that the European internal market would bring great benefits, including an estimated 2 million new jobs in the medium run.

In the progress report the Commission said the following about the relation between the completion of the internal market and economic and monetary policies:

Economic and monetary policies have both a direct and an indirect impact on the completion of the internal market. The directive on liberalisation of capital movements, which will come into effect in July 1990, constitutes an integral part of the White Paper Programme and now forms a fundamental basis for the establishment of a genuine internal market for financial services. Moreover, unstable exchange rates hamper free movements between national markets. The European Monetary System should therefore be strengthened in order to enhance the unity of the internal market.

'Stable exchange rates' and a 'high degree of capital mobility' will make it impossible for a small open economy like that of the Netherlands – and to a lesser extent for the large European countries such as the UK, West Germany and France – to pursue an independent monetary course. It is true that exchange rates can be kept stable in the short term by means of interest-rate policies, but in the long run the real cost of a higher interest rate will be considerable in an integrated market. At the moment, interest rates in the capital market are strongly influenced by governmental fiscal policies. In the context of greater capital mobility or fixed exchange rates, fiscal policies may become more effective, provided that European countries do not adopt contrary policies.

Owing to the increased interdependence of economies in general, and in the EC in particular, there is also a chance that, as seen within the community context, the outcome of a restrictive fiscal policy (in terms of increased production and employment) is overrated and that of an expansive fiscal policy underrated.

In the 1980s a gap developed between the reach of national macro-economic policies and the starting-points of Community policies. This is represented by the operational economic policy models of the Netherlands Central Planning Bureau, Freia and FREIA KOMPAS, in that they are highly resistant to national policy instruments which might stimulate growth and employment, and very sensitive to exogenous impulses.[1] This phenomenon, to which the draining-away of domestic ability to act is central, is also called the Padoa-Schioppa theorem (Padoa-Schioppa, 1985; 1987). In other countries however, such as France, this development has occasioned the planning bureau and economic institutes to use European policy models besides national ones '*pour raisonner en européen*', or '*prendre en compte l'Europe dans le raisonnement économique*'.[2]

As the subsidiarity principle[3] lays down, the Community should not assume powers which national governments and market parties can very well exercise themselves. Or, in positive terms, the Community should see to it that national governments and market parties are enabled to carry out their tasks as well as possible. Only where their ability is wanting may the Community step in to make good the shortfall.

12.3 LIMITS OF NATIONAL MACRO-ECONOMIC POLICIES AND LOSS OF NATIONAL ABILITY TO ACT

Macro-economic and monetary coordination

European national governments redistribute a large share of national income, which in principle gives them the tools to pursue macro-economic policies. So it is fair to say that, given the distribution of the actual ability to intervene and coordinate, the primary competence for macro-economic and monetary policies lies with the member states. The question is, however, whether this competence can still be exercised in fact, as the former Governor of De Nederlandsche Bank, Zijlstra (1966), wondered. National macroeconomic policies can be upset by:

1. monetary policies
2. the macro-economic policies of other countries
3. the draining-away of policy effects to other countries

French experience indicates that a simultaneous occurrence of these three factors greatly lessens the ability of national governments to pursue macro-economic policies (Knoester, Kolodziejak and Muijzers, 1990, p. 25–7). When the Mitterrand government took office in 1981, it launched an ambitious policy plan to boost the economy. This policy was upset by the EMS monetary policies, the macro-economic policies of other member countries – in particular, of the then West Germany – and the draining-away of the effects of France's policies to other countries. It will be clear that the increasing mobility of goods, services, labour and capital throughout the Community will enhance such drainage, especially under a regime of increasingly stable or fixed exchange rates. National ability to intervene can be restored through coordination of the member states' macro-economic policies. This coordination problem will be discussed in Section 12.4.

The prescription for macro-economic policy cooperation, however, is connected with many other problems, as is illustrated by the huge body of literature published on the subject, especially in America.[4] Even if there is consensus on the need for coordinated government intervention, the question remains how governments should intervene. The question can be divided into four subquestions:

1. What is the analysis of the economic process?
2. What goals are selected?
3. What is our economic model for linking instruments to objectives?
4. What policy instruments are employed?

In general terms, there will be consensus on both the objectives and the need for a balanced development without a great deal of inflation, without major unemployment and without surpluses or deficits in the current account of the balance of payments. The precise quantification of the objectives, the weight to be given to each of them and the choice of policy tools, however, depend closely on the analysis made of the economic process and the political context. In the current constellation, a coordination of macro-economic policies imposed by the Community stands a chance only if the member states decide to let themselves be constrained – as Odysseus did when sailing past the Sirens – in their freedom of macro-economic policy action, as has happened to some extent within the EMS.

The loss of national macro-economic and monetary autonomy

The draining-away of the ability of the member states to pursue effective macro-economic and monetary policies on their own is the more a problem because it is *not* being made good at the Community level. For the achievement of major economic policy intentions, such as the curbing of unemployment, the government has in recent years proved to be highly dependent on developments abroad and the cooperation of foreign countries. In the following a brief quantitative analysis is given by way of example of the possibilities for the Netherlands to pursue independent macro-economic or fiscal policies and monetary or money-supply and exchange-rate policies. We also take a look at the macro-economic and monetary autonomy of the larger economies in the Community. The importance of insight into the loss of macro-economic and monetary autonomy should not be underrated. National politicians are still too prone to believe that they have got the whole macro-economic world in their hands. Yet this loss of autonomy should not be confused with loss of sovereignty.

The illusion of national autonomy is still widespread and is widely confused with national sovereignty. The latter concerns the formal ability of a nation to act on its own rather than under the instruction of another nation. That remains undiminished. National autonomy in contrast, is the ability of a nation to attain its objectives through unilateral action. That is heavily constrained in an environment of high interdependence. Economic cooperation may restore some effectiveness in pursuit of objectives. Far from undermining national sovereignty, such cooperation often represents wise exercise of that sovereignty.[5]

In Cooper's view coordination can thus compensate to some extent for diminishing autonomy and – given the high degree of interdependence – it represents a wise exercise rather than an undermining of sovereignty. We shall see in Section 12.4 that the concept of an economic cooperation and coordination *without* consequences for national sovereignty reflects a typically American approach, which does not fit the achievements of European integration to date. It is important to keep in mind the connection between growing international interdependence and the diminution of national policy autonomy. On the basis of fourteen multi-country models, Kolodziejak (1988) surveyed the quantitative extent of the macro-economic and monetary interdependence within the EC and between the EC countries, on the one hand, and other countries and blocs of countries in the world economy, on the other. He also clearly demonstrated the limited national autonomy of individual countries. In Knoester, Kolodziejak and Muijzers (1990) we highlighted more precisely the restricted autonomy which already exists apart from the *de facto* or *de jure* international constraint of national monetary policy and a domestic money policy, accommodating or not. In other words, what is important here is the extent of the *involuntary restriction* of national autonomy. Using the Netherlands as an example, we focused on dependencies which are indicated by several multi-country models (Kolodziejak, 1988).

The draining-away of policy effects to other countries

The ineffectiveness of isolated national policies: the Dutch case

All relevant models show that the so-called first-year GDP fiscal multiplier for the Netherlands is relatively small and at any rate does not exceed 1. This multiplier represents the percentage increase in Gross Domestic Product (GDP) as a result of an increase in autonomous domestic expenditure of 1 percentage point of GDP. The OECD estimated this multiplier at about 0.7 for the Netherlands, compared with more than 1 for virtually all other countries. The low value for the Netherlands shows that in this country the effects of an expansionary fiscal policy largely drain away to other countries.

Say the Dutch fiscal authorities propose to reduce direct taxes, which could fit both a demand-side and a supply-side económic policy vision: how far would Holland get by its own efforts? An indication is obtained by comparing the results after 1 and 4 years of a once-and-for-all tax *increase* (in which case the signs have to be reversed) of 1 per cent of Net National Income (NNI), computed with five Dutch economic policy models and one multi-country model, the Atlas model of the French Direction de la Prévision. Two variants have been calculated with this Atlas model: one in which the Netherlands, as with the five Dutch models, takes this action alone, and one in which Belgium, West Germany, France, Italy and the UK carry out the same fiscal action simultaneously. The results should be seen as cumulated deviations, expressed in percentages or percentage points, from the central projection (Figure 12.1).

It is found that the results for the various models mesh as regards direction and also, *grosso modo*, as regards the size of the effects. In the case of an isolated action by the Netherlands, the results of the calculation by means of the Atlas model accord with those obtained with the other models. Although the results of the policy action can be termed limited as regards changes in production volume and rate of unemployment, a tax reduction or increase has a fairly strong impact on the current account of the balance of payments and certainly on the government's budget deficit. So if a tax cut is not accompanied by a cutback in government spending, the result as shown by the models is unattractive. This confirms what Knoester has argued in various writings about the inverted Haavelmo effect and the validity of the Laffer curve (Knoester, 1983, 1988a, 1988b; Knoester and Kolodziejak, 1988).

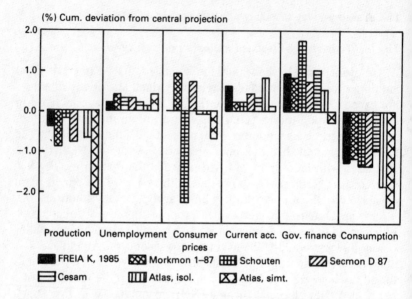

Figure 12.1   Increase in direct taxes in the Netherlands by 1 per cent of
NNI; results after 4 years (3 years for Atlas variants)

A comparison of simulations of an increase in direct taxes, this
time – contrary to the previous simulations – accompanied by an
increase in government spending of 1 per cent of NNI, *does* reveal
essential differences between the models: after 4 years the balanced
budget multiplier is for the Netherlands Central Planning Bureau's
Freia Kompas model +0.5, for the De Nederlandsche Bank's Mork-
mon model −0.4 and for the Secmon model of the University of
Amsterdam 0. Then the Keynesian Haavelmo effect (Haavelmo,
1945), the supply-side economic inverted Haavelmo effect (Knoester,
1983) and classical neutrality (Ketellapper and Osinga, 1981) would
respectively apply. Although these models are so different among
themselves they agree as far as their difference from the results with
Atlas's simultaneous run is concerned.

The effectiveness of simultaneous European policies

If we see what happens if the other countries (Belgium, West Germany, Italy, France, and the UK) also change their tax rates, a
completely different picture emerges (Figure 12.2). The outcomes of
relevant multi-country models other than Atlas, such as the Oxford

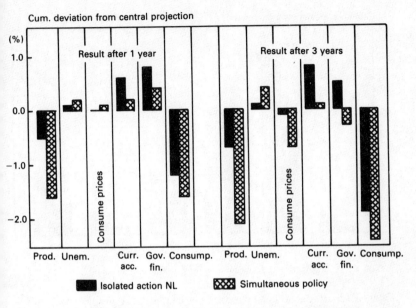

Figure 12.2 Increase in direct taxes of 1 per cent of NNI: effects for the
Netherlands of isolated and simultaneous action respectively;
results obtained with the Atlas model after 1 and 3 years

Economic Forecasting Model, the Mimosa model of the Centre
d'Etudes et d'Informations Internationales (CEPII) and the Obser-
vatoire Français des Conjunctures Economiques (OFCE) and the
Hermes/Comet model of the European Commission, all point in the
same direction. The Albert and Ball report mentioned in section 12.2
certainly deserves praise for pointing out that this 'impotence of
states', or the impossibility of 'going it alone' holds good for all the
countries of the Community, even if the small countries, as for
instance the Netherlands, are more vulnerable than the large ones.
The effect on foreign employment – that is the overall effect on
Belgium, West Germany, France, Italy and the UK – of an isolated
Dutch fiscal action or tax cut is almost twice as large as the domestic
effect after 3 years. The absolute effect on German employment
alone, in terms of persons employed, is as large as the effect on Dutch
unemployment (+ 12,000). If these six EC member countries take
the same fiscal measure simultaneously, the lever effect for the
Netherlands is relatively large. The impact of a tax cut on employment, as computed with the Atlas model, is then 2.5 times as big as in

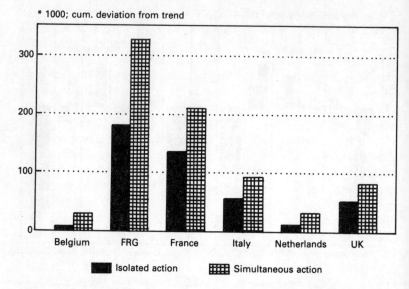

Figure 12.3 Reduction of taxes of 1 per cent of GDP in 6 EC countries: effects on employment with an isolated versus simultaneous action; results obtained with the Atlas model after 3 years

the event of an isolated action, that is to say + 32,000 persons (see Figure 12.3). For Belgium, too, the lever or simultaneity factor is large, namely 3.8. For the other countries it is:

West Germany 1.8 (1.2)   France   1.5 (1.4)
Italy   1.6 (1.2)   UK   1.6 (1.1)

The simultaneity factors in brackets are those computed with the aid of the comparable Oxford Economic Forecasting Model.

These are on average one-quarter point lower than the Atlas figures, which is mainly due to the fact that the OEF model, unlike the Atlas model, assumes flexible exchange rates and limited capital mobility, which results among other things in weaker foreign effects.

Loss of ability to act through self-constraint in the Community

European policy coordination: le défi américain[6]

We do not see the EC, or more particularly the EMS, as an *ad hoc* integration to regain national ability to act. This ability is rather oppressed by the negative European integration, the achieved market integration and the deficit of *communautaire* ability to act. The hallmark of European policy coordination is now precisely the pre-commitment *ex ante*. It is not only the loss of national macro-economic autonomy which is gradually pulling us into the European order. The point is far more to preserve the conscious commitment, which is a major cause of the loss of national autonomy, and not to endanger the *acquis*. A member state wishing to quit the Community today, whether it be large or small, would incur the suspicion that it wished to wipe itself off the world map. The American outlook on these things, and monetary coordination in particular, is fundamentally different, judging by many scientific analyses and political comments. The EMS is particular treated far too much in terms of the theory of games and partial analyses, as in 'Who should join and who should leave' (Melitz, 1986). As if there were no Treaty of Rome and the EC were a sort of 'summer alliance' instead of 'an ever closer union', as the preamble to the Rome Treaty strikingly expresses the crux of European unification.

Technical and political loss of autonomy: France 1981–3

France's macro-economic policies between 1981 and 1983 are a case in point. When the Mitterrand government took office in 1981, it launched an ambitious plan for economic stimulation, which was upset by EMS monetary policies, especially by the macro-economic policies of the then West Germany and the draining-away of French policy effects – read 'the extra impact on demand and employment' – to other countries (Sachs and Wyplosz, 1986). As a rule the French *retour* is explained by pointing to the 'external constraints' to which interdependent economies are liable. The result would then be an involuntary technical and economic loss of ability to act. This can at best be only a partial explanation of the French turnabout.

Albert and Ball said in their report (1983) that it was also true for France that these:

> policies for stimulating the economy by reflating demand, when pursued in isolation, have therefore been self-defeating. They have had the opposite effect to the one intended: instead of providing a boost to growth, the ultimate outcome was a net decline in growth.

Albert and Ball stressed that the two comparable French stimulation experiments of 1974 and 1982 underlined the harsh truth that in Europe even the 'big countries' must submit to external constraints as soon as they have stepped up their rate of growth.

This was true in the case of France which, after taking steps to expand consumption in 1981–1982 which enabled the growth rate to be increased by 0.2 % in 1981 to 1.8 in 1982, was obliged to adopt restrictive counter-measures equivalent to a reduction in growth of at least 3 to 4 % of GDP.

According to Albert and Ball, France, like the UK in 1973, assumed that the introduction of flexible exchange rates following the collapse of the Bretton Woods system in that year would offer a release from the external constraints – that is to say a protection against a substantial drop in the value of the currency. It was wrong, as was the UK, which quickly developed a balance of payments deficit exceeding the OECD average by 4 percentage points, and had to pay for a 1.5 point acceleration of growth in 1973 with a 1978 growth rate falling no less than 6 points short of the OECD average. A closer look at what happened in France over the 1981–3 period makes it clear that the abandoning of the isolated macro-economic action, besides the internal balances created, was in fact prompted by loss of national ability to act (Knoester, Kolodziejak and Muijzers, 1990, pp. 24–7). Analogously to what we have said earlier about the Netherlands, a distinction should be made as to the following components of this loss:

1. *Loss of autonomy in the technical economic field* through the increased openness and international interdependence of the economies, whereby the constraints of competitiveness, payments balance situation and/or the rate of exchange play a major role. Albert and Ball have made this quite clear.
2. *Loss of autonomy in the political economic field* because, in the event of isolated action, a national economy undergoes the constraints of economic policy commitments, such as that of an exchange-rate arrangement (the EMS) to ensure stability of exchange rates and prices. The French political attitude made it clear that, on joining the exchange-rate arrangement, France came to regard the commitment as indissolubly linked with membership of the EC.

12.4 COORDINATION OF MACRO-ECONOMIC AND MONETARY POLICIES AS A EUROPEAN CHALLENGE

Policy coordination; panacea or Pandora's box?

How do we go on from here with macro-economic coordination and monetary cohesion? Technically speaking, national states have lost a great deal of the macro-economic and monetary policy autonomy which national regulations and administration still assume to be present. For instance the promotion of adequate employment, social security of the population, distribution of wealth, the monetary system: all these things are listed in, for example, the Dutch Constitution as matters of government concern.[8] As we have explained, the loss of autonomy rests on two factors:

1. Increased international interdependence
2. The absorption of member states into the EC; to the extent the response to these two factors is international coordination of macro-economic and monetary policies, restoration of the national ability to act or creation of ability to act by the Community may occur, as we have already explained

The term 'to coordinate' is defined by the Oxford English Dictionary as 'to place or arrange [things] in proper position relatively to each other and to the system of which they form part: to bring into proper combined order as parts of a whole'. In international economic parlance the term is used with several different connotations. No wonder that to some coordination is a panacea, and to others Pandora's box, the source of all evils.[9] The confusion is compounded by the fact that American authors commonly speak of (international) policy coordination when referring to cooperation, whereas European authors sometimes use the term in the less important sense of 'exchange of information' or 'more or less free consultations', etc., and at other times with the weightier meaning of 'cooperation governed by rules' (Fieleke, 1988; Frankel, Goldstein and Masson, 1988; Schouten, 1986; Scharrer and Wessels, 1987). The vagueness of the term is a godsend to many politicians and policy-makers.

Coordination of macro-economic and monetary policies

Definition

The *communautaire* context may help to arrive at a more precise definition. The Rome Treaty already mentioned economic policy coordination as a goal, alongside convergence of the economic developments of the member states. These principles were developed by Council decisions, in particular Council decision 74/120/EEC of 18 February 1974, amended by decision 75/787/EEC of 18 December 1975. The Treaty terms macro-economic and exchange-rate policies 'matters of common interest' and calls for policy coordination in these fields. 'Coordination' relates to the choice of mutually reconcilable target values and the choice, size and timing of the fitting economic policy instruments. If in the domestic economy coordination means concerted use of various policy instruments (e.g., compatibility of fiscal and monetary policies), in the multi-country economy of the Community coordination demands that national policies take proper account of the policies and goals of other countries.

In the Community context, coordination is often mentioned alongside convergence and harmonisation. In this context, 'convergence' means reducing differences between national goals, such as reduction of differences between rates of inflation and possibly attainment of the most desirable feasible target level. The term 'harmonisation' is applied to the fixing of rules to lessen the scope for free policy-making and arrive at greater uniformity of economic structures. Steinherr (1987) rightly observed that 'convergence', 'harmonisation' and 'coordination'could supplement or be substituted for each other. He mentioned the EMS as an example of complementarity of harmonisation and coordination: a system of rules requiring policy coordination if it was to work properly. The present paper uses the term 'coordination' as a *pars pro toto*, covering – in accordance with policy practice – all forms of macro-economic and monetary alignment and cooperation, either through 'rules' or through 'discretion' (Kydland and Prescott, 1985). It does not, therefore, attempt to make a consistent distinction between coordination, on the one hand, and convergence and harmonisation on the other – or 'positive integration', to use the terminology of the Netherlands Scientific Council for Government Policies (WRR).

In the Community context, the eventual goal of policy coordination is to curb integration and coordination deficits and restore *communautaire* and national ability to act, with the ultimate goal of helping pave the way for a common market which should in turn make possible convergence of economic developments such as standard of living and inflation at the highest possible level of prosperity. A synthesis of the thinking of Cézanne (1987) and Kolodziejak (1988) yields a relationship between interdependence, autonomy, coordination and convergence as represented in Figure 12.4.

Increased interest in international policy coordination

The problems attaching to the prescription of macro-economic policy coordination are legion, as is evinced by the volume of literature on the subject. Szász (1986) gave a correct explanation of the sudden huge American interest in international policy coordination. Lack of policy coordination caused the collapse of the global system of fixed exchange rates – Bretton Woods – in 1973. Until 1985, the American authorities took the view that, when rates of exchange were flexible, every country should pursue exclusively its own internal objectives. According to Szász (1986), 'Good internal policies would then automatically engender a reasonable measure of exchange-rate stability. This view ruled out any furthergoing international policy coordination'. The Dutch Central Bank took a different view. It argued not only that flexible exchange rates would cause the fundamental striving for restoration of equilibrium to vanish, but also that the exchange-rate movements, once set in motion, would tend to be self-reinforcing and that an appreciation which had got out of control could not but lead to a strong urge towards protectionism (DNB, 1986). In September 1985, the American authorities changed their tack, precisely in response to the protectionist urge following the appreciation of the dollar.

If before they had believed that judging exchange rates was best left to the market, they then came round to the view, laid down in the Plaza agreement, that rates of exchange should reflect competitiveness better than they had done hitherto. External goals, and the consequent awareness of the need for international policy coordination, made a comeback.

From 1984 on, American and American-domiciled European economists have produced a large body of literature about coordination of macro-economic policies, using the term 'coordination' in the sense defined by Wallich (1984) as 'a significant modification of national policies in recognition of international economic interdependence'.[10]

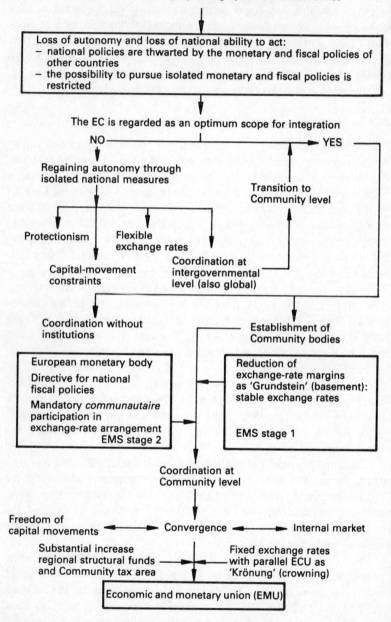

Figure 12.4   The relationship between independence, autonomy, coordination and convergence

The new approach adopted in the (so far rather theoretical) literature on coordination was the use, in addition to the usual optimalisation techniques, of the theory of games in international economics: coordination as a 'cooperative game',[11] for which the work of von Neumann and Morgenstern (1947) and Nash (1950: 1951), among others, served as a basis. Another important innovation was the combination of this approach with the use of empirical multi-country models, such as Interlink and MCM.[12] One of the pioneering studies in this area was that by Oudiz and Sachs (1984). Knoester and Kolodziejak (1988) used the same instruments for their analysis of *extracommunautaire* coordination – doing their computations with the Compact model of the European Commission – although from a more policy-oriented angle. Their analysis reflected an endeavour to make sure that their conclusions of a technical economic nature did not end in a policy vacuum.[13]

The various authors – producing in the aggregate an impressive effort – have tried to meet the greatest possible number of theoretical and practical objections in order to answer not only the question whether international coordination was feasible and necessary but also many related questions. Frankel and Rockett (1988) have even come to grips with the phenomenon of various countries or blocs using different models of the economic correlations and yet a different model turning out to be the 'correct' one. A comparison of the monetary and fiscal multipliers of multi-country models, some of which were also presented by Frankel (1987) and Knoester and Kolodziejak (1988), and those obtained through a special theme meeting of the Brookings Institution in 1986, makes clear that this is in fact an important point.

Looking over the literature on coordination, one cannot escape the conclusion that it certainly does not provide ready-made answers to the problems of *communautaire* macro-economic and monetary coordination. Among the far-reaching stylisation, extreme casuistry and political sterility – that is to say the abstraction of the *communautaire* context – which is found in a large part of the literature, it is hard to find any handholds of value for reality.[14] One is as it were caught up in the games model and confronted with the 'fallacy of misplaced concreteness' (Whitehead, 1964). The theoretical analyses in respect of coordination often reveal a deplorable lack of information applicable to economic policy. A point worth keeping in mind, however, is the finding that cooperative equilibria can be achieved, which are better in terms of a target function than the non-cooperative equilibrium, the Nash solution. This holds true also where different countries or regions have different target functions, as Knoester and Kolodziejak (1988) have shown.

Policy coordination in a communautaire and global framework

In the international coordination of macro-economic and monetary policies which is already taking place, a distinction should be made between global policy coordination and coordination in the Community context, including the EMS, although this is not, strictly speaking, a Community institution. Global coordination is taking place mainly between the 'Big Five' (G-5) or the 'Big Seven' (G-7), also between the USA, Japan and the former West Germany, and in various other international bodies such as the OECD.[15] In this coordination a small country like the Netherlands has little say, at any rate not as long as the EC is not taking part in such talks as a single bloc. Moreover, this policy coordination has so far been for the most part verbal, even though results have been achieved such as the halting of the dollar rise (by the Plaza agreement of 22 September 1985) and the slowing down of the dollar's fall (by the Louvre agreement of 22 February 1987).

The *intracommunautaire* macro-economic and monetary alignment should be seen as a precondition for a successful *extracommunautaire* alignment. Present imbalances – notably America's double deficit in the budget and the balance of trade – illustrate the importance of this. It is vital, moreover, for target zones and indicators to be agreed for the USA, Japanese and European currencies and macro-economic key variables, in accordance with the proposals put forward by Williamson (1985), Williamson and Miller (1987) and Kyriazis and Chryssanthou (1986) and others, once European monetary cooperation has been strengthened. A symptom of the feeble global coordination is the enhanced significance acquired by flexible exchange-rate regimes since the collapse of the Bretton Woods system.

Coordination of macro-economic and notably fiscal policies in the EC has not yet got very far, mainly because the member states keep clinging to their sovereignty in this area. Yet, as we have said before, it is doubtful whether the national governments are still able to make good their competence in this respect. Under the Convergence decision of 1974, the European Commission makes macro-economic policy recommendations to the member states in its economic report at least once a year, but these are not mandatory. The lack of macro-economic convergence and coordination is currently exerting a negative influence on monetary integration. In line with the so-called monetarist theory, the (semi-fixed) EMS parities have a certain convergent effect on macro-economic policies: monetary policy is to some extent laying the foundations for economic integration. De Nederlandsche Bank has in general emphasised rather the so-called *economistic* standpoint, saying that monetary integration is the result – or crown if you prefer – of macro-economic convergence. This is then mainly convergence of price movements towards a stable low level.[16] There is consensus in theory that economic and monetary integration must proceed side by side, so that the one may strengthen the other, which is called 'parallelism'. It is found in practice, however, that (for example) fiscal coordination is much more difficult to achieve than monetary coordination, because the fixing of budgets, taxes and deficits strikes at the heart of the national welfare states. Growing European market and financial integration will make more demands on fiscal policy coordination than the current coordination instruments are is capable of meeting.

12.5 POLICY COORDINATION THROUGH THE EMS AND BEYOND

The European Monetary System

The EMS has since 1980 become a major pillar of European macro-economic and monetary integration. Hence the EMS must also be the starting-point for the necessary strengthening of the European policy coordination for which European countries should strive. The EMS has its origin in a political initiative taken by the then German Federal Chancellor, Helmut Schmidt, and the French President, Valéry Giscard d'Estaing. The Bundesbank was not enthusiastic, to put it mildly. The western world's determination to fight inflation played a major part in the establishment of the EMS, as did also the persistent weakness of the US dollar (Hellman, 1979). The aim of the EMS is to create a zone of monetary stability. Its two chief goals are exchange-rate stability and price stability, although no direct instrument was created for the latter – internal stability. Underlying objectives are freedom of intra-Community payments and contributing to the whole process of European integration (Kleinheyer, 1987). The building-blocks of the EMS are the European currency unit (Ecu), the exchange-rates scheme with bilateral parity bands, the

Table 12.1   EMS realignments: bilateral central-rate changes as compared with stable currencies (blank spaces)

	BLF	DKR	FF	DM	IRL	LIR	NGL
24.09.79		–2.86		2.00			
30.11.79		–4.76					
23.03.81						–6.00	
05.10.81			–3.00	5.50		–3.00	5.50
22.02.82	–8.50	–3.00					
14.06.82			–5.75	4.25		–2.75	4.25
21.03.83*	1.50	2.50	–2.50	5.50	–3.50	–2.50	3.50
22.07.85**						–7.84	
07.04.86	1.00	1.00	–3.00	3.00			3.00
04.08.86					–8.00		
12.01.87	2.00			3.00			3.00
05.01.90						–3.70	

Notes: *   Realignments as officially presented.
           ** For presentational considerations' in the form of a -6% devaluation, with simultaneous revaluation of the other currencies by 2%.

reserve and intervention system, the Ecu deviation indicator, the credit and assistance mechanism and the European Fund for Monetary Cooperation (van Ypersele and Koeune, 1985; European Commission, 1979).

In its 10-year life and in 1989–90 especially, the EMS has done good work,[17] even if the initial years were marred by frequent and extensive realignments. Table 12.1 overviews the EMS realignments. Since the famous 1983 realignment, it has been comparatively quiet on the currency front, thanks in part to the falling rate of inflation on a global scale. The conclusions to be drawn from Figure 12.5 may well be that the EMS has had a disciplinary effect not only on external but also on internal stability. Owing to the greater stability of the German Mark and the Dutch guilder in particular, the other currencies have more or less continually depreciated against them. The depreciation of the other EMS currencies against the guilder and the German Mark has been only in nominal terms. In real terms, it is rather that the German Mark has depreciated (Table 12.2) and also the guilder (Knoester, 1986). This is an important issue in the expansion of the EMS in support of the *acquis*, of which more will be said Section 12.6.

Edison and Fisher (1989) tested whether there had been stable,

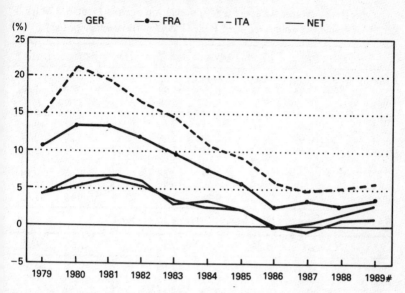

Figure 12.5 Consumer price indexes: annual growth for (West) Germany, France, Italy and the Netherlands

bilateral real exchange rates for the EMS in the 1980s. They found such stability – that is to say a true trend towards PPP in only a few cases. They confirmed the statistical correctness of the argument advanced by Giavazzi and Pagano (1986) that *real appreciation* by participants in the EMS exchange-rate mechanism with relatively high inflation rates was a characteristic of the EMS and helped to impose discipline on those countries. The implication of this view is that the realignments meet the inflation-rate differentials only in part, and that shifts occur in competitiveness. The burden of adjusting is imposed on the countries with relatively high inflation rates, which contributes to what is called in Eurospeak the *asymmetry* of the EMS. Edison and Fisher have furnished statistical proof that the likelihood of cointegration between exchange rates and prices during the EMS period has been smaller than during the preceding period.

The extension of macro-economic and monetary integration

This paper has considered three factors in favour of an extension of macro-economic and monetary integration in the EC context.

1. The macro-economic and monetary integration lag threatens the

Table 12.2   Nominal versus real appreciation against Deutsche Mark

A   *CIP growth as compared with West Germany (percentage points)*

	BEL	DEN	FRA	IRE	ITA	LUX	NET
1979	0.28	6.42	6.49	9.08	10.73	0.38	0.05
1980	1.24	5.98	8.00	12.83	15.84	0.90	1.12
1981	1.30	5.40	7.10	14.10	13.20	1.80	0.40
1982	3.47	4.85	6.55	11.84	11.22	4.08	0.64
1983	4.39	3.60	6.31	7.19	11.28	5.32	−0.47
1984	3.93	3.89	4.99	6.18	8.42	3.26	0.85
1985	2.65	2.53	3.56	3.24	6.97	1.86	0.05
1986	1.53	3.87	2.78	4.06	6.10	0.53	0.33
1987	1.30	3.77	3.09	2.88	4.50	−0.46	−0.98
1988	−0.18	3.16	1.29	0.78	3.67	0.23	−0.64
1989*	0.31	2.03	0.73	1.35	2.99	0.58	−1.66

B   *Nominal appreciation (+) * against Deutsche Mark (%) of:*

	BF	DKR	FF	IRL	LIR	LF	NGL
1979	−1.98	−4.35	−3.20	−2.66	−6.79	−1.98	−1.58
1980	−0.57	−7.43	−0.15	−0.32	−3.78	−0.57	−0.06
1981	−2.08	−1.63	−3.33	−2.33	−6.33	−2.08	−0.94
1982	−12.75	−8.21	−11.21	−5.55	−9.75	−12.75	0.33
1983	−5.98	−4.13	−9.26	−7.65	−6.30	−5.98	−1.56
1984	−1.37	−1.58	−2.80	−2.93	−3.65	−1.37	−0.86
1985	0.67	1.11	0.61	1.40	−4.81	0.67	−0.06
1986	−1.96	−3.40	−4.31	−7.14	−5.53	−1.96	−0.01
1987	−0.96	−2.09	−4.62	−8.18	−4.79	−0.96	0.11
1988	−0.79	−0.72	−1.41	0.20	−2.71	−0.79	0.13
1989	−0.11	−1.42	−0.05	−0.46	1.55	−0.11	−0.22

C   *Real appreciation (+) against Deutsche Mark (%) (= A + B) of:*

	BF	DKR	FF	IRL	LIR	LF	NGL
1979	−1.70	2.07	3.30	6.42	3.94	−1.60	−1.53
1980	0.67	−1.44	7.85	12.51	12.06	0.33	1.19
1981	−0.78	3.77	3.77	11.77	6.87	−0.28	−0.54
1982	−9.28	−3.36	−4.66	6.30	1.47	−8.67	0.97
1983	−1.59	−0.52	−2.95	−0.46	4.98	−0.65	−2.03
1984	2.56	2.31	2.19	3.25	4.77	1.89	−0.01
1985	3.32	3.63	4.18	4.64	2.16	2.53	−0.01
1986	−0.43	0.47	−1.53	−3.08	0.57	−1.43	0.32
1987	0.34	1.68	−1.54	−5.30	−0.29	−1.42	−0.87
1988	−0.97	2.44	−0.12	0.98	0.96	−0.56	−0.51
1989*	0.20	0.61	0.68	0.89	4.54	0.47	−1.88

Notes: *   Figure 1989, Italy, on basis of QII.
          ** Calculated on the basis of $ rates (annual averages).
Source: Calculations on IMF basis, *International Financial Statistics*.

acquis; the second stage of the EMS had been scheduled to commence as early as 1981

2. Growing capital mobility, stable rates of exchange, trade integration and involvement in the Community are causing a loss of national ability to act, which must be made good at the Community level

3. National European economies cannot contribute to the necessary coordination of the world economy on its own but only through the EC

The EMS is the appropriate starting-point for such an extension. However, the strengthening of the EMS through the *'petite réforme'* of September 1987 – the Basel-Nyborg package – was no adequate response to the macro-economic and monetary integration challenges mentioned in the present paper.[18] It seems to us that the German monetary authorities have meanwhile changed their policies:[19] they are waiting for political decisions, and seem to be coming round to the more monetarist way of thinking to the chairman of the Delors committee. The Germans have taken a close look at their situation and understood that they cannot just go on playing the part of a *de facto* key-currency country, as they have so far been able and obliged to do. Germany will have less political scope for this role in the future, since its economy is too small in relation to the whole Community and the world economy. For Germany, too, coordination is becoming more important as the effectiveness of its monetary policies diminishes further under the influence of more fixed exchange rates and growing capital mobility. EMU, however, is not attainable in one big leap, but has to be achieved step by step. What is needed is to compile a simultaneous package – in line with the present market-integration situation – to serve as an intermediate step towards a European economic and monetary union.

1. As for monetary policies, the important thing is to reach agreement on a *communautaire* inflation target and potential production growth at the European level, but within a global monetary objective. From this results a money-volume growth rule for the EMS as a whole to the effect that money-volume growth must equal the sum of the desired price rises and the desired real production growth ($\dot{m} = \dot{p} + \dot{y}$). To this must be added individual domestic credit targets on condition of non-sterilisation of interventions and a nominal income target for each

participant. Demand, however, must be steered only in a coordinated *communautaire* context. Whenever the set inflation target is exceeded, monetary policies must be tightened in a coordinated manner.

2. As indicated in Figure 12.6, institutionalisation of stage two of the EMS must contain the following central elements:

   (a) mandatory participation of all member states in the exchange-rate arrangement
   (b) creation of a European monetary body to serve intra- and extra-*communautaire* coordination
   (c) a directive for national fiscal policies

3. The UK, Portugal and Greece will have to be persuaded to take part in the exchange-rate arrangement in the same way as the other EC member states are already doing. At the five-yearly EMS evaluation in September 1989, Spain saw fit to decide to join, whereas Italy said it would be able to agree to join with a 2.25 per cent band instead of the 6 per cent one. Membership of the Community and full participation in the EMS should be linked by 1993 at the latest. Article 52 of the European Parliament's draft European Union treaty provides for such a link under the EC Treaty. Like other parliaments, both chambers of the Dutch parliament signified approval in resolutions passed on 7 and 29 May 1985. The Dooge Committee (Spaak II) report termed it a necessary strengthening of the EMS, which notion prompted inclusion of Article 20 in the Single European Act. The procedure for the link in the Treaty has thus been included in Article 102A (2) of the new EC Treaty.

4. Article 102A says, moreover, that a European monetary body must be created to take the place of the Committee of Governors of the Central Banks, which was set up by the Council decision of 8 May 1964 (64/300/EEC). The existing committee must develop into a Community bank system. A new *ad hoc* committee should be set up before 1993 as a follow-up to the Delors committee, to prepare the statute of a European – i.e., *communautaire* – Central Bank. The transfer of national monetary powers will concern mainly the instruments used to control money volume, interest rates and rates of exchange. Its institutionalisation should in the first instance fulfil the following conditions:

   (a) This European monetary body can best be shaped along the lines of the US Federal Reserve System (see Figure 12.6). We

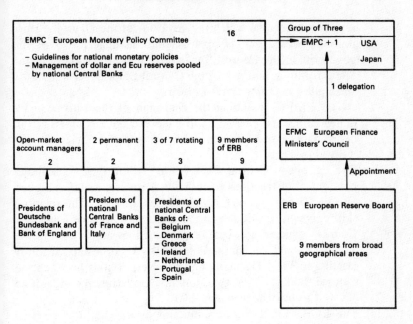

Figure 12.6 A plan for an ECBS

propose a European Reserve Board, consisting of nine members, to be appointed by the European Finance Ministers' Council (EFMC), on nominations by the European Commission, for an eight-year term, observing a certain geographical spread. The Commission's nomination of the – re-eligible – President of the Board will be binding. The Board will take its decisions by majority. There will moreover be a European Monetary Policy Committee (EMPC) to issue directives for national monetary policies as mentioned in 1 above. The Policy Committee will moreover administer the pool of dollar and Ecu reserves fed by the national Central Banks. This will guarantee further growth of the Ecu in the 'optional stage'.

The EMPC will be composed of the nine members of the Board, the governors of the Central Banks of France, West Germany, Italy and the UK (of which the Deutsche Bundesbank and/or the Bank of England could act as 'open-account manager' analogously to the Federal Reserve Bank of New York), and three of the governors of the Central Banks of the seven other member states in turn. Thygesen's proposal differs from this approach. In his view the Board would consist of seven members, of which the governor of the Deutsche Bundesbank would act as open-account manager, two of the governors of the Central Banks of France, Italy, the UK and Spain rotating, and two of the Central Bank governors of the six smaller member states in turn.

The EMPC, including the chairman of the European Finance Ministers' Council, will have exclusive competence to coordinate *extracommunautaire* monetary policies in the 'Group of Three'.

(b) The European Central Bank (ECB) would have to be independent of instructions by individual governments, as argued also by Eizenga in his farewell address in 1987. The relationship between the ECB and the European Finance Ministers' Council, which might best be governed by a provision in the Treaty, should be comparable to the relationship currently existing in West Germany and the Netherlands between the Central Banks and the governments. Governments will not be allowed to borrow from the ECB.

(c) The ECB should aim at simultaneous internal and external stability.

5. Progress with monetary integration can have lasting effect only if a better fiscal policy coordination is established. This goes in particular for the size and manner of funding of the national budget deficits.

6. National current expenditure budget deficits should be gradually built down to zero, at the latest by the time when the 2.25 per cent bands are reduced to close to zero and the Community's public spending, notably on regional redistribution, has been raised from about 1 per cent to at least 6 per cent of the total EC product, in accordance with the proposals made in the MacDougall report (MacDougall *et al.*, 1977). The deadline recommended for this in the above step-by-step plan is 1997.

12.6   SUMMARY AND CONCLUSIONS

EC countries have lost a great deal of macro-economic and monetary autonomy. To the extent that this is a consequence of their membership of the EC, they have consciously opted for this in the past (Section 12.2). Since the ensuing loss of ability to act has not been

made good at the Community level, deficits in the ability to act have
arisen. Coordination may be a remedy, provided it takes place in the
Community context. This means that further steps need be taken,
especially in the EMS context, towards macro-economic and monetary integration. This is not an aim in itself but serves to support
integration in other areas where it is assuming new dynamics, in
particular through the liberalisation of the capital market as of 1990
and of the goods and services markets after 1992 (Section 12.3). In
the meantime, managers in the EC consider monetary cooperation to
be an area in which progress is urgent in order to safeguard what has
already been achieved by means of the integration process, and is
scheduled to be achieved in 1992. This means that coordination of
macro-economic and monetary policies is needed (Section 12.4). The
step-by-step strengthening of the macro-economic and monetary
integration should consist of a Community directive imposing low
ceilings on the national budget deficits. Furthermore, a European
monetary body must be set up, which will gradually assume Central
Bank functions under a federal system after the example of the US
Federal Reserve System (Section 12.5). Moreover, membership of
the EC cannot and must not be divorced from participation in the
exchange-rate arrangement. This also means that no country should
join the arrangement without being an EC member state. This
applies, for instance, to Norway and the Alpine States. National
states should be prepared to give up their traditional instruments in
given areas – in particular, monetary policy and to a less but not
insignificant extent fiscal policy – to surrender a – mainly specious –
macro-economic and monetary autonomy in exchange for policies
shared with other European countries. In today's practical situation,
individual European countries do not have an alternative. In this
respect, too, they are gradually being pulled into the European
order.

The main conclusions of this paper can be summarised as follows:

- The present situation of European integration can be characterised as 'limping integration', meaning that to date the positive
integration (i.e., harmonisation of the policies of national governments) has lagged behind the negative integration (i.e., abolition
of intra-European constraints). Progress towards a full economic
and monetary union requires as a first step the strengthening of
cooperation of the national governments' macro-economic and
monetary policies.

- Such a strengthening of policy coordination should in the first place consist of a strengthening and extension of the EMS.
- National authorities should see the macro-economic and monetary development of their countries primarily in the EC context. National ability to act in these areas has become *de facto* restricted, and will be restricted further by the new dynamics of European integration. The subsidiarity principle should be the starting-point for the relationship between the Community and the national states.
- The Fleming–Mundell analysis makes clear that there is little scope for autonomous national monetary policies in most European countries, given the EMS exchange rates, which can be termed 'fixed' in an operational sense, and capital mobility. The ineffectiveness of monetary policies or the loss of monetary autonomy for member states will be strengthened, but not caused, by the free movement of capital. Yet capital mobility does strengthen fiscal policies, provided that they are coordinated.
- The vitally important internal market can emerge and be maintained only if steps are taken in the direction of a European monetary and economic union. Such steps cannot wait until after 1992. Completion of the internal market is not only a matter of market integration but also of supportive macro-economic and monetary policy integration. Inadequate coordination of these policies will threaten the internal market and make its drawbacks outweigh its benefits.
- Various surveys have shown that European and national industries desire substantial progress towards monetary integration. Industry (and, in consequence, the citizens) is the main victim of integration and coordination deficits in the area of macro-economic and monetary unification. A single European currency (the Ecu) is high on the list of priorities of European and national industries, and for the citizens it rates just below a European environmental policy.
- Growing European market and financial integration will make bigger demands on fiscal policy coordination than can be met by the existing coordination instruments.
- In the monetary policy area, a common inflation target and corresponding national directives should be prepared. This will entail a transfer of national powers to control money volume, rates of interest and exchange rates, to Community bodies.
- The institutional shaping of these bodies might be on the lines of

the US Federal Reserve System. The present Committee of Governors of the Central Banks will develop into a Community bank system. Such a European Central Bank should aim at internal and external stability. It should carry out its duties independently of instructions by individual governments. The relationship between the ECB and the Council of Ministers might follow the example of the Dutch situation. In addition, a European Reserve Board, appointed by the Council of Ministers, should be part of the monetary policy body responsible for the directives relative to national policies, as mentioned under 5 above (p. 274).

- Preparation of a European fiscal policy directive binding the national government budget deficits structurally is conceivable. It should be possible for national governments to depart from this directive briefly or for a longer time in the event of extraordinary circumstances, but such exemptions should be restricted to a minimum. Formulation of a European directive for the size of national budget deficits should take place on the basis of financial and economic conditions permitting a sound and stable development of the European economy. It seems a reasonable policy to aim at the classical rule for budget deficits – a zero deficit for current government expenditures – and to allow deficits only for the government capital account (i.e., for government investments).

- In considering these recommendations for macro-economic and monetary coordination, it should be borne in mind that European market integration will meanwhile ease the demands made upon policy integration in the Community. The national governments will have to consider that, in pursuing investment, economic-growth and employment targets, they will have to do their wages and prices fixing in a European context. A supply-strengthening policy aimed also at removing labour-market rigidities is of growing importance in this context for the 'harmonious development of economic activities' mentioned in Article 2 of the Rome Treaty.

- It is preferable for the desired progress towards a full economic and monetary union to be simultaneous in all twelve member states, because of its correlation with the common market. A link between EC membership and participation in the EMS exchange-rate arrangement is desirable. On past experience, political contrasts may, however, appreciably slow down further progress towards European integration. In that case, it deserves serious recommendation, in the interest of the further integration progress and conservation of the *acquis*, to opt for a two-speed Europe in the form of what Delors called '*géometrie variable*' rather than acquiescing in minimum progress or even stagnation.

Notes

1. On policy mania and policy resistance see, for example, Crombag (1986); Van Gunsteren (1976); Lubbers (1984); Pen (1983).
2. See, for example, *Rapport d'Information au nom de la délégation du Sénat pour la planification (1) sur les résultats de projections macroéconomiques*, pp. 21–9.
3. Subsidiarity is a key conception of Roman Catholic social teaching, first mentioned as a principle in Pius XI, Encyclical Letter Quadrogesimo Anno, *A.A.S. 23*, 1931, pp. 177–228.
4. See the list of references in Knoester and Kolodziejak (1988).
5. R.N. Cooper, in Jones and Kenen (1984), pp. 1229–30.
6. Cf. Servan-Schreiber (1967).
7. The growth figure published by the OECD is 0.5 per cent.
8. Art. 19, par 1 Constitution or Coinage Act 1948, the Bank Law 1948, the Credit System Control Law (1978), the Law concerning the exchange rate of the guilder (1978).
9. A negative position towards coordination is held by, for example, Vaubel (1983; 1986) and Feldstein (1987).
10. See for a summary and evaluation of this literature, for instance, Artis and Ostry (1986); Fisher (1987); Kenen (1987); Cooper (1987); Fieleke (1988); Frankel, Goldstein and Masson (1988); Horne and Masson (1988).
11. Von Neumann and Morgenstern (1947); Nash (1950; 1951); McMillan (1986).
12. Bryant and Portes (1987); Frankel (1987); Kolodziejak (1988).
13. See Frey (1981); Borner (1981); Bonus (1982).
14. We consider, for instance, Giavazzi and Pagano (1986) and Edison and Tryon (1988) as being relevant for policy questions.
15. The Big Five consist of the USA, Japan, West Germany, France and the UK. The Big Seven include Italy and Canada as well.
16. For the important discussion between 'economists' and 'monetarists' with respect to the building of a economic and monetary union, see, for instance, van Esch (1975) and the Werner report of 1970.
17. Guitian (1988); Giavazzi, Micossi and Miller (1988); Schlüter (1989); Stoltenberg (1989); De Cecco and Giovannini (1989).
18. See also Sénat (1987), pp. 18–19.
19. See, for instance, K.-O. Pöhl in *Börsenzeitung* (10 March 1989).

References

Albert, M. and Ball, R.J. (1983) *Towards European Economic Recovery in the 1980s*, report presented to the European Parliament, European Parliament Working Documents 1983–4.

Artis, M. and Ostry, S. (1986) *International Economic Policy Coordination*, Chatham House Papers, no. 30, Royal Institute of International Affairs, London.

Association for the Monetary Union of Europe (1988) *European Business and the Ecu, Results of a survey carried out by Faits et Opinions among 1036 business leaders in the European Community*, with the help of the Ecu Banking Association and the European Commission, Paris.

Ball, R.J. (1988) *After Albert and Ball; The progress of the European Community*, London Business School Discussion Paper, no. 29–88, London.

Bonus, H. (1982) 'Information und Emotion in der Politikberatung – Zur politischen Umsetzung eines wirtschaftstheoretischen Konzepts', *Zeitschrift für die gesamte Staatswissenschaft*, 138.

Borner, S. (1981) 'Die wissenschaftliche Beratung der Politik', in Timmerman, M. (ed.), *Nationalökonomie morgen*, Stuttgart, Verlag W. Kohlhamme.

Bryant, R. and Portes, R. (1987) *Global Macroeconomic Policy Conflict and Cooperation*, London, and Macmillan.

Cecco, M. de and Giovannini, A. (eds) (1989), *A European Central Bank? Perspectives on Monetary Unification after the Years of the EMS*, Cambridge, Cambridge University Press.

Cecchini, P. (1988) *The European Challenge 1992. The Benefits of a Single Market*, Brussels, EC.

Centraal Planbureau (1987) *The FREIA-KOMPAS model for The Netherlands, a quarterly model for the short and medium term* (P. van den Berg, G. Gelauff and V.R. Okker) Occasional Paper, no. 39, The Hague.

Cézanne, W. (1987) '*Begriffe und Optionen der wirtschaftspolitischen Koordinierung in der EG*', in Scharrer, H.-E. and Wessels, W. *(eds), Stabilität durch das EWS. Koordination und Konvergenz im Europäischen Währungssystem*, Bonn, Europe Union Verlag.

Chouraqui, J.C., Driscoll, M. and Strauss-Kahn, M.-O. (1988), *The effects of Monetary Policy on the Real Sector; An overview of empirical evidence for selected OECD economies*, OECD Department of Economics and Statistics, Working Papers, no. 51, Paris, OECD.

Commission of the European Communities (1979) 'The European Monetary System – Commentary, Documents', *European Economy*, no. 3. (July).

Commissie van de Europese Gemeenschappen (1985) *De voltooüng van de interne markt: het Witboek van de Commissie aan de Europese Raad*, COM (85) 310 def., Luxembourg.

Commissie van de Europese Gemeenschappen (1988) *Voltooüng van de interne markt: een ruimte zonder binnengrenzen*, Verslag over de voortgang van de werkzaamheden overeenkomstig artikel 8B van het verdrag, COM (88) 650 def. (Brussels, 17 November).

Committee for the study of Economic and Monetary Union (Delors committee) (1989) *Report on Economic and Monetary Union in the European Community*, (April).

Cooper, R. (1987) *International Economic Cooperation. Is it desirable? Is it likely?*, Lecture presented at the International Monetary Fund, N.J..

Crombag, H. (1986) 'De eeuw van het beleid', *Intermediair*, no. 22.

De Nederlandsche Bank (DNB) (1968), *Jaarverslag 1968*, Rotterdam International Müller NY.

Edison, H. and Fisher, E. (1989), *A long-run view of the European Monetary System*, Board of Governors of the Federal Reserve System, International Finance Discussion Paper, no. 339, Washington, D.C.

Edison, H. and Tryon, R. (1988) 'An empirical analysis of policy coordination in the United States, Japan and Europe', in Motamen, H. (ed.), *Economic Modelling in the OECD Countries*, London and New York, Chafman & Hall.

Esch, J. van (1975) *Economische en Monetaire Unie*, Deventer, Kluwer.

European Commission (1979) The European Monetary System – Commentor, Documents', *European Economy*, N.J. (July).

Europees Parlement (1984) *Ontwerp tot Verdrag tot oprichting van de Europese Unie*, Luxembourg.

Feldstein, M. (1987) *Rethinking International Economic Coordination*: A Lecture on the Occasion of the fiftieth anniversary of Nuffield College, Oxford.

Fieleke, N. (1988) 'Economic Interdependence between Nations: Reason for Policy Coordination?', *New England Economic Review* (May–June).

Fisher, S. (1987) *International Macroeconomic Policy Coordination*, NBER Working Paper, no. 2224, Cambridge, Mass.

Frankel, J. (1987) *Obstacles to International Macroeconomic Policy Coordination*, IMF Working Paper, WP/87/29, Washington, D.C.

Frankel, J. and Rockett, K. (1988) 'International Macroeconomic Policy Coordination When Policymakers Do Not Agree On The True Model'; *American Economic Review*, vol. 78, no. 3 (4 June).

Frankel, J., Goldstein, M. and Masson, P. (1988) *International Coordination of Economic Policies: Scope, Methods, and Effects*, IMF Working Paper, WP/88/53, Washington, D.C.

Frey, B. (1981) *Theorie demokratischer Wirtschaftspolitik*, Munich, Franz Wotlen.

Giavazzi, F. and Pagano, M. (1986) *The Advantage of Tying One's Hands: EMS Discipline and Central Bank Credibility*, CEPR Discussion Paper, no. 135, London, CEPR.

Giavazzi, F., Micossi, S. and Miller, M. (eds) (1988) *The European Monetary System*, Cambridge, Cambridge University Press.

Gros, D. and Thygesen, N. (1988) *The EMS. Achievements, current issues and directions for the future*, CEPS, no. 35, London, CEPS.

Guitian, M. (1988) *The European Monetary System: A Balance Between Rules and Discretion*, Part I of 'Policy Coordination in the European Monetary System', IMF Occasional Paper, no. 61, Washington, D.C.

Haavelmo, T. (1945) 'Multiplier effects of a balanced budget', *Econometrica*, 13.

Hellman, R. (1979) *Das Europäische Währungssystem*, Baden-Baden, Nomes Verlagsgesellschaft.
Horne, J. and Masson, P. (1988), *Scope and Limits of International Economic Cooperation and Policy coordination*, IMF Staff Papers, vol. 35, Noth-Hillun.
Jones, R.W. and Kenen, P.B. (1984) *Handbook of International Economics*, Amsterdam and New York.
Kenen, P. (1987) *Exchange Rates and Policy Coordination*, Brookings Discussion Papers, no. 61, The Brookings Institution, Washington, D.C.
Ketellapper, R.H. and Osinga E. (1981) 'De balanced budget multiplier in macro-economische modellen, *Maandschrift Economie*, jaargang 45, no. 9.
Kleinheyer, N. (1987) *Die Weiterentwicklung des Europäischen Währungssystems*, Ueberlegungen zur stabilitätsorientierten Ausgestaltung der 'Zweiten Stufe', Berlin, Durke & Humbodlt.
Knoester, A. (1983) 'Stagnation and the Inverted Haavelmo Effect: Some International Evidence', *De Economist*, vol. 131, no. 4.
Knoester, A. (1986) 'Wisselkoersen en economische politiek' (Exchange Rates and Economic Policy), in *Wisselkoersen in en veranderende wereld* (Exchange rates in a changing world). Preliminary report for the Royal Dutch Economic Association, Leiden and Antwerp, H.E. Stenfert Kroese.
Knoester, A. (1988a) 'Supply-side Policies in four OECD Countries', in Motamen, H. (ed.), *Economic Modelling in the OECD Countries*, London and New York, Chohmu & Hall,.
Knoester, A. (1988b) 'The Haavelmo Effect Revisited', *Finnish Economic Papers*, vol. 1, no. 1 (Spring).
Knoester, A. (1989) *Economische politiek in Nederland*, Leiden/Antwerp. H.E. Stenfeit Kroese.
Knoester, A. and Kolodziejak, A. (1988) *Economic Growth in Europe, Japan, and the United States: Policy options for the 1990s*, Research Memorandum 8804, Katholieke Universiteit Nijmegen.
Knoester, A., Kolodziejak, and Muijzers, A. (1990) *Economic Policy and European integration*, paper presented at the 'Exchange Rate Regimes and Currency Unions' conference of the Confederation of European Economic Associations, Deutsche Bundesbank, Frankfurt/Main (22–24 February).
Kolodziejak, A.M.M. (1986) *Policy-mania and policy-resistance in economics. Preparing a model for economic policy of the European Community*, Luxembourg (mimeo).
Kolodziejak, A.M.M. (1988) *Meerlandenmodellen met betrekking tot de Europese Gemeenschap*, Katholieke Universiteit Nijmegen.
Krugman, P. (1985) 'Economic integration in Europe: some conceptual issues', in *Efficiency, stability and equity. A strategy for the evolution of the economic system of the European Community*, a report by T. Padoa-Schioppa, European Perspectives Series, Brussels.
Kydland, F.E. and Prescott, E.C. (1985) 'Rules rather than discretion: The inconsistency of optimal plans', *Journal of Political Economy*,

Kyriazis, N. and Chryssanthou, N. (1986) *US-EC Monetary Relations'*; Secretariat of the European Parliament, Directorate General for Research, Economic Series, no. 8, Luxembourg.

Lubbers, R. (1984) *Vermeende beleidsresistentie en 'scheppende ontwikkeling'*; Lezing bij gelegenheid van de opening van het Academisch Jaar en de start van de Economische Faculteit aan de Rijksuniversiteit Limburg (4 September 1984).

MacDougall, G.D.A. *et al.* (1977) *Report of the Study Group on the Role of Public Finance in European Integration*, CEC, Economics and Finance Series, vol. 1, Brussels.

McMillan, J. (1986) *Game Theory in International Economics; Fundamentals of pure and applied economics*, vol. 1, International trade section, Chur., Harvard.

Melitz, J. (1986) *The prospect of a depreciating dollar and possible tension inside the EMS*, Board of Governors of the Federal Reserve System, International Finance Discussion Papers, no. 279, Washington, D.C.

Muijzers, A. (1989) *Het EMS en de Interne Markt. Over symmetrie van monetair beleid en de Europese integratie*, Nijmeegse Studies, no. 14, Katholieke Universiteit Nijmegen.

Nash, J. (1950) 'The bargaining problem', *Econometrica*, 18.

Nash, J. (1951) 'Non-cooperative games', *Annals of Mathematics*, 54.

OECD (1987) 'Statistiques Rétrospectives 1960–1985', *Perspectives économiques de l'OCDE*, Paris, OECD.

Oudiz, G. and Sachs, J. (1984) 'Macroeconomic Policy Coordination among the Industrial Countries', *Brookings Papers on Economic Activity*, 1, The Brookings Institution, Washington, D.C.

Padoa-Schioppa, T. (1985) *Money, Economic Policy and Europe*, European Perspectives Series of the Commission of the European Communities, Brussels.

Padoa-Schioppa, T. *et al.* (1987) *Efficiency, Stability and Equity, A Strategy for the Evolution of the Economic system of the European Community*, Oxford, Blackwell.

Pen, J. (1983) 'De rechten van de homo politicus en de plichten van de wetenschap', in Maks, A.H. and Wester, E. (eds), *Met het oog op de werkelijkheid*, Leiden and Antwerp, H.E. Sterfeit Kroesa.

Pöhl, K.-O. (1988) 'Ein europäisches Notenbanksystem ist nur föderalistisch strukturiert vorstellbar', *Handelsblatt Wirtschafts- und Finanzzeitung*, 30–31 December 1988, Düsseldorf and Frankfurt.

Pöhl, K.-O. (1989) 'Vom Währungssystem zur Währungsunion', *Börsenzeitung*, 10 March 1989.

Rapport d'Information fait au nom de la Délégation du Sénat pour la planification (1) sur les résultats de projections macroéconomiques, par Bernard Barbier, Sénateur, Président de la délégation, no. 39, Sénat, première session ordinaire de 1988–1989.

Rapport d'Information fait au nom de la Mission d'Information (1) désignée par la Commission des Affairs Economiques et du Plan (2) chargée d'étudier les conséquences pour l'économie française de l'achèvement du marché interieur européen en 1992, par Jean François-Poncet et Bernard

Barbier, Sénateurs, no. 59, Sénat, première session ordinaire de 1988–1989.

Sachs, J. and Wyplosz, C. (1986) 'The Economic Consequences of President Mitterrand', *Economic Policy*, 2 April.

Scharrer, H.-E. and Wessels, W. (1983) 'Eine Zukunft für das EWS? Optionen künftiger Währungspolitik der Gemeinschaft', in Scharrer, H.-E. and Wessels, W. (eds), *Das Europäische Währungssystem. Bilanz und Perspektive eines Experiments*, Bonn, Europa-Asia Verlag.

Schlüter, P.-W. (1989) *10 Jahre Europäisches Währungssystem*, Deutsche Bundesbank, Heft 108, Frankfurt.

Schouten, D. (1986) *Het wankele evenwicht in de economie (Coordination versus fragmentation of national and international economic policies)*, Leiden and Antwerp.

Sénat (1987), Délégation Parlementaire pour les Communautés Européennes no. 182/87, *La libération des mouvements de capitaux et l'intégration financière de la Communauté Européenne*, Rapport par Guy Cabanel, Sénateur, Paris (21 October).

Scharrer, H.-E. and Wessels, W. (eds) (1987) *Stabilität durch das EWS? Koordination und Konvergenz im Europäischen Währungssystem*, Servan-Schreiber, J.J. (1967) *Le déti americain*, Paris, Bonn, Aithème Fayars.

Steinherr, A. (1987) 'Nutzen und Grenzen einer Koordinierung der Wirtschaftspolitik im EWS', in H.-E. Scharrer, and W. Wessels, (eds) *Stabilität durch das EWS? Koordination und Konvergenz im Europäischen Währungssystem*, Bonn, Aithème Fayars.

Stoltenberg, G. (1989) Zehn Jahre Europäisches Währungssystem – Bilanz einer erfolgreichen Zusammenarbeit, *Die Welt*, 13 March.

Szász, A. (1986) 'Internationale beleidscoördinatie', Voordracht ter gelegenheid van het 50-jarig bestaan van Beleggingsmaatschappij OBAM N.V., Amsterdam (31 October), zoals weergegeven in De Nederlandsche Bank, *Kwartaalberichten* 1986/3.

Van Gunsteren, (1976) *The Quest for Culture*, Lava, Wiley.

Vaubel, R. (1983) 'Coordination or Competition Among National Macroeconomic Policies?', in Machlup, F. *et al.* (eds), *Reflections on a Troubled World Economy* London, Macmillan.

Vaubel, R. (1986) *Internationale coördinatie van beleid*, Rotterdamse Monetaire Studies.

Von Neumann, J. and Morgenstern, O. (1947) *The Theory of Games and Economic Behaviour*, Princeton, Princeton University Press.

Wallich, H. (1984) 'Institutional Cooperation in the World Economy', in Freukel, J. and Musson, H. (eds), *The World Economic System: Performance and Prospects*, Wert Feit, Conn., Greenwood.

Werner Report (1970) Verslag aan de Raad en aan de Commissie van 8 oktober 1970 betreffende de verwezenlijking in etappes van de Economische en Monetaire Unie in de Gemeenschap, Publicatieblad van de Europese Gemeenschappen, no. C 136/1.

Wetenschappelijke Raad voor het Regeringsbeleid (1986) *De onvoltooide Europese integratie*, rapport no. 28, The Hague.

Whitehead, A. (1964) *Science and the Modern World*, New York, Capricorn.

Williamson, J. (1985) *The Exchange Rate System*, Institute for International Economics, Policy Analyses in International Economics, no. 51, Washington, D.C.

Williamson, J. (1987) *Options for Improving the International Coordination of Economic Policies*, Marcus Wallenberg Papers on International Finance, International Law Institute, Georgetown University, Washington, D.C.

Williamson, J. and Miller, M. (1987) *Targets and Indicators: A Blueprint for the International Coordination of Economic Policy*, Institute for International Economics, Policy Analyses in International Economics, 22, Washington, D.C.

Ypersele, J. van and Koeune, J.-C. (1985) *The European Monetary System; Origins, Operations and Outlook*, European Perspective Series, Luxembourg.

Zijlstra, J. (1966) *Economische politiek en concurrentieproblematiek*, Serie 'Concurrentie' no. 2, Brussels.

Discussion

Hans-Werner Sinn

This paper is a revised and improved version of that presented at the Conference. The new version takes much of the discussant's criticism into account; basically, it is a plea for policy coordination and a more speedy development of the European monetary system.

I would like to make two comments at this stage of the discussion.

The first concerns the reason for policy coordination. Knoester, Kolodziejak and Muijzers point to the fact that significant fractions of Keynesian multiplier effects spill over to other countries when the country carrying out the policy is small – as, for example, the Netherlands. Citing the example of the Mitterrand experiment and the results of a number of macro-economic models, they make the case for a coordination of fiscal policies to avoid the spillovers and to internalise the presumably beneficial effects of multiplier policies.

While I do not deny the validity of this argument, I find allocative reasons for policy coordination between the members of the EC much more important. Unlike short-run Keynesian policies, allocative policies can have a much more profound and lasting effect on people's well-being, and indeed unbridled competition of economic policies may be very harmful. There are many examples for this.

- *Environmental regulation* In the presence of international spillovers of waste and pollution via commonly-owned media such as air and water, it is in a single country's interest to impose less rigid pollution controls than is efficient from the viewpoint of all countries together.
- *Quality Standards* When there is asymmetric information on product quality (as in the Akerlof model), countries have an incentive overly to relax their quality and safety regulations, for this reduces their industries' production costs without deterring ignorant foreign consumers.
- *Income redistribution* When factors of production (or simply legal tax bases) can easily be moved across national boundaries, competitive governments cannot carry out redistributive tax policies. Each government has an incentive to undercut its rivals' taxes

on the rich and benefits granted to the poor until a situation of
mere benefit taxation is reached.

• *Public goods*   Public goods, which are defined by decreasing or
even zero marginal costs with regard to the number of users,
cannot be supplied by competitive governments since the tax prices
charged on the users cannot exceed the marginal costs and are thus
insufficient to finance intra-marginal costs.

In all of these examples, policy coordination would be useful to
avoid the devastating effects of fiscal competition. Common European environmental standards, equal quality standards or at least a
common system of well-defined and popularised quality categories,
an extended social charter, and harmonised tax systems seem necessary; but all of this has little to do with Keynesian multiplier effects.

My second comment refers to the requirements the authors believe
to be necessary for a workable European currency union. Among the
requirements and aims of official policy listed are external stability
and balanced government budgets. If these postulates are to be
understood as proscriptions of borrowing and lending activities by
countries and governments, I find them highly objectionable.

I do not see any particular reason why countries should not be
allowed to exploit the welfare gains from intertemporal trade in
economic resources which come along with extended periods of
current-account imbalances. Why should a rapidly-growing country
not borrow to smooth its international consumption pattern or to
finance its investment projects? There are certainly moral hazard
problems involved, but they should not be put forward completely to
forbid current account deficits.

My reservation against the proscription of public borrowing has a
similar motivation. Borrowing can help shift the burden of long-
lasting public investment projects to those who benefit from them; it
is a way of overcoming the markets' liquidity constraints against
private borrowing; and, as the Domar formula tells us, it can, in a
growing economy, continue indefinitely without ever creating bankruptcy problems.

Apart from this criticism I fully share the other postulates the
authors establish for a European Currency Union. The independence
of the Central Bank from national governments, including the full
independence of the national governors delegated to the European
Reserve Board, is a necessary requirement for a credible commitment to a policy of price level stability, a point of view I am pleased
to see shared and further developed in the paper.

Index of Subjects

interest super-neutrality 219
International Bank for Economic
    Cooperation 99
International Monetary System 171
international transmission-channels 85
intertemporal opportunity costs 73
intervention equation 63
intervention
    Central Bank 4, 160, 167
    coordinated 5, 131, 140, 146, 150,
        253
    effectiveness of the Bundesbank and
        the Federal Reserve 143, 149, 158
    effects of 114
    exchange market 5, 132, 133, 149,
        157, 179
    forward market 69, 70, 74
    fully anticipated 114, 119
    initial 140, 141, 146, 149, 150
    in the exchange market 70
    measuring the effects of
        unsterilised 123
    money market 73, 74, 82
    non-coordinated 5, 131, 140, 146,
        150
    non-sterilised or unsterilised 4, 23,
        74, 76, 82, 110, 112, 122, 123, 128,
        130, 133–6, 271
    official 131, 132
    spot market 137, 138
    sterilised or sterilising by the Central
        Bank 21, 69, 70, 74, 77, 82, 133,
        135, 136, 161, 167
    subsequent 140, 141, 146
    unanticipated 123, 129
investments
    direct 14, 29
    foreign 20, 92
    imported 14, 16
    portfolio 29
Ireland 189
Italy 39, 43, 62, 184, 186, 235, 239,
    255, 256, 269, 270, 272–4

Japan 141, 192, 266

Keynesian
    model 73
    multiplier effects 285, 286
    philosophy 234
    policies 285

labour
    costs 184, 197

market 3, 8, 64, 73, 187, 188, 190,
    192–4, 198, 201, 202, 277
migration 192
mobility 189, 193, 198
productivity 18, 197
Laffer curve 255
liberalisation
    of capital 1, 275
    of capital movements 86
    of convertible currency imports 93
    of external trade 91, 104
    financial 3, 62, 63
    of foreign economic relations 92/93
    of imports 92, 98–100
    of international trade 86
liquidity constraints 286
loans
    in domestic currency 15, 24, 29
    in foreign currency 14, 15, 20, 21
Louvre agreement (Summit,
    1987) 143, 149, 266

MacDougall report 274
Madrid Conference 183, 189, 248
Mark V version (of a continuous
    macroeconometric model) 40
Marshall plan 4, 89, 104
mint conventions 200
Mitterrand government 252, 259, 285
model
    Akerlof 285
    Atlas 255–8
    Black–Scholes 210
    CAPM portfolio balance 161
    Cesam 255
    Djajic 110
    fourteen multi-country 254
    Freia K'85 255, 256
    of the French Direction de la
        Prévision (Atlas) 255–8
    Hermes/Comet 257
    Interlink 265
    Keynesian 73
    macroeconomic 3, 285
    MCM 265
    Mimosa 257
    monetary 217
    monetary growth 218
    Morkmon 1–87 255
    operational economic policy of the
        Netherlands Central Planning
        Bureau 251
    Oxford Economic Forecasting
        (OEF) 256, 258

Index of Names